The Economic Psychology of Tax Behaviour

Tax evasion is a complex phenomenon which is influenced not just by economic motives but by psychological factors as well. Economic-psychological research focuses on individual and social representations of taxation as well as decision-making. In this book, Erich Kirchler assembles research on tax compliance, with a focus on tax evasion, and integrates the findings into a model based on the interaction climate between tax authorities and taxpayers. The interaction climate is defined by citizens' trust in authorities and the power of authorities to control taxpayers effectively; depending on trust and power, either voluntary compliance, enforced compliance or no compliance are likely outcomes. Featuring chapters on the social representations of taxation, decision-making and self-employed income tax behaviour, this book will appeal to researchers in economic psychology, behavioural economics and public administration.

ERICH KIRCHLER is a Professor in the Faculty of Psychology at the University of Vienna. His research interests include economic psychology, household financial decision-making and tax behaviour, and he has written several books in these areas.

The Economic Psychology of Tax Behaviour

Erich Kirchler
University of Vienna, Austria

CAMBRIDGE UNIVERSITY PRESS
Cambridge, New York, Melbourne, Madrid, Cape Town, Singapore, São Paulo

Cambridge University Press
The Edinburgh Building, Cambridge CB2 8RU, UK

Published in the United States of America by Cambridge University Press,
New York

www.cambridge.org
Information on this title: www.cambridge.org/9780521876742

First published 2007

Printed in the United Kingdom at the University Press, Cambridge

A catalogue record for this book is available from the British Library

ISBN 978-0-521-87674-2 hardback

Contents

Figures

Tables

Foreword

Valerie Braithwaite

This book brings together research that has traditionally been fragmented into camps of legal, economic and social-psychological scholarship. Each camp acknowledges the need to be aware of the others' findings, but few books have been as inclusive and successful in creating a coherent framework that can house these different bodies of research. Kirchler describes the various research traditions in detail, setting out the building blocks for the reader to survey at close range. These parts are then assembled to provide an integrated account of how some taxpayers take the path down the slippery slope of non-compliance, while most stay on the high ground. Kirchler acknowledges that some individuals are less willing to say no to evasion than others, that some are less committed and able, and that varying social contexts can make it easier to comply or harder. But the spotlight is not only on the strengths and weaknesses of individual taxpayers and their immediate environment. Tax authorities play their part too and can adopt enforcement policies that are likely to push taxpayers down the slippery slope. Too often tax authorities fail to communicate respect and trust to the taxpayer, instead playing the 'cop' who is single-mindedly in pursuit of the 'robber' taxpayer.

This book provides a new frame for analysing tax compliance research. Classic economic theory depicting taxpayers as rational cost–benefit analysts has long provided the benchmark for evaluating new developments in tax research. In this book, Kirchler reinvents the frame. The classic economic view is no longer the standard but rather one of many possible social representations of taxpaying. Kirchler examines the role of individuals' perceptions of gains and loss, opportunities and obstacles as they appraise taxpaying demands. The lens is then broadened to incorporate sociological and psychological understandings of social context and cultural setting, and the part such factors play in determining how taxpayers approach and deal with tax authorities. Kirchler integrates the various theories and models of tax compliance as different kinds of social representations, and through a meticulous review of the literature presents a question that he both answers and poses for future tax compliance work: what are the circumstances in which these different models have most leverage for changing behaviour?

To read this book is to enter a treasure trove of research on taxation compliance. Consecutive chapters present accumulated knowledge in the different worlds of taxpayers as rational actors and trusting citizens, as self-employed business owners and taxpaying employees, as willing, reluctant or inaccurate payers and as calculating avoiders and evaders. The recurring theme is that the social representations of individuals matter and shape how taxpayers approach the demands made by tax authorities. Recognising disparities not only in types of taxpayers but also in intellectual traditions and analytic methods, Kirchler tracks the tax compliance story across taxpaying groups, academic disciplines and countries with divergent laws, norms and traditions. This book is a timely and invaluable contribution to a field that has for more than a decade been seeking a positive account of why people pay taxes.

VALERIE BRAITHWAITE
Regulatory Institutions Network
Australian National University
Canberra, Australia

Preface

This book seeks to collect and integrate economic-psychological research on tax compliance in general, focusing specifically on tax evasion. Research findings are integrated into a model based on two dimensions: originating from the interaction climate between tax authorities and taxpayers, the dimensions are defined by citizens' trust in authorities and the power of authorities to control taxpayers effectively. Depending on trust and the use of power, either voluntary compliance, enforced compliance or no compliance are likely to result. While economic studies on tax evasion have been growing immensely in the past decades, only about 10% of publications assume an economic-psychological perspective, i.e., one that focuses mainly on individual and social aspects of tax representations, decisions and behaviour. Thus, this book aims to fill the present gap by reviewing the accumulated economic-psychological knowledge and mapping the field.

After a brief introduction, the increasing concerns with the complexity of tax law and the growth of the shadow economy are described, and definitions of tax compliance, avoidance and evasion are presented. As a psychologist, I choose to approach tax behaviour from an individual and social-psychological perspective. The available research focuses on individual and the collective (social) representations of taxation as well as on tax morale, and decision-making. I have chosen to afford the majority of attention to income tax, with special attention to self-employed taxpayers' behaviour. More recently, interest has been shown in tax authorities' orientations towards taxpayers and the interactions between tax officers and taxpayers. This book picks up and expands upon this important research trend.

After the introductory chapters, research findings on social representations are presented. Essentially, the chapter on social representations collects information on taxpayers' knowledge about taxation and subjective constructs, or lay theories of tax issues. Second, attitudes towards fiscal policy and taxation are reviewed. The chapter proceeds by focusing on norms, especially on personal norms (conceived as a belief that there is a moral imperative with which one should deliberately comply); social norms (conceived as prevalence of tax evasion among a reference group); and societal norms. Next, behaviour control, defined as perceived opportunities not to comply, is described. Moreover, fairness considerations are of special importance: as shown, distributional, procedural and retributive justices are frequently found to have lasting effects on tax behaviour. After addressing subjective understandings, attitudes, norms and perceived opportunities, as well as fairness considerations, the focus is directed towards tax behaviour via discussions on motivational postures at the individual level and tax morale at the collective level.

Literature on income tax behaviour often rests upon the assumption that taxpayers deliberately decide whether or not to pay their share of taxes. While it can be argued that taxpayers may often spontaneously cooperate and comply rather than deliberating on their decisions, the economic approach almost exclusively addresses tax behaviour as a (rational) decision outcome. If taxpayers make decisions with the aim of maximising their individual profit, the dominating economic approach suggests that they face a risky decision. One must decide between paying taxes correctly or opting for the risky alternative, which is accompanied by a possibility of saving money, as well as the possibility of audit, detection and, in the case of evasion, fines. Depending on audit, as well as detection probability and fines, taxpayers choose the alternative that promises the most favourable outcome. The description of rational decision-making is followed by considerations of effects of repeated audits. Finally, it is argued that decision-makers often depart from rational decision-making by applying heuristics and falling victim to biases. Prospect theory, which addresses risk bias, has been successfully applied to tax behaviour.

The next chapter is dedicated to the tax behaviour of self-employed and entrepreneurial individuals. The obligation to collect various taxes for the tax office, paying taxes out of pocket and having various opportunities to cut income declarations or exaggerate expenditures makes the tax situation of the self-employed unique. Throughout the book, the focus is on individual income taxpayers. Therefore, payment of other taxes is rarely addressed, nor are corporations' tax engagement and corporate crime explicitly addressed.

The next section of the book deals with the interaction processes between tax authorities and taxpayers as a central theme. The approach tax authorities and tax officials take, their beliefs about taxpayers' behaviour and the respective interaction styles are of paramount importance in determining the tax climate. I argue that taxpayers react in accordance with the approach taken by the tax authorities. A 'cops and robbers' approach is likely to breed distrust, corrupting voluntary cooperation. However, 'trust is an important lubricant of the social system,' wrote Kenneth Arrow (1974, p. 23). 'It is extremely efficient; it saves a lot of trouble to have a fair degree of reliance on other people's word ... it [is] essential in the running of society.' In a climate of distrust, authorities resort to control and punishing misbehaviour and must enforce citizens' compliance. On the other hand, a 'service and client' approach, which is characterised by supportive and respectful treatment of taxpayers, transparency of procedures and acceptance of authorities, is likely to enhance trust and a cooperative atmosphere leading to voluntary compliance. Whereas a 'cops and robbers' or 'command and control' approach establishes a climate of distrust, a 'service and client' approach is assumed to reduce the 'social distance' (Bogardus, 1928; V. Braithwaite, 2003a) between taxpayers and tax authorities, thus creating a climate of mutual trust and voluntary cooperation.

The final section offers conclusions that are to be taken cautiously. Firstly, economic-psychological research is still in its infancy, providing merely isolated results rather than an integrative model of tax behaviour. Secondly, research on tax behaviour faces a bulk of methodological problems, vague conceptualisations of phenomena and heterogeneous operationalisation of assumed determinants of tax behaviour. Unsurprisingly, effects of determinants (or consequences) of tax behaviour were sometimes found to be strong, sometimes weak and sometimes insignificant or even in the opposite direction to expectations. Contradictory findings may be due either to methodological idiosyncrasies or to the neglect of relevant differentiating variables. Furthermore, tax behaviour has not been systematically studied in different political and tax systems, nor have cultural differences been satisfactorily explained. I argue that the tax climate predominantly results from the interaction style between authorities and taxpayers, which might be a crucial differentiating variable: in case of a 'cops and robbers' approach, a hostile, non-cooperative climate may result. In a system of hostility and non-acceptance of authorities, taxpayers may seek to maximise their individual profit, make (rational) decisions, and comply only if the authorities have the power to command and control taxpayers and to enforce compliance by effective audits and severe fines. On the other hand, a 'service and client' approach should create a basis for mutual trust and a cooperative tax climate, with taxpayers accepting the authorities and being spontaneously willing to contribute to the collective good.

I argue – and summarise in the 'slippery slope model'[1] – that trust in the authorities and voluntary compliance integrate favourable social representations, that is, basic comprehension of tax laws, favourable tax mentality, favourable personal, social and societal norms and a perceived fairness with regard to distribution of tax burden, benefits and procedures. Trust depends on cooperation and favours cooperation. A cooperative climate is based on and favours compliance, which is derived from commitment as a motivational posture and from high tax morale in the society. Rather than guaranteeing compliance, audits and fines may have opposite effects in a trustful climate and thus corrupt voluntary compliance. Trust can spiral downwards to reduced levels when authorities respond to low levels of cooperation with control and punishment. Audits and fines may be highly effective in a completely distrustful climate with high social distance between authorities and taxpayers. In such a climate with no voluntary compliance, compliance can be enforced by the power of the authorities. However, audits and fines as the 'tools' to command and control taxpayers will not be suitable to create a cooperative tax atmosphere.

If interaction between tax authorities and taxpayers is a crucial variable, future research should consider tax climate as a variable that moderates the effects of both audits and fines and social representations. If the climate is characterised by distrust, but the state has the legitimate and expert power to control and fine non-compliant citizens, compliance can be enforced. However, if the climate is characterised by trust, authorities' power is of less importance: citizens will comply voluntarily. If the tax authorities' approach to taxpayers proves to be of crucial importance to establish mutual trust and voluntary compliance, the practical consequences are, among others, to aim for more simple tax laws comprehensible to ordinary taxpayers, better information detailing the distribution of tax burden and benefits, guaranteed procedural and retributive justice and efficient communication of social norms in order to promote taxpayer collaboration and enhance tax morale.

Acknowledgements

I would like to express thanks to numerous friends, colleagues and institutions that have supported this work. In particular, I wish to thank the University of Vienna, Austria, for permitting a sabbatical leave enabling

---

[1] The term 'slippery slope model' was introduced by Henk Elffers at a conference in Leiden, The Netherlands, on 'Managing and maintaining compliance' (10–11 April 2006), where I had the opportunity to talk about 'Why people comply'.

me to research, select and review hundreds of scientific articles for the writing of this book. The Australian National University at Canberra and the University of Sydney, Australia, deserve special gratitude for the invitation to spend six months with them and for all the necessary support for conducting this work. Enormous thanks go to Valerie and John Braithwaite and their research teams at the Research School of Social Sciences (Centre for Tax System Integrity, Regulatory Institutions Network), Australian National University for their collegiality and extraordinary generosity in providing material and scientific support, for invitations to join their workshops on tax compliance and regulatory justice and discussing research on tax compliance. I owe many thanks to Erik Hölzl and Stephan Mühlbacher, and many other research fellows at the University of Vienna, who cast a critical eye over the text and made many suggestions for improvements, and to Elisabeth Höllerer, Eva-Maria Holy and Christine Talker for their attention to compiling the references, creating tables and drawing figures, and to Kate Connery for language correction and excellent assistance in editing the original manuscript of this book.

And last but not least, I thank Carrie Cheek, Rosina dï Marzo, Andrew Peart, Jackie Warren and David Watson from Cambridge University Press for their interest in the topic of this volume and their support, guidance and editorial skills.

ERICH KIRCHLER
Vienna, Austria, September 2006

1 Introduction

Is tax evasion a hot topic in economics and social sciences? A search for citations in the 'Web of Science' (January 2006; SSCI, SCI and A&HCI) yielded confirming results: from the beginning of documentation in 1945 to 1980, 75 citations were produced when the key words 'tax', 'taxes', 'taxation' and 'evasion' or 'compliance' were entered. In the following decade, 1981 to 1990, the number increased to 141, and reached 372 in the years spanning 1991 to 2000. Even faster growth is seen from 2001 to 2005, with 278 new publications registered. In 1986, Freiberg wrote that little is known about the extent of tax evasion, and even less is known about the criteria for enforcement of the law, or why some cases are selected for prosecution and others are not. Andreoni, Erard and Feinstein (1998) observed that from the beginning of the 1980s until the completion of their tax compliance review in the late 1990s there was an increasing tide of research on tax compliance. This tide has continued to grow into the present. As most of the publications are in the field of economics, an overwhelming majority refers to the influential models of tax evasion developed by Allingham and Sandmo (1972) and Srinivasan (1973) on the basis of Becker's 1968 theory of crime, which is tested by econometric modelling and analyses of empirical data, and further refined by adding specific variables which are assumed to influence tax compliance (cf. Franzoni, 2000).

The terms 'psychology' or 'psychological' appear in only 10% of the titles and abstracts of publications, with little variation over the years: from 1981–1990, 1991–2000 and 2001–2005, the respective percentages are 12%, 9% and 11%. From the beginning of registration (1945) to 1980, the term 'psychology' appeared in only 1% of the publications. Clearly, the field is dominated by economics. Nevertheless, the increase of publications relating to psychological aspects of taxes, from 1 to 17, 33, and 32 publications in the periods from 1945 to 2005, looks promising.

Niemirowski, Baldwin and Wearing (2001) presented a historical overview of thirty years of tax compliance research in economics and social sciences, beginning with its development in the late 1950s with the early

1

work of Schmölders (1959). The overview centred on attitudes and social norms in the 1970s (e.g., Vogel, 1974), and included knowledge as a determinant of compliance (e.g., Eriksen and Fallan, 1996; Wärneryd and Walerud, 1982). Additionally, Niemirowski and colleagues covered the analyses of justice perceptions and tax ethics (e.g., Song and Yarbrough, 1978; Spicer and Lundstedt, 1976), the analyses of anomalies in compliance decisions (e.g., Schepanski and Shearer, 1995) and finally, the study of cooperative interaction between tax authorities and taxpayers (e.g., V. Braithwaite, 2003b). The accumulated volume of knowledge is impressive. Indeed, by the late 1970s, the US Internal Revenue Service (IRS) had already identified more than sixty factors likely to determine taxpayer behaviour. Yet, important recent additions like gain and loss framing of tax dues and withholding phenomena were not included (IRS, 1978, quoted in Chang and Schultz, 1990). The field has seen several literature reviews (e.g., Andreoni, Erard and Feinstein, 1998; Brandstätter, 1994; Franzoni, 2000; Hasseldine and Bebbington, 1991; Hasseldine and Li, 1999; Jackson and Milliron, 1986; James and Alley, 2002; Lewis, 1982; Milliron and Toy, 1988; Richardson and Sawyer, 2001; Slemrod, Blumenthal and Christian, 2001; Torgler, 2002; Webley *et al.*, 1991; Weigel, Hessing and Elffers, 1987), as well as collections of research in taxation such as the annual publication 'Advances in Taxation', edited by Thomas M. Porcano, and, since 2004, Suzanne Luttman, or special journal issues (e.g., *Journal of Economic Psychology*, 1992, edited by Paul Webley and Dick J. Hessing). This accumulated knowledge provides insight into taxpaying behaviour and is of practical relevance for fiscal policy (cf. OECD, 2004). However, research has yet to be integrated into a comprehensive model of taxpayer behaviour. Thus, the fast-growing evidence on tax behaviour and the still widely neglected psychological determinants of tax behaviour in economic models call for a review and for a model integrating the most recent findings in the social sciences.

This volume provides an overview of studies on income tax behaviour as related to psychological aspects and keeps purely economic approaches on the margin. It aims to summarise and integrate findings of tax research and present conclusions that are both scientifically cutting-edge and practically applicable. Tax behaviour has been investigated from a political perspective, mainly focusing on tax law complexity and shadow economy, and from an economic perspective, with the focus on rational decision-making and the impact of tax audits, fines, tax rates and income on compliance. Tax behaviour researched from a behavioural economic and economic-psychological slant has focused on various attitudinal variables, norms and fairness and decision anomalies. Taking all of this

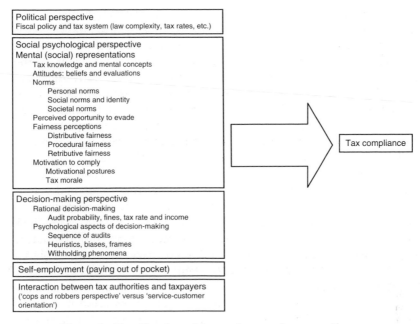

| Political perspective |
| Fiscal policy and tax system (law complexity, tax rates, etc.) |

Social psychological perspective
Mental (social) representations
    Tax knowledge and mental concepts
    Attitudes: beliefs and evaluations
    Norms
        Personal norms
        Social norms and identity
        Societal norms
    Perceived opportunity to evade
    Fairness perceptions
        Distributive fairness
        Procedural fairness
        Retributive fairness
    Motivation to comply
        Motivational postures
        Tax morale

Decision-making perspective
    Rational decision-making
        Audit probability, fines, tax rate and income
    Psychological aspects of decision-making
        Sequence of audits
        Heuristics, biases, frames
        Withholding phenomena

Self-employment (paying out of pocket)

Interaction between tax authorities and taxpayers
('cops and robbers perspective' versus 'service-customer orientation')

Tax compliance

Figure 1: Classification of determinants of tax compliance

into account, the present work classifies this research into two main thematic fields: social representations of taxation and decisions to comply. Two additional sections focus on the specificity of tax behaviour of the self-employed and entrepreneurs, and on the interaction between taxpayers and tax authorities. The latter topic has predominantly been studied from a social psychological perspective. Figure 1 displays the various perspectives and variables under consideration.

To help guide the reader through this material, the following maps the course of this book: before summarising research on social representations, decision processes, self-employment and tax compliance, and interaction dynamics, first, the complexity of tax laws is discussed. Second, statistics on the shadow economy in general, and tax non-compliance in particular, are presented. Third, tax compliance and evasion are defined. In the section on social representations of taxes, first, research on subjective tax knowledge and subjective concepts of taxation is presented; second, research on attitudes towards tax non-compliance is summarised; third, norms are addressed; and fourth, opportunities of non-compliance are addressed; fifth, fairness and justice considerations are considered; sixth, motivation to comply and tax morale are discussed. In the section on decision-making, rational decisions and decision anomalies are presented. In the remainder, evidence on the tax compliance of self-employed taxpayers and entrepreneurs of small or medium businesses is presented. The final section is dedicated to models of cooperation between taxpayers and tax authorities. The volume ends with a reflection on the difficulty of assessing tax behaviour and advantages and disadvantages of widely used research methods and a summary of presented research. In the last chapter, a model is proposed to integrate research findings as well as for serving as a base to develop interaction strategies with taxpayers. The model is based on tax authorities' perception of taxpayers as 'robbers' or 'clients' and the taxpayers' compliance reactions. Whereas a 'cops and robbers' approach is assumed to evoke mistrust and non-cooperation, a 'service and client' approach is assumed to excite cooperation and voluntary compliance. In a climate of distrust, taxpayers are assumed to deliberately take decisions to optimise their own profit. They are assumed to consider whether it pays to evade, given a certain audit probability and fine in case of detected evasion, or whether it is too risky not to comply. In a climate of trust, taxpayers develop favourable representations of taxation and feel less social distance to tax authorities; thus, voluntary compliance is likely to result. In the former case compliance can be enforced if the state has the power to control tax behaviour and fine evasion; in the latter case compliance is the result of spontaneous cooperation.

2 Tax law, the shadow economy and tax non-compliance

2.1 Complexity of tax law

Tax laws are not always clear. As Slemrod and colleagues put it, 'although one can assert that legality is the dividing line between evasion and avoidance, in practice the line is blurry; sometimes the law itself is unclear, sometimes it is clear but not known to the taxpayer, sometimes the law is clear but the administration effectively ignores a particular transaction or activity' (Slemrod, Blumenthal and Christian, 2001, p. 459).

The concern of legality grows in parallel with the increasing globalisation of business, the increasing complexity of business structures, the nature of financing and transactions and tax flight by establishing businesses off shore, tax havens and money laundering (Owens and Hamilton, 2004). Bartelsman and Beetsma (2003) and Yaniv (1990) present suggestive evidence of income shifting in response to differences in corporate tax rates for a large selection of OECD countries. Modern organised non-compliant businesses act within the law, exploiting the law's shortcomings and loopholes. In Cyprus alone, an estimated 37,000 companies have been established using the advantages of a tax haven, and the number is increasing steadily (Courakis, 2001). Businesses take advantage of loopholes in the law and find more sophisticated ways to reduce tax payments when new regulations and laws are established in response to aggressive avoidance. Businesses also respond symmetrically to tax changes, moving into the underground economy if taxes increase, and out when they decrease (Christopoulos, 2003). In addition to businesses, individuals are also 'tax savvy' and avoid paying more if they can do so legally (Barber and Odean, 2004), or make their creative tax designs sound legal to tax authorities. Rawlings (2004) reports an event which demonstrates how difficult it is to decide what is legal behaviour corresponding to 'the letter of the law', although it is clear what behaviour would have been in line with 'the spirit of the law':

In 1999, the Federal Court of Australia ... was told of a family who had not filed a tax return for 20 years, but had $A 13 million on term deposit with a Swiss bank managed

5

by trustees in Vanuatu. The two applicants in this case, Doreen and Barry Beazley, had in the mid-1970s sold a successful business in New Zealand for an undisclosed sum and placed the proceeds in what was then the Anglo-French Condominium of the New Hebrides. They did not move to the New Hebrides with their funds, but relocated to Australia ... Between 1989/90 and 1995/96, these investments generated $A 4,322,968, which was channelled through Vanuatu managed trusts, offshore corporations, captive insurance companies and debentures. (p. 325)

On the basis of documents seized by the Australian National Crime Authority, it was alleged that Mr and Ms Beazley had each failed to declare income of $A 1,080,742 between 1989 and 1996. However, the Beazleys claimed that these funds were not income, but the progressive repayment and receipt of 'loans' to and from Vanuatu. To meet their day-to-day expenses the family used Bank of Hawai'i credit cards with entities in Vanuatu paying off the resulting debts. They affirmed that these arrangements were part of 'a sophisticated but lawful taxation structure'. Even though the court found that the documents suggested 'a guilty mind', it conceded that the structure might be 'entirely legal' (ibid., p. 325).

In their collection of experiences and innovations in taxation in various countries, Owens and Hamilton (2004) state that in OECD countries one of the major problems in tax administration is understanding what has to be administered, namely the tax laws and how to interpret them. An impressive example can be found in the Australian legislation. The quote below is an uncut selection from the Australian GST Legislation (http://law.ato.gov.au/pdf/ps05_024.pdf; retrieved 7 February 2007). Plain English or clarity are very much lacking. In fact, it verges on the ridiculous and was awarded The Plain English Campaign's 'Golden Bull' Award (see http://www.plainenglish.co.uk/bull05.htm; retrieved 7 February 2007):

Australian Taxations Office for its Goods and Services legislation:
"For the purposes of making a declaration under this Subdivision, the Commissioner may:
a) treat a particular event that actually happened as not having happened; and
b) treat a particular event that did not actually happen as having happened and, if appropriate, treat the event as:
   i) having happened at a particular time; and
   ii) having involved particular action by a particular entity; and
c) treat a particular event that actually happened as:
   i) having happened at a time different from the time it actually happened; or
   ii) having involved particular action by a particular entity (whether or not the event actually involved any action by that entity)."

A half-century ago, in 1959, Schmölders tested politicians in the German parliament and members of its finance committee on their economic knowledge and found poor understanding of fiscal policy. Tax authorities face the problem of the complexities of public finance and the law, as well as ambiguities in interpreting and executing it. Another trend shows that expert tax lawyers are increasingly specialising in particular domains as the complexity renders it impossible to be an expert in general tax law. Tax practitioners investigated in Australia claimed that maintaining an appropriate level of professional competence by ongoing development of their knowledge and skills is a main problem with regard to correctly filing income tax (Marshall, Armstrong and Smith, 1998). Tax laws have become so intricate that even experts, such as accountants, lawyers and tax officers, have difficulty interpreting many of the law's provisions.

Complex tax law is even more difficult to understand for ordinary taxpayers. In 1994, Moser undertook a linguistic analysis of tax laws and identified several problems that make it difficult for ordinary tax-payers to understand the law. Examples of unnecessary complexity are the high level of abstraction in the language, long and complex sentences, use of abbreviations, and reference to experts rather than to ordinary readers. Lewis (1982) reports that the necessary education to understand tax laws is unreasonably high. According to a formula to assess reading age necessary to comprehend the laws, which is based on length of sentences, complexity of words, etc., the British tax law required, at the time of analysis, thirteen years of school education, while the average citizen had nine years of schooling. The US tax law required twelve and a half years, and the Australian seventeen years. Reading and understanding of a 'quality' journal requires less school education. Complexity of tax laws and trends of increasing complexity in the past fifty years are well illustrated in a USA tax foundation graph depicting the increasing number of words used in the US IRS Code from 1955 to 2000 (see figure 2).

In response to this increasing complexity, many countries have endeavoured to simplify the law, although without much success. For instance, New Zealand's tax law was set into plain English, but still faces the same administrative and compliance problems as before the attempt to make it simpler. 'And if the law cannot be made simple, then it is inevitably going to be difficult to understand and administer,' conclude Owens and Hamilton (2004, p. 350), quoting a review of the simplification efforts in New Zealand (www.businesscompliance.govt.nz/reports/final/final-11.html):

From 1989 to 2001, eleven tax simplification/compliance cost reduction policy documents have been published. Eight of these have been released in the last five years. Despite their relative frequency, and their effort to simplify various taxes and processes, the initiatives have had little impact on the volume of tax regulation, its complexity, and the compliance loading on business taxpayers ... Businesses considered taxation their most significant business compliance cost ... Individuals expressed their anger, frustration, confusion, and alienation about

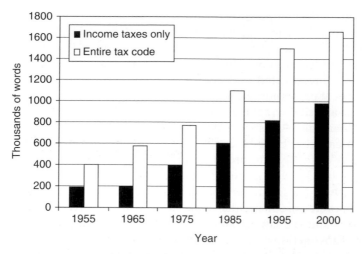

Figure 2: Growth in number of words in the US IRS Code from 1955 to 2000 (adopted from www.taxfoundation.org/compliancetestimony.html; quoted in Owens and Hamilton, 2004, p. 349)

their attempts to meet their tax commitments ... There was a great deal of support for the basic tax system itself, but very high levels of frustration in the way it was implemented. Business people told us that the complexity of the law made compliance difficult and very time consuming. (p. 351)

Experiences in Australia were similar. The Tax Law Improvement Project aimed at rewriting the law into plain English. And while a readability test on Australia's simpler Tax Act showed some improvement, the level of readability remained much too high for the general public, as it required a university education to understand it. Also, the length of the text had increased: eleven lines of one key section were increased to five paragraphs in the new legislation.

'I hold in my hand 1,379 pages of tax simplification,' said USA congressman Delbert L. Latta (*US News and World Report*, 23 December 1985), satirising endeavours to reduce tax complexity on the part of tax administrators and politicians. In Australia, the *Sydney Morning Herald* (9–10 July 2005) published a memorable report about many innovations leading to no substantial changes:

Taxes giveth as GST taketh away
Ross Gittins
Gittins on Saturday
Everyone who's socially aware knows the introduction of the goods and services tax – as it happens, exactly five years ago last week – made the tax system a lot more regressive.

Except that everyone is wrong.

Associate Professor Neil Warren of Atax at the University of NSW and Professor Ann Harding and Rachel Lloyd of Natsem at the University of Canberra have just produced a study of "GST and the changing incidence of Australian taxes", which reaches some surprising conclusions. It's published in the eJournal of Tax Research.

A "progressive" tax is one that takes a progressively bigger proportion of people's incomes as incomes rise. A "regressive" tax is the opposite: it takes a progressively smaller proportion of people's incomes as incomes rise.

The popular conviction that the GST caused the tax system to become more unfair is based on a simple logic: the GST is an indirect tax, all indirect taxes are regressive, therefore the system has become more regressive.

But that logic was always too simple. For a start, the GST was replacing various old indirect taxes that were regressive also. For another thing, the decision not to tax food made the GST a lot less regressive than it could have been. For a third, there were many other changes in the tax reform package – including increases in welfare benefits and huge cuts in income tax – so what effect did they have?

Clearly, the effect of the GST package isn't something you can work out in your head. You have to study the figures very carefully. Which is just what Warren & Co did. They compared the position in 1994–95 (the Labor government's second last year) with the position seven years later in 2001–02 (after the GST had been going two years).

They found that the GST was indeed a bit more regressive than the indirect taxes it replaced. On the "progressivity index" (where anything above zero is progressive, anything below zero is regressive and zero is "proportional" – that is, neither progressive nor regressive), the GST scored minus 0.17, whereas the previous taxes scored minus 0.16.

Don't forget, however, that how regressive a tax happens to be is just one dimension of its effect. The other is whether you use the regressive tax to raise a lot of money or a little. (This is known as the "height" of the tax.)

Over the seven years to 2001–02, household pre-tax income rose by 36 per cent in nominal terms, while collections from indirect taxes rose by 59 per cent.

So not only was the GST a bit more regressive than the taxes it replaced, but the Government used it to raise more revenue than before. This meant that the proportion of their income paid in indirect tax by all households rose from 9.3 per cent to 9.7 per cent.

But that's just the first part of the story – and the first step in the sum. Warren & Co found that the progressivity index for income tax rose a fraction from 0.223 to 0.225. So while the GST was making indirect taxes a bit more regressive, income tax was becoming a fraction more progressive.

What's more, the Government was using it to raise a lot more revenue. While household income rose by 36 per cent, revenue from income tax rose by well over 60 per cent.

In consequence, the proportion of income paid in income tax by all households rose from 18.6 per cent to 19.5 per cent.

What was it that caused income tax to become a fraction more progressive? The same thing that caused income-tax collections to grow so strongly: bracket creep.

In other words, the huge income-tax cut that accompanied the introduction of the GST in July 2000 wasn't sufficient to outweigh the Government's failure to index the tax scales every year.

Income tax became a fraction more progressive because the absence of tax indexation hit higher income-earners a bit harder than it hit lower income-earners. Finally, if we lump together all the other federal and state taxes – but particularly company tax – we find that they're mildly regressive. But their score on the progressivity index improved a bit from minus 0.08 to minus 0.07.

This favourable development, however, was pretty much offset by the fact that these taxes, too, were used to raise a lot more revenue. The proportion of income paid in "other taxes" by all households rose a little from 15.9 per cent to 16.1 per cent.

Now, let's start putting it all together. Because income tax and other taxes became a bit more progressive at the same time as the GST was making indirect taxes a bit more regressive, and because income tax raises about twice as much revenue as indirect taxes do, the combined effect was actually to make the whole tax system a little more progressive.

The system's score on the progressivity index rose from 0.035 to 0.037. (Note, however, that this very low score – not far above zero – means the total tax system is only just progressive. It's a bit more redistributive than if it was only proportional – that is, if everyone was losing the same percentage of their income – but not by much.)

So far, we've been looking at how progressive the tax system is and then, by taking account of the increase in the amount of revenue raised by it, at how much redistributing of income from rich to poor it's doing.

But now let's look at what happened to the distribution of income over the seven years to 2001–02 and what part the tax system played in the change.

The most common way of summarising the inequality of incomes between households is to use the "Gini coefficient". If the coefficient was zero, that would mean income was divided perfectly equally between all households, if it was 1, that would mean one household had all the income.

According to Warren & Co's figuring, the distribution of pre-tax income became a bit more unequal over the period, with the Gini rising from 0.33 to 0.36.

But the distribution of after-tax income hardly moved, with the Gini virtually unchanged at 0.33.

So, notwithstanding the introduction of the evil GST, the tax system became a little more progressive and redistributive, and this was sufficient to counteract a worsening in the distribution of pre-tax income, leaving the distribution of after-tax income essentially unchanged.

Warren & Co conclude that, despite all the changes during the seven-year period – in the tax and transfer system, the economy and the characteristics of households – the distribution of the tax burden and the distribution of household income were remarkably stable. (p. 70)

Several countries (e.g., Austria, Australia, France) have put particular effort into simplifying tax law for the self-employed and small business owners. Nevertheless, concerns with complexity remain. In 'Markets in Vice, Markets in Virtue', J. Braithwaite argues for a complete reformation of the law and proposes to integrate specific rules into principles. Actually, the prescription of relatively specific acts leads to creative tax compliance or, in other words, savvy tax avoidance. Taxpayers who engage in such behaviour make use of the many loopholes in very specific tax laws. They construct complex business structures in the global market that are extremely difficult to understand and evaluate by tax officials, and often it is impossible to say whether they are legal or not legal. According to J. Braithwaite (2005), '[a] smorgasbord of rules engenders a cat-and-mouse legal drafting culture – of loophole closing and reopening by creative compliance' (p. 147). The prescription of principles as highly unspecific actions which should serve to clearly guide behaviour would prevent many such 'games'. He continues, arguing for a principled integrity of rules, and suggests that:

tax law can list rules for transactions that are common, leaving judicial enforcement of the principles and in particular, a general anti-avoidance principle to mop up when unusual transactions are in contest. This hybrid of rules and principles would put the brakes on economically wasteful legal entrepreneurship to manipulate the rules. It is a strategy for reaping the benefits of rules – clear guidance to taxpayers in common situations – while limiting their pathologies: exponential growth in legal complexity, burgeoning compliance costs, expanding waste of private and public resources on legal game playing and countering it, a tax system that ordinary people cannot comprehend and therefore has low legitimacy, and reduced prospects of voluntary compliance. (p. 149)

He proposes the following integration of rules and principles in tax law:

1. Define the overarching principles that are to be binding on taxpayers.
2. Include amongst the overarching principles a general anti-avoidance principle which states that schemes are illegal when their dominant purpose is a tax advantage, even if the scheme 'works' as a shelter from detailed tax rules.
3. Define a set of rules to cover the complex area of tax law.
4. Legislate, perhaps through an Acts Interpretation Act, that in contest between a rule and overarching principle, it will not be the rule that is binding. That is, the principle is not merely used to assist in interpreting the rule. Rather it is the reverse. The principle is binding, with the rules to be used only to assist in applying the principle . . .
5. Write specific sets of rules for the most commonly used types of transactions or business arrangements. This might involve a dozen different sets of rules to regulate concrete arrangements. Such rules are not exhaustive; they are introduced explicitly as no more than examples of how the principles apply.
6. Follow each of the dozen sets of illustrative rules with the explanation that the reason for the rules being this way in this concrete situation is to honor the overarching principles. This is a way for the legislature to make it clear to judges, practitioners and taxpayers, that it is the principles that are the binding feature of the law and that should a legal entrepreneur attempt to get around the law by re-engineering financial product number 11 as '11A',

or corporate structure 9 as '9A', judges must go back to the principles to decide what to do.

7. Enact, should judges revert to old habits of privileging rules, a simple statute that says that 11 A shelter violates named principles in the tax law and should be disallowed in future. Its effect is simply to strike down the court's precedent in the 11 A case and to engage the judiciary in a conversation with the legislature on the clarity of its intention to have a principle-driven tax law.

8. Foster educative dialogue with judges, company directors and the community about the principles in the tax law in the hope that conversations among judges and tax practitioners, around the boardroom table and around the table of dinner parties will develop shared sensibilities on what those principles mean. (pp. 149–50)

Uncertainty in the tax law makes it difficult for both taxpayers to follow the law and tax authorities to decide unequivocally what is legal and what is at the fringe of tax law. In the area of 'tax avoision', to use the term coined by Seldon (1979), it is relevant that taxpayers comply with the spirit of the law. Guidance of tax behaviour by principles may be an improvement on specifying narrow rules that are likely to be eluded by creative financial engineers. Financial engineering is just a newer modality of a long tradition of multinational corporations who have the capacities to escape liability, and also of individuals who have the money to pay for artful advice. Thus, the complexity and ambiguity of tax law lends itself to exploitation without actual violation of the law. It goes without saying that the self-employed and owners of small businesses, without strong financial backing, cannot purchase advice to contrive such clever schemes and risk being condemned for aggressive non-compliance. In the meantime, it is the rich offenders who are avoiding and getting away with it, inflicting the greatest losses on the community (J. Braithwaite, 2005).

Thus far, we have seen that even with simplified tax regulations, ordinary wage and salary earners, retired people, self-employed and owners of small businesses find tax laws hard to understand and have difficulty complying. 'How should the tax affairs of small businesses be dealt with – people who cannot hire a bevy of tax accountants or lawyers to ensure that they get things right? These are people who generally are so caught up in running their business, often until late each night, that they have little time for the seemingly costly bureaucratic processes required to comply with tax obligations,' write Owens and Hamilton. The authors continue by demanding: 'You have to make the system a lot simpler for such people if you expect them to be able to comply easily' (Owens and Hamilton, 2004, p. 357).

If the tax law is too complex for ordinary taxpayers' comprehension, and if the complexity offers high-income earners the possibility to hire creative experts to find loopholes to reduce their tax liability, it is not surprising that ordinary taxpayers perceive the tax law as unjust and therefore devalue it. Moreover, how can ordinary taxpayers have control over the correctness of their respective filing behaviour? If incorrect behaviour is punished – as was frequently practised in order to promote future compliance – and taxpayers lack control over the correctness of their behaviour, feelings of helplessness emerge, eventually leading to frustration (Seligman, 1992). Consequently, negative attitudes towards taxes and jurisdiction may result, leading to low tax morale, the perception of unfair exchange between one's own contributions to and benefits from the community and reduced participation in contributing to public goods. Eventually, non-compliance may be justified as a means to balance out the inequitable exchange relationship. At least in retrospect non-compliance may be rationalised by referring to one's disadvantaged taxpaying position (Falkinger, 1988). It is, thus, not surprising that shadow economy and tax non-compliance are substantial and have had periods of rapid increase, particularly in transitional economies.

2.2   Shadow economy

Most societies attempt to control the shadow economy and, in particular, tax evasion. Efficient control is based on reliable statistics that profile who is likely to engage in the shadow economy. However, if tax laws are so difficult to understand that variations exist even in tax authorities' interpretations, control is difficult. Measures of evasion and shadow work remain vague. The problem is defining what activities adequately capture the activities of the shadow, or underground, economy. Shelak's (1997) definition of shadow economy includes activities involving illegal production of trademarked goods, drug dealing, commercial vice and prostitution, loan sharking, illegal gambling, barter, employment of illegal aliens, do-it-yourself projects, skimming of business revenue and tax evasion. V. Braithwaite et al. (2003) recognise the difficulties in defining non-observed economic activities and refer to components of the economy identified by OPEC in 'The Handbook of the Organisation for Economic Cooperation and Development' as non-official economic activities, namely underground production (activities that are legal and productive, but concealed from public authorities), illegal production, informal sector production and production of households for their own final use.

The size and impact of these components will differ across countries, and estimations of shadow activities are often based on different definitions of which components should be measured. Schneider and colleagues attempt to periodically measure the shadow economy in countries across

Table 1: *Taxonomy of types of underground economic activities (Alm, Martinez-Vazquez and Schneider, 2004, p. 16)*

Type of activity	Monetary transactions	Non-monetary transactions
Illegal Source	Trade with stolen goods; drug dealing and manufacturing; prostitution; gambling; smuggling; fraud; etc.	Barter of drugs, stolen goods, smuggling etc. Produce of growing drugs for own use. Theft for own use
	Tax evasion Tax avoidance	Tax evasion Tax avoidance
Legal Source	Unreported income from self-employment; wages, salaries and assets from unreported work related to legal services and goods Employee discounts; fringe benefits	Barter of legal services and goods All do-it-yourself work and neighbour help

the world (Alm, Martinez-Vazquez and Schneider, 2004; Schneider, 2003; Schneider and Klinglmair, 2004). According to Schneider and Klinglmair, the shadow economy comprises all currently unregistered economic activities that contribute to the official or observed Gross National Product. Schneider and Enste define shadow economy as including income unreported to the tax authorities, but generated from the production of legal goods and services, often by means of clandestine labour, involving monetary or barter transactions by agents who are not registered or do not pay taxes (Schneider and Enste, 2000). In table 1, Alm and colleagues present a taxonomy of underground economic activities. It is shown that the shadow economy includes all economic activities that would generally be taxable when reported to the tax authorities (Alm, Martinez-Vazquez and Schneider, 2004; Schneider and Klinglmair, 2004). In estimating the size of the shadow economy, these activities – usually excluding do-it-yourself activities and the production of goods in private households for members' own use – are considered.

As shadow activities are hidden from law, it is difficult to assess their occurrence. Schneider (2003) summarises direct and indirect methods and modelling approaches for assessing the shadow economy. (a) Direct methods are either interview and questionnaire techniques asking people to report on their economic activities, or audits by tax authorities, and extrapolations of detected evasion to the national economy. It is unlikely that direct assessment methods detect all shadow activities. Therefore, estimations by direct methods should be considered as lower bound estimates. (b) Indirect methods are based on the discrepancy between income and expenditures. National accounts of income measures should yield results equivalent to expenditure measures. The gap between income and expenditure indices can be used as an indicator of the size of the shadow economy. Another indirect approach is based on the discrepancy between the official and de facto labour force participation rate. Assuming that the total labour force participation remains constant, a decrease in official participation would indicate that people move into hidden economic activities. A frequently used indirect approach to assess the size of the shadow economy is the currency demand approach, which rests on the assumption that shadow activities are cash transactions. Increased demand for currency is taken as an indicator of increasing shadow activities. Another indirect method is the transaction approach, which assumes that there is a constant relation between the volume of transactions and official gross net product (GNP). The discrepancy between official GNP and nominal GNP, which is based on the value of total known transactions in the national economy, should indicate the size of shadow activities. An appealing method due to its easy application relates electricity consumption to GNP. It is assumed that an increase in electricity consumption is correlated with growth of overall, official and unofficial GNP. The difference between this proxy measure for the overall economy and estimates of official GNP indicates the amount of unofficial economic activities. While all listed methods have serious shortcomings in so far as they derive an index of shadow economy size from one single indicator, the (c) model approach considers multiple causes leading to and indicating the existence and growth of the shadow economy. Developed by Frey and Weck-Hannemann (1984), this approach uses structural equation models to estimate unobservable behaviour – shadow economic activities – on the basis of causes and indicators. Causes are, for instance, the burden of direct and indirect taxes, the burden of regulation by the state, citizens' attitudes towards taxes and tax morale. It is assumed that shadow economy activities are higher with higher actual and perceived tax burdens, more state regulation of economic activities and lower tax morale. Indicators of shadow economy activities are, for instance, the development of monetary (cash) transactions, and decreasing participation of workers in the formal sector.

Schneider and colleagues used various methods to estimate the size of the shadow economy all over the world (Alm, Martinez-Vazquez and Schneider, 2004; Schneider, 2003; Schneider and Klinglmair, 2004). Table 2 shows that the highest rates of hidden economic activities are estimated in developing and transitional countries. In Africa and in South America, 41% of economic activities are hidden. In European transitional countries, shadow activities amount to 38%. In Asia, the calculated amount is 26%. In OECD countries it reaches the lowest level of slightly less than 17%. The countries with lowest shadow economy activities are Switzerland, the United States and Austria, whereas Bolivia and Georgia lead the list with more than 66%.

Although some shadow economy activities result in positive outcomes, there is little doubt that the negative outcomes outweigh the positive ones. On the positive side, for instance, it must be acknowledged that activities carried out in the 'shadow economy', such as neighbourly help, would probably not be carried out if they were official jobs which involved paying taxes or forgoing social security. However, hidden economic activities produce wealth, and most of the income earned in the shadow economy flows back to the official economy. For Austria, it has been shown that 70% of income earned in the shadow economy returns in the official sector (Schneider, 2003). Bracewell-Milnes (1979) argues that a national economy may need to 'breathe through the holes in the tax law'. Nevertheless, the negative effects outweigh possible positive consequences: the massive losses of taxes and social security lead to reduced

Table 2: *Relative size of the shadow economy around the world in 2000 (percentage of GNP, 1999/2000) (Alm, Martinez-Vazquez and Schneider, 2004, p. 22; Schneider and Klinglmair, 2004, pp. 42–4)*

Continent	Shadow Economy 2000	Country	Shadow Economy 2000
Africa	41.0	1. Algeria	34.1
		2. Benin	45.2
		3. Botswana	33.4
		4. Burkina Faso	38.4
		5. Cameroon	32.8
		6. Egypt	35.1
		7. Ethiopia	40.3
		8. Ghana	38.4
		9. Ivory Coast	39.9
		10. Kenya	34.3
		11. Madagascar	39.6
		12. Malawi	40.3
		13. Mali	41.0
		14. Morocco	35.4
		15. Mozambique	35.8
		16. Niger	41.9
		17. Nigeria	57.9
		18. Senegal	43.2
		19. South Africa	28.4
		20. Tanzania	58.3
		21. Tunisia	38.4
		22. Uganda	43.1
		23. Zambia	48.9
		24. Zimbabwe	59.4
Asia	26.0	1. Bangladesh	35.6
		2. China	13.1
		3. Hong Kong, China	16.1
		4. India	23.1
		5. Indonesia	19.4
		6. Iran	18.4
		7. Israel	21.9
		8. Japan	11.3
		9. Jordan	19.4
		10. Korea, Republic	27.5
		11. Lebanon	34.1
		12. Malaysia	31.1
		13. Mongolia	18.4
		14. Nepal	38.4
		15. Pakistan	36.8
		16. Philippines	43.4
		17. Saudi Arabia	18.4

Table 2: (*cont.*)

Continent	Shadow Economy 2000	Country	Shadow Economy 2000
		18. Singapore	13.1
		19. Sri Lanka	44.6
		20. Syria	19.3
		21. Taiwan	19.6
		22. Thailand	52.6
		23. Turkey	32.1
		24. United Arab Emirates	26.4
		25. Vietnam	15.6
		26. Yemen	27.4
South America	41.0	1. Argentina	25.4
		2. Bolivia	67.1
		3. Brazil	39.8
		4. Chile	19.8
		5. Colombia	39.1
		6. Costa Rica	26.2
		7. Dominican Republic	32.1
		8. Ecuador	34.4
		9. Guatemala	51.5
		10. Honduras	49.6
		11. Jamaica	36.4
		12. Mexico	30.1
		13. Nicaragua	45.2
		14. Panama	64.1
		15. Peru	59.9
		16. Uruguay	51.1
		17. Venezuela	33.6
Europe Transformation Countries	38.0	1. Albania	33.4
		2. Armenia	46.3
		3. Azerbaijan	60.6
		4. Belarus	48.1
		5. Bosnia-Herzegovina	34.1
		6. Bulgaria	36.9
		7. Croatia	33.4
		8. Czech Republic	19.1
		9. Georgia	67.3
		10. Hungary	25.1
		11. Kazakhstan	43.2
		12. Kyrgyz Republic	39.8

Table 2: (*cont.*)

Continent	Shadow Economy 2000	Country	Shadow Economy 2000
		13. Latvia	39.9
		14. Lithuania	30.3
		15. Moldova	45.1
		16. Poland	27.6
		17. Romania	34.4
		18. Russian Federation	46.1
		19. Slovak Republic	18.9
		20. Slovenia	27.1
		21. Ukraine	52.2
		22. Uzbekistan	34.1
		23. Yugoslavia	29.1
OECD Countries	16.8	1. Australia	14.1
OECD Countries (European Countries only)	18.0	2. Austria	9.8
OECD Countries (Non-European Countries only)	13.0	3. Belgium	22.2
		4. Canada	16.0
		5. Denmark	18.0
		6. Germany	16.0
		7. Finland	18.1
		8. France	15.2
		9. Greece	28.7
		10. Ireland	15.9
		11. Italy	27.1
		12. Japan	11.2
		13. Netherlands	13.1
		14. New Zealand	12.8
		15. Norway	19.1
		16. Portugal	22.7
		17. Sweden	19.2
		18. Switzerland	8.6
		19. Spain	22.7
		20. United Kingdom	12.7
		21. USA	8.7

quantity and quality of public goods, and the fairness of the tax system is challenged in principle.

What are the principal causes of shadow economy work? According to Schneider and Klinglmair (2004), the official tax and social security contributions, as well as subjectively felt tax pressure, are among the most important causes for working outside the official economy. Sweden provides an example of high tax pressure and unintended effects of tax design, as during the 1970s and 1980s, the government imposed the industrialised world's most steeply progressive income tax schedule. The marginal tax wedges for some broad categories of employees reached 80% to 90%. The high pressure of taxes led to high levels of tax avoidance, as the tax system no longer redistributed income fairly, and thirty years of egalitarian tax policy came to a dead end (Agnell and Persson, 2000). Also, the increase of government regulations, expressed as laws and regulations, requirements for licences, etc., may be perceived as a reduction of individuals' freedom to engage in official economic activities, which can be circumvented by moving to underground activities. In 2002, Brosio, Cassone, and Ricciuti argued that shadow economy and tax non-compliance were also possible expressions of disagreement with state provision of public goods. The authors investigated tax evasion across Italian regions and found that in the poorer South tax evasion was significantly higher than in the richer North. The results were interpreted as poorer areas possibly preferring a combination of lower taxes and lower levels of public services. This may be especially true when income and wealth levels differ among the regions and the demand for publicly provided goods is correlated to these levels. Moreover, tax complexity, unclear understanding of tax law, the 'anonymity' of government and policy and the feeling of not being heard are causes for non-cooperative behaviour. Taking the example of Switzerland, with a high degree of direct democracy, Frey and Eichenberger (2002) and Kirchgässner, Feld and Savioz (1999) argue that the more extensive the political participation rights of citizens are, the more satisfied they are with their lives, and they show higher levels of cooperation with the community. Political participation is a means for governments to receive the citizens' mandate for their activities. Without support for political and economic principles and purposes, citizens' cooperation is likely to corrode. Besides causes located at the state level, societal and individual causes should be considered, such as perceptions of fairness and attitudes of cooperation towards the government and the society.

Data shows that the shadow economy has increased over time. In 1975, the shadow economy was estimated to amount to 5.75% in Germany, 2.04% in Austria, and 3.20% in Switzerland. Ten years later, the estimated sizes were 11.20%, 3.92%, and 4.60%, respectively. In 1995, the shadow economy reached 13.90%, 7.32%, and 6.89% of those countries' GNP. For the year 2003, Alm and colleagues, along with Schneider, have estimated shadow economy amounts reaching approximately 17% for Germany and 10% for Austria and Switzerland. The shadow economy is estimated to be most common in the construction sector, in which estimations for Germany reach 38%. In trade and commerce it is estimated to reach 17%, and the same amount in the service and entertainment sector (restaurants, hotels, etc.; Alm, Martinez-Vazquez and Schneider, 2004; Schneider, 2003).

Although shadow economy has increased over time, most people claim not to be involved. V. Braithwaite's research group asked over 1,000 Australian citizens whether they were or are supplying cash-in-hand work or services in the years 2000 and 2002 (V. Braithwaite *et al.*, 2003). The vast majority claimed not to be involved at either time (90.4%). Only 7.6% admitted that they had supplied labour either in 2000 or 2002, and the remaining 2.0% admitted to supplying labour in both years. These figures suggest that only a few people are in the shadow economy, and of those only a minority remains, while the others move in and out. Suppliers of cash economy labour admitted being more disengaged from the tax system and expressed a relative lack of commitment to the system. They expressed less concern, shame and remorse for tax evasion than non-participants. In short, tax morale was lower among cash economy workers.

2.3   Tax compliance versus non-compliance

2.3.1   *Definitions of tax compliance, avoidance and evasion*

Just as the shadow economy has increased in the past, tax evasion has also risen, creating a problem of growing concern. 'In the real world, people often do their best to evade or avoid taxes, and most governments fight a constant battle against these activities,' assert Balestrino and Galmarini (2003, p. 51). The authors exaggerate. As will be shown below, most taxpayers do not engage in income tax evasion. Nevertheless, tax compliance is less than perfect.

At this point the meaning of tax evasion or tax avoidance and tax compliance versus non-compliance should be clarified. Tax compliance is probably the most neutral term to describe taxpayers' willingness to pay their taxes. Non-compliance represents the most inclusive conceptualisation referring to failures to meet tax obligations whether or not those failures are intentional. The degree of compliance varies, however, and non-compliance does not necessarily imply the violation of law. James and Alley (2002) perceive the meaning of compliance as a continuum of definitions, which ranges from the narrow law enforcement approach to wider economic definitions and on to versions of taxpayer decisions to conform to the objectives of tax policy and cooperation with the society.

While at the one end of the continuum non-compliance is illegal, at the other end, non-compliance can conform to the law.

McBarnet (2001) distinguishes between different forms of compliance: (a) committed compliance is taxpayers' willingness to pay their taxes without complaints; (b) capitulative compliance refers to reluctantly giving in and paying taxes; whereas (c) creative compliance is defined as engagement to reduce taxes by taking advantage of possibilities to redefine income and deduct expenditures within the brackets of the law. This book draws an important distinction between taxpayers who voluntarily comply with the tax law and taxpayers who comply as a result of enforcement activities.

In most countries there is a legal distinction between tax avoidance and tax evasion. As Webley put it in 2004, tax avoidance is not illegal, as attempts are made to reduce tax liability by legal means, taking advantage of loopholes in the law and the 'creative designing' of one's own income and deductions. On the other hand, tax evasion is illegal, as it involves deliberately breaking the law in order to reduce the amount of taxes due. Evasion can involve acts of omission (e.g., failing to report certain assets) or commission (e.g., falsely reporting personal expenses as business expenses). Similarly, Elffers, Weigel and Hessing (1987) describe 'tax evasion behaviour' or 'tax cheating' as a deliberate act of non-compliance that results in the payment of less tax than actually owed whether or not the behaviour eventuates in subsequent conviction for tax fraud. Tax evasion excludes inadvertent non-compliance resulting from memory lapses, calculation errors, inadequate knowledge of tax laws, etc. With respect to income tax, evasion behaviour usually takes the form of deliberately under-reporting income or claiming unwarranted deductions. King and Sheffrin (2002) quote the US IRS Code, Section 7201: 'tax evasion occurs when an individual knowingly and wilfully fails to declare taxable income' (p. 505). Sandmo (2003) defines tax evasion as:

[a] violation of the law: When the taxpayer refrains from reporting income from labour or capital which is in principle taxable, he engages in an illegal activity that makes him liable to administrative or legal actions from the authorities. In evading taxes, he worries about the possibility of his actions being detected. Tax avoidance, on the other hand, is within the legal framework of the tax law. It consists in exploiting loopholes in the tax law in order to reduce one's tax liability ... In engaging in tax avoidance, the taxpayer has no reason to worry about possible detection. (p. 4)

However, he adds, many people may have difficulties in seeing the difference between tax evasion and tax avoidance from a moral perspective. He argues:

The house painter who does a bit of extra work in the black economy violates the law, while the wealthy investor who engages a tax lawyer to look for tax havens does not. From a moral point of view their behaviour may not seem to be all that different. Clearly, the borderline between what seems morally right and wrong does not always coincide with the border between what is legal and illegal. (p. 5)

Wolfgang Gassner (1983) at the Department of Austrian and International Tax Law, Economic University of Vienna, interprets Austrian tax law as distinguishing between tax avoidance, tax circumvention and evasion. In principle, taxpayers are not deterred from designing their income in order to pay the minimum taxes. The freedom to present one's income within the legal range in such a form that the least tax is to be paid is defined as tax avoidance, which results in tax savings. The principle of freedom of income presentation ends where taxes are circumvented, that is, where 'creativity' of designing taxes is against the spirit and purpose of the law. While tax circumvention will not be fined, taxpayers are obliged to modify their tax files and pay taxes. Tax evasion results if tax law is deliberately violated. Evasion implies conscious illegal tax reduction, which is liable to prosecution and fines, ranging from financial sanctions, which frequently can be up to double the evaded sum, to prison sentences.

   On James and Alley's continuum-concept, one pole would be defined as committed, voluntary compliance, followed by capitulative compliance or compliance due to threats and harassments. Then would follow creative compliance, which, in the case where taxable income is designed against the spirit and purpose of the law, would result in tax circumvention and tax flight, and end in deliberately illegal actions, defining the other pole of evasion. They propose to define compliance in terms of following both the letter and the spirit of the law (James and Alley, 2002).

2.3.2   Diffusion of income tax evasion

Quoting Porcano (1988), the US IRS, which has developed the Taxpayer Compliance Measurement Program, estimated 10–15% of underreported income in 1983. Five years later the tax gap was about 17% of true liability. Andreoni, Erard and Feinstein (1998) estimate that over 25% of all US taxpayers underpaid their taxes in 1988. In developed countries, tax evasion is estimated to reach 20% of the level of tax revenues, while in developing countries the percentages are even higher (Orviska and Hudson, 2002). These facts are even more impressive if absolute amounts of tax that have failed to be reported are presented, and if these reports are compared to the respective state's deficit. Collins and Plumlee (1991), for instance, calculate that non-reported income and tax loss equalled 40% of the United States' federal deficit in 1986.

Slemrod, Blumenthal and Christian (2001) explain that much of this gap refers to non-filers and estimates of undetected non-compliance. The detected rate of non-compliance is 7.3% but varies widely across types of gross income and deductions. In 1988, voluntary reporting was 99.5% for wages and salaries, but only 41.4% for self-employed income. Similar percentages were estimated in the following years. In 2002, King and Sheffrin reported that, according to the US IRS, 99% of wage income was correctly reported, but less than 70% of income from unincorporated businesses was correctly reported. At the end of the 1990s, estimated income tax losses in Germany amounted to 34% (Lang, Nöhrbass and Stahl, 1997).

The fraction of reported income varies with the size of income. Christian (1994) reports that taxpayers with audit-adjusted incomes over $100,000 in 1988 reported, on average, 96.6% of their true income to the US IRS. Those with incomes below $25,000 reported only 85.9%. Yitzhaki (1974) also comes to the conclusion that tax evasion declines with income growth. On the other hand, it was found that tax non-compliance increases with income (Anderhub et al., 2001; Clotfelter, 1983). In Germany, this results in an effective marginal tax rate 16% below the legislated rate for the highest income groups (Lang, Nöhrbass and Stahl, 1997). Vogel (1974) found that taxpayers who reported improvement of their economic status also reported participating in tax non-compliance and evasion more than those who reported deterioration in economic status. Generally, there is evidence that tax evasion declines with age and is more common among men than women. It varies also between occupations, with car dealers and store and restaurant owners evading the most, while those in finance, insurance and agriculture evade less. It varies also between salaried and self-employed workers (Andreoni, Erard and Feinstein, 1998).

Under-reporting reduces the tax revenues of the state, affects public provision of goods and services, undermines tax effects on fair income redistribution, corrodes feelings of fair treatment and creates disrespect for the law. Therefore, there is little doubt that non-compliance should be contained, and evasion, in particular, needs to be combated. It is, however, wrong to assume that the majority of people try to evade or avoid paying taxes. Long and Swingen (1991) write that some taxpayers are not predisposed to evade and do not search for ways to cheat. Survey studies and experiments on income tax behaviour show that honesty characterises a majority of participants (e.g., V. Braithwaite, 2003d; James and Alley, 2002; Kirchler et al., 2005). Elffers (2000) reports, 'the gloomy picture of massive tax evasion is a phantom'. Antonides and Robben found that 4.2% of participants in their study corrected their tax files to their disadvantage, whereas 23.8% corrected them to their advantage

(Antonides and Robben, 1995). Assuming that those negatively correcting their files made unintentional mistakes, and an equal percentage of those who positively corrected their files also did so undeliberately, then less than 20% were intending to cheat. On the basis of 1982 US IRS audit data, Alexander and Feinstein (1987; quoted in Erard and Feinstein, 1994a) report that approximately one-quarter of all taxpayers make accurate tax reports. According to their analysis, 13.5% overstate their taxes, presumably due to errors in completing tax returns. If the same percentage understates their taxes due to errors, then more than half of taxpayers tend to be honest. Similar results were obtained in analyses of 1988 data of the American Taxpayer Compliance Measurement Program, which led to the finding that middle-income earners understated tax in 60% of the cases, while 26% reported correctly, leaving 14% that overstated tax (Christian, 1994; quoted in Slemrod, Blumenthal and Christian, 2001). Assuming again that the latter were not cheating deliberately, and an equal percentage of those underreporting their income also did not intend to evade taxes, 54% of taxpayers intended to report honestly. Hessing, Elffers and Weigel (1988) estimate that more than two-thirds of taxpayers declare their income honestly. A survey in Sweden found that 14% of participants admitted not having declared some income, 7% admitted having made illegal deductions, 18% admitted having received 'black money', and 18% admitted having paid someone 'black money' (Wahlund, 1992). In a representative survey in Australia, more than 90% of participants were committed to the tax system in principle (V. Braithwaite, 2003a), and in a study by the Australian Taxation Office, less than 2% of non-business taxpayers were identified as high compliance risks (Niemirowski *et al.*, 2002).

The assumption that taxpayers are generally compliant is challenged by the wide use of tax preparers and studies contending that taxpayers generally demand aggressive advice (Duncan, LaRue and Reckers, 1989; Jackson, Milliron and Toy, 1988; Milliron, 1988). These studies were conducted from tax preparers' view, but investigations from taxpayers' perspectives reveal a different picture. The use of a tax practitioner does not seem primarily driven by the desire to avoid paying taxes, but by uncertainty about the tax law and the motivation to report correctly. Niemirowski and Wearing (2003) found a high level of agreement among taxpayers to the following statement: 'Because I do not want to make any mistakes, I use a tax professional to prepare my tax return,' and to similar statements. Sakurai and Braithwaite (2003) found that the idealised tax practitioner is a low-risk, no-fuss practitioner who is honest and risk averse. Some respondents found that engagement in cautious minimisation of tax was acceptable. However, tax practitioners assume that their clients demand aggressive tax planning. Yet, only a minority of the respondents in the study indicated a desire for creative, aggressive tax advice, while the majority of people prefer their tax practitioners to declare taxes correctly.

Studies by Collins, Milliron and Toy (1990) and Tan (1999) also found evidence that taxpayers aim for a practitioner who correctly prepares the tax return. Even if taxpayers are presented with an ambiguous tax situation in which their tax advisor provides aggressive or conservative advice, there is no preference for aggressive tax filing in general (Hite and McGill, 1992). Only about one-fifth of tax practitioners investigated in Australia agreed that their peers engage in unethical activities, although more than half of the practitioners participating in the survey agreed that there exist many opportunities for practitioners to engage in unethical activities (Marshall, Armstrong and Smith, 1998).

In 2001, Schmidt added a differential aspect to taxpayers' expectations by applying Kahneman and Tversky's (1979) prospect theory. Participants read a scenario in which they were involved in an ambiguous tax situation and had the opportunity to claim a deduction of business-related travel expenses, thus saving a certain amount of tax. If the tax preparer suggested claiming the deduction in a situation of tax prepayment with refunds due, the aggressive advice was followed less often compared with accepting the advice in a balance-due prepayment position. Tax practitioners believe their clients' primary motive is to have their taxes minimised while the majority of taxpaying clients believe that practitioners' primary responsibility is to prepare their tax returns accurately.

Hite and Hasseldine (2003) investigated tax preparers' aggressiveness by examining whether there are more audit adjustments and penalty assessments on tax returns with paid-preparer assistance than on tax returns without paid-preparer assistance. By comparing the frequency of adjustments on US IRS office audits, they found that there are significantly fewer tax adjustments on paid-preparer returns than on self-prepared returns.

The level of tax compliance generally appears to be quite high in most countries, regardless of the incentives to cheat, and much higher than expected by most economists relying on the rational choice model (e.g., James and Alley, 2002). This evidence seems to contradict the fact that the amount of US federal income tax evaded equals the US federal deficit (Porcano, 1988) as well as the assertion that shadow economy and tax evasion are of growing concern. We are left with seemingly contradictory findings on tax evasion: on the one hand, the amount of evaded tax and the size of the shadow economy have increased. On the other hand, most studies find that only a minority of taxpayers evades taxes; the majority complies. The interpretation favoured here is that, while the number of people evading is still small, the amount (or sum) of evaded tax is increasing, and corporate crime is alarming (Simpson, 2002). In other words, the few people evading evade higher amounts and corporations engaging in tax evasion and avoidance represent an increasing problem, while the quantity of people evading may remain constant. That being said, the absolute financial value of shadow work and tax avoidance is increasing at an alarming rate.

3   Social representations of taxes

> How is the state mirrored in citizens' minds? This is the question with which any investigation about the discipline that citizens exercise over their tax paying behaviour must start. Consciousness about the state leads to citizens' civic and tax 'sentiments' and to a fundamental attitude with regard to problems of 'their' state. (Schmölders, 1960, p. 38)

Tax laws are difficult to understand and are of little interest to the ordinary taxpayer. This attitude can result from the belief that taxes are to be paid, taxes are unavoidable as income is taxed at source, or that attempting to understand the law is not worth the frustration due to its complexity. For instance, Calderwood and Webley (1992) investigated hypothetical work reactions to a tax rate decrease or increase. The majority of respondents thought they would not change their workload at all, while one-third thought they might work more, independent of a decrease or increase, and less than 10% would reduce the amount of their work. The authors concluded that taxation is simply not salient in the daily lives of most people.

While taxes might not be a frequently disputed issue in day-to-day conversations, people do try to make sense of their contributions to the community when taxes are due or whenever government spending is contested or new taxes are introduced. Moreover, people discussing taxation issues evaluate fiscal policy, tax rates and the use of taxes for the provision of public goods, as well as the interaction between themselves as taxpayers and tax authorities. Eventually, motivation to comply or not to comply develops, and this shapes subsequent behaviour. Cullis and Lewis highlight the importance of subjective sense-making and the social construction of the taxation phenomena as guidelines for behaviour:

Talk about social constructionism is everywhere in the wind like pollen and rather than merely being fashionable the ideas are highly relevant to tax compliance. Economists tend to see (construct) tax evasion as a technical problem; social scientists (including psychologists) as a social problem. Following the social constructivist line the whole notion of tax compliance can be viewed as socially constructed by the principal actors. Tax 'enforcement' officers have beliefs about tax evaders, who they are, what they are like. Taxpayers (including evaders) likewise have notions about tax officers, their beliefs and how they will behave. None of these beliefs need to be 'true' in any 'objective' sense but if the players in the game believe them to be (and act as if they do) then the reality is constructed. It follows from this that any analysis must examine these constructions and that the rhetoric of 'rational economic man' is far from an abstract idea and can become instead the guide and map for dealing with everyday life and social problems. If we believe taxpayers are selfish utility maximisers, taxpayers will behave like selfish utility maximisers. If we believe taxpayers have a moral nature, a sense of obligation or civic duty, taxpayers will reveal this side of their nature. (Cullis and Lewis, 1997, p. 310)

When people discuss issues that are socially relevant (e.g., religion and science topics, environment protection, economic issues or taxes in particular), they are not usually experts in the field, but rather exchange lay knowledge, trying to understand and evaluate the issue at stake. An example of a 'phenomenon' that was unfamiliar but relevant for people was the introduction of the Euro in twelve countries of the European Union, first as book money in 1999, and, 1 January 2002, as cash. Despite most people's limited knowledge, they engaged in hot disputes about the single currency, trying to understand and evaluate the new money. They were engaged in building a concept able to be understood by themselves and others, which enables social communication and behaviour (el Sehity, Kirchler and Muehlbacher, 2003; Meier and Kirchler, 1998).

Serge Moscovici (1961, 2001) termed the concepts which are constructed in social interaction 'social representations' and developed a theory that describes and explains processes which lead from unfamiliar phenomena to familiar concepts. His 'théorie des représentations socials', based on Durkheim's (1976 [1898]) work on 'représentations collectives', offers explanations in terms of a series of social phenomena, such as attitudes, values and norms, stereotypes and attributions, and myths and ideologies. Although individuals are the holders of social representations, it is important to highlight that social representations emphasise the shared social construction process rather than individual cognitive processes.

The main function of social representations is to create a homogeneous, familiar environment for everyday discourse. Unknown contents need to be disclosed, sense has to be made, and they need to be integrated in the field of socially shared and individual knowledge and evaluations. To fulfil this function, social representations are created (Abric, 1984). The structure of social representations is organised by elements forming the nucleus and elements forming the periphery. The nucleus defines the relevance and particularity of a representation. It is the main content-base in everyday discussions. Peripheral elements are positioned at the border of a representation and function as links to other concepts. The periphery protects the nucleus of a representation, while, at the same time, taking a mediating position if representations in general change, allowing for the adaptation of a specific concept to the ever-changing knowledge and evaluations of individuals and the society.

Whenever unfamiliar contents enter everyday discourse, these contents are confronted with the existing stock of representations. New contents are compared with the existing knowledge and integrated. The cognitive processes that achieve integration are the anchoring and objectivation processes. Anchoring controls ordering processes. Representations that are stored in memory are scrutinised with the aim to classify the new contents on the base of already existing categories and to name these new contents. For instance, when psychoanalysis became a phenomenon discussed in society, an already existing representation with which to compare the new contents might have been the Christian institution of confession. In the linking of psychoanalytic techniques with the representation of confession, both concepts underwent a dynamic process of adaptation. Tax audits may be linked to a judicial hearing with the risk of condemnation, or to socialisation and learning at school with the associations of detection of failures and teaching improvement.

Objectivation, on the other hand, defines the process of visualising a concept. Unknown contents are by definition in the abstract and lack an intuitive 'picture', and are, thus, difficult to understand and communicate. While anchoring creates a context in which to place the new contents, objectivation leads from the abstract content to a concrete representation. It transforms the abstract content to a 'figurative' object. For instance, the Christian objectivation of God resulted in the picture of a father; the psychoanalyst became the modern priest. Tax auditors may be perceived as 'cops' searching for the 'robbers' who are to be prosecuted and punished, while the interaction between taxpayers and tax authorities may result in the analogy of 'cat and mouse games' or in more benevolent teacher–pupil, supervisor–student relationships. Concepts described in such figurative language show the result of objectivation.

In this book, the concept of social representations serves as a frame to integrate a manifold of variables discussed in the literature as determinants of tax compliance. At a societal level, these determinants are ethics and values, social norms and tax morale, defined as intrinsic motivation to comply, as well as a sense of civic duty (Frey, 1997). Also, cultural aspects are discussed, mainly in studies comparing tax non-compliance across countries (e.g., Alm and Torgler, 2006; Torgler and Schneider, 2004). At an individual level, subjective knowledge and perceptions of taxes and tax non-compliance are part of social representations, as well as attitudes and behaviour intentions. Attitudes, binding norms, and the control over one's own behaviour in terms of opportunities to comply or not to comply can be discussed in the language of Fishbein and Ajzen's theory of reasoned action and theory of planned behaviour (Ajzen, 1991; Fishbein and Ajzen, 1975). In developing these theories, attitudes towards the government were measured, such as trust in the government and in government spending. More specifically, attitudes were measured towards non-compliance, overstating expenditures and non-filing of income. Findings revealed that an important variable determining compliance is fairness perceptions. Closely related to behaviour intentions, motivational postures (V. Braithwaite, 2003a) are also integrated in this section. Overall, the concept of social representations is closely related to what Schmölders (1960) defined as tax morale, integrating knowledge about taxes, socially shared concepts, evaluations, norms and opportunities to comply or not to comply, fairness considerations, and the motivation to pay one's taxes. While motivational postures are perceived to steer individual tax behaviour, tax morale is perceived to operate at the aggregate collective level.

In the following section, research findings regarding social representations are reviewed; that is, findings regarding subjective knowledge are discussed first, followed by thoughts and concepts about taxes. In the frame of the theory of planned behaviour, attitudes, personal, social and societal norms and perceived opportunity to avoid taxes are discussed. The section on social representations continues with a discussion of fairness issues, and ends with reference to tax morale, the motivation to comply and, as a sense of civic duty, to cooperate at the aggregate, societal level.

3.1   Subjective knowledge and mental concepts

3.1.1   Subjective knowledge

The tax literature studying subjective tax knowledge is poor, although it can be assumed that people's knowledge and concepts of taxation form the basis of their judgments, evaluations, perceptions of fairness and willingness and ability to comply with the law. Subjective tax knowledge – i.e., ordinary people's understanding of taxation – is important in understanding why people behave as they do. When taken as part of social representations, subjective understanding does not focus on whether the knowledge is correct with regard to existing laws and administration of laws, but focuses instead on what knowledge people have and how this knowledge is organised to form a meaningful representation (Moscovici, 2001).

Many people do not feel competent with regard to taxes. Indeed, it is in this arena of economic understanding, writes Furnham (2005), that young people seem most ignorant. The adult population also lacks understanding (e.g., McKerchar, 1995). Sakurai and Braithwaite (2003) surveyed more than 2,000 Australian taxpayers and found that a relatively small percentage of respondents described themselves as fully competent: 36% denied fully the statement 'I feel competent to do my own income tax return', 26.3% indicated feeling a little competent, 24.9% a fair bit, 12.4% very much. It is not surprising that more than three-quarters rely on tax agents, 6.5% on tax office staff, and one-fifth on other people such as family members or friends (Sakurai and Braithwaite, 2003). According to research by Blumenthal and Christian (2004), the use of tax preparers by individual income taxpayers grew by 26.4% over the past decade, compared to an overall growth of 13.7% in the number of returns filed. Close to 60% of the 128 million individual US income tax returns in 2001 were signed by a preparer. Moreover, tax decision support systems have been developed to help individual taxpayers file their taxes as well as aid tax practitioners who face increasing intricacy and need advice by computer programs (Noga and Arnold, 2002).

People blame the complexity of the tax law for their feelings of tax incompetence and lose interest in the system (McKerchar, 2001). Lewis (1982) found that for most people, fiscal policy is not an important issue. Similar results are reported by Schmölders (1960) in a survey on policy and public finances carried out at the Cologne Research Institute for Economic Behaviour in the 1950s. Approximately two-thirds of the respondents indicated they would hardly ever talk about politics because they did not have time or did not understand much about it (22%), or indicated that it made no sense because of limited influence (14%), or they had had bad experiences talking about politics at home or in public. More than half of the respondents thought they could not do anything if they were dissatisfied with the government, fiscal policy or taxation; an after-thought of resignation.

Governments are aware of problems associated with the complexity of tax law both for tax authorities and ordinary taxpayers, and are investing considerable energy to simplify the laws and bolster public support for the proposed changes. Public opinion polls and surveys are used to gain insight into citizens' preferences and acceptance levels, discussing topics such as the advantages and disadvantages of flat tax rates as opposed to progressive tax rates and the related issue of fairness (e.g., Lenartova, 2003; see discussions in most European countries, particularly in Germany in the run-up to the elections in 2005: Grimm, 2005). However, Roberts, Hite and Bradley (1994) convincingly demonstrated how problematic results of opinion polls can be if respondents do not have a thorough understanding of the concepts. They examined the knowledge on progressive taxation by comparing participants' choices of fair tax rate structures in response to questions framed in both abstract and concrete terms. Participants were presented with either abstract or concrete questions asking their opinions about differences in types of income tax rates of the following format (p. 187; answering scales ranging from 1, 'much less fair', to 9, 'much more fair'). Examples of abstract questions were the following:

(a) Are progressive tax rates (where the tax rate increases as income increases) more or less fair than flat tax rates (where the tax rate is the same for all income levels?)

(b) Are progressive tax rates more or less fair than regressive tax rates (where the tax rate decreases as income increases)?

Examples of concrete questions (p. 187; answering scales ranging from 1, 'the same', to 9, 'five times') were the following:

(c) Andy and Bob are the same age. Andy has taxable income of $40,000 per year. Bob has taxable income of $20,000 per year. In terms of fairness, how much more income tax do you think Andy should pay than Bob?

(d) Frank had taxable income of $16,000 last year. This year Frank has changed jobs, and his taxable income has increased to $24,000. In terms of fairness, how much more income tax do you think Frank should pay this year as compared to last year?

In the surveys of the general public using abstract questions, Roberts and his colleagues found that a majority of participants preferred progressive taxation. More than 75% preferred progressive tax rates when progressive rates were compared both to flat taxes and to regressive taxes (items (a) and (b)). This preference, however, was reversed in the situation with concrete questions, where participants favoured flat tax, that is, proportional tax rates to income. As regards item (c), only 12% assigned progressive taxes to the higher income of Andy, while a majority of 61% found it fair if Andy paid twice as much as Bob; 27% preferred a regressive tax by indicating that Andy should pay more than Bob but less than twice as much. Answers to item (d) were similar: only 18% selected progressive tax rates, while the majority of two-thirds favoured a proportional tax rate. This preference reversal is hypothesised to be associated with participants' lack of understanding of progressive taxation.

A majority of participants interpreted a tax rate as progressive when a higher-income taxpayer paid a higher amount of money than a lower-income taxpayer, but not a higher percentage of the income. Similar results of preference reversals are reported in studies by McCaffery and Baron (2003, 2004). However, in Sweden, Edlund (2003) found that, irrespective of whether abstract or concrete measures were applied, progressive taxation was favoured.

Low understanding of flat tax and progressive tax was also confirmed in a study on New Zealanders' preference concerning a fair tax structure. Although Kemp (2004) presented detailed explanations of flat, progressive and regressive tax, respondents' preferences for flat and progressive tax, suitable for the provision of various services, varied substantially. Many responses were given at the mid-point in the answering scales, indicating unpronounced preferences and indecision, probably due to lack of knowledge, in indicating a clear preference. Seidl and Traub (2001, 2002) found, in a German sample, that respondents' preferences for different forms of taxes are inconsistent. However, in general, flat-rate taxation and lump-sum taxes à la Margaret Thatcher did not enjoy much support.

Since tax laws are criticised for being too complex to be fully understood by ordinary taxpayers, it can be expected that knowledge about taxes is generally low. People in Great Britain were asked what they think the income tax rates are for people in income brackets ranging from £0 to £6,000, from £6,001 to £7,000, etc, to income over £21,000, and what they consider as fair tax rates (Lewis, 1978). The results showed that mean estimates are inaccurate to the extent that they are about 11% below the actual marginal tax rates at that time. Additionally, people thought fair rates would be about 27% lower than what they estimated the marginal tax rates were, which, in turn, was about 35% lower than the actual rate. These differences varied little from one income bracket to another. People with income below £6,000 were significantly more accurate in assessing the rates of the lower income brackets. Also, 50–65-year-old respondents were significantly more accurate in their estimates. It is also interesting to note that 65% of the respondents thought that people with higher incomes should pay a larger proportion of their earned income in tax than those with lower incomes paid. Thus, 65% of the respondents were expressing a preference for progressive tax rates; 31% were for the same proportion as those lower paid, and 3% favoured a smaller proportion. Wealthier respondents advocated greater reductions for themselves than did people with lower incomes as they had a more accurate appreciation of the rates they actually paid. The estimates given by people of different political party affiliation did not differ within any single income bracket; and overall Conservative and Liberal supporters advocated much greater tax reductions than did Labour supporters and those politically uncommitted. Older people considered fair rates to be lower than younger people, and a comparison between their estimates and preferences revealed that this group advocated the greatest overall reductions in tax.

In one of the earliest surveys on subjective concepts and evaluations of taxes, Schmölders (1960) found German citizens had vague knowledge about taxes. Although the majority had an approximate understanding of their income tax (however, they exaggerated their tax burden), they only made vague guesses about the overall taxes they paid in their household. Dornstein (1987) attempted to examine perceptions and attitudes regarding taxes and the tax system in Israel. The research focused on tax consciousness of income taxes, property taxes, taxes on goods and services, capital gains taxes, etc., satisfaction with the fiscal system and specific taxes within it, as well as perceptions of equitability of the tax system. The issues investigated were found to be much more complex than assumed in the prevalent literature. Tax consciousness is not simply a result of the technicalities of tax collection as is often assumed. Satisfaction with taxes – which was low, as only 28% of the participants were satisfied with the tax system – is not so much affected by their visibility or by their level of equitability as it is by social factors; also perceptions of equitability are affected by social factors rather than by objective equitability.

Poor understanding or misunderstanding breeds distrust. It is usually assumed that higher tax knowledge is correlated with compliance. Several studies used education as a proxy for knowledge and assumed that knowledge about taxation increases with the length of education (Kinsey and Grasmick, 1993; Song and Yarbrough, 1978; Spicer and Lundstedt, 1976; Vogel, 1974). In Schmölders's (1960) influential study on tax morale in Germany, he reports that agreement with governmental activities and fiscal policy was higher in higher-educated groups. While 75% of respondents with a secondary school diploma agreed with actual policy and evaluated the 'state' positively, 58% of respondents with a primary school diploma did so. He argues that knowing more about policy goes with better understanding the aims of governmental strategies and higher approval. Generally, it was found that higher education is positively associated with compliance. This approach, however, has serious shortcomings as it does not consider the content of education, rather assuming that higher education goes hand-in-hand with better knowledge of tax issues.

The assumption of a positive relationship between tax knowledge and subjective understanding and tax attitudes has received support in a survey in Australia (Niemirowski *et al.*, 2002) in which subjective evaluation of tax knowledge was significantly linked to tax-related values, attitudes towards compliance and behavioural intentions. The positive effect of reduced complexity and higher knowledge was found in several studies in various countries (Clotfelter, 1983; Groenland and van Veldhoven, 1983; Kirchler and Maciejovsky, 2001; Park and Hyun, 2003; Wahlund, 1992; Wärneryd and Walerud, 1982). It is acknowledged in the tax evasion model proposed by Weigel, Hessing and Elffers (1987; see also Webley *et al.*, 1991). Moreover, O'Donnell, Koch and Boone (2005) found that tax preparers favour less aggressive recommendations if they have high procedural knowledge in dealing with complex tax tasks.

A study by Carnes and Cuccia (1996) found complexity perceptions to be negatively and significantly related to equity perceptions. In an experiment participants were assessing the equity of a potential tax provision under the conditions of either low or high compliance complexity, tax authorities' pressure to increase revenues by either eliminating exemptions or doubling the amount for all taxpayers, and justifications for the complexity or no justifications. In this experiment, Carnes and Cuccia (1996) found that complexity negatively affects equity assessments. This was, however, only the case when no explicit justifications for complexity were provided. In 2003, Kirchler, Maciejovsky and Schneider assessed tax knowledge of fiscal officers, students of economics and business administration, business lawyers and entrepreneurs using a ten-question multiple-choice test, and correlated subjects' knowledge with fairness judgments of tax avoidance, tax evasion and tax flight. Unsurprisingly, fiscal officers scored highest on the knowledge test, followed by business students, and business lawyers. Entrepreneurs achieved the poorest results. Tax knowledge was correlated neither with the perceived fairness of tax evasion nor with the perceived fairness of tax avoidance. However, for business lawyers and entrepreneurs it was found that profound tax knowledge is positively correlated with perceived fairness of tax avoidance, indicating that the better the knowledge, the fairer tax avoidance was perceived. For the sub-sample of fiscal officers, on the other hand, it could be shown that tax knowledge is negatively correlated with perceived fairness of tax evasion, indicating that the higher the knowledge about taxes, the less likely officers were to consider evasion fair.

Eriksen and Fallan (1996) examined the connection between attitudes towards taxation and specific tax knowledge, which combines information about tax rules and the financial knowledge necessary to calculate economic consequences. Their question was whether increased knowledge would lead to more favourable attitudes. They tested two student groups on their tax knowledge and their attitudes towards taxes and tax evasion both before and after taking a class in either marketing or tax law. While tax law knowledge of students in the marketing course remained invariant, those students taking the tax course had increased knowledge. Moreover, attitudes towards tax evasion had become stricter after knowledge was gained in the course on tax law. Specific tax knowledge improved tax ethics and, in turn, increased tax compliance and reduced the propensity for tax evasion. A related study reports the importance of gender differences in tax attitudes after improving tax knowledge (Fallan, 1999). The author argued that male students were more exposed to tax knowledge in a way that made them reconsider their own attitudes towards tax evasion, i.e., tax ethics, than are their female peers. In other words, male students developed stricter attitudes toward their own tax evasion. However, female students were more exposed to tax knowledge in a way that made them reconsider their attitudes towards other people's tax evasion than are their male peers. As a consequence, women developed a stricter attitude towards others' tax evasion. Improved tax knowledge significantly changed both male and female students' attitudes towards the fairness of the tax system. After increasing their tax knowledge, they considered the tax system to be fairer than they did before. Similar results are reported by Grasso and Kaplan (1998) who found that students who completed an introductory tax course had higher ethical standards for issues involving tax than professionals and students exposed to a general course on ethics. Also, females had higher ethical standards regarding tax compliance than did males.

So far, little doubt has emerged regarding the positive relationship between tax knowledge and compliance. It could, however, be argued that lack of knowledge leads to uncertainty and people might be less inclined to take risks in situations of uncertainty. In view of the standard economic assumption that frequent audits and serious sanctions lead to increased taxpayer compliance, it could be argued that taxpayer uncertainty about these enforcement prescriptions could lead to increased honest behaviour. Indeed, Beck, Davis and Jung (1991) found that income uncertainty can increase reported income. The effect of uncertainty was, however, related to penalty rates and audit rates. A reduction in uncertainty led to higher levels of reported taxable income when penalty rates or audit probabilities were decreased. On the other hand, a reduction in uncertainty led to lower levels of reported income when penalty rates or audit probabilities were increased. Snow and Warren (2005) showed that an increase in taxpayer uncertainty about the amount of tax evasion that would be detected if an audit was undertaken increased compliance for prudent taxpayers. In a laboratory experiment, Alm, Jackson and McKee (1992a) endowed participants with an income of

Table 3: *Average compliance rates depending on uncertainty about fines, taxes and detections probability, and provision of public goods (Alm, Jackson and McKee, 1992a, p. 1,024)*

	Mean compliance rate	
Experimental session	No provision of public goods	Provision of public goods
Base case	.262	.557
Fine uncertainty	.374	.501
Tax uncertainty	.370	.398
Detection uncertainty	.481	.519

which only the individual knew the amount. Based on voluntary reporting, income taxes had to be paid. Fine rates were uncertain, as were tax rates and detection probability. Moreover, either public goods were provided on the base of paid taxes or no public goods were distributed. The authors found that there was substantial compliance that did not decay as the experimental periods proceeded, and there was generally more compliance if public goods were provided. Mixed results were found regarding uncertainty: if no public goods were received, uncertainty increased compliance. If, however, a public good was received in exchange for taxes, uncertainty lowered compliance (see table 3).

In a system with educated taxpayers who are confident in their knowledge and aware of the use of public finances, transparency is not only a question of fairness and consideration to taxpayers as mature citizens, but also a prerequisite of citizens' cooperation (Torgler, 2002). In a 1990 publication, Alm, Jackson and McKee provide evidence that tax compliance increases when taxpayers are aware of a direct link between their tax payments and the provision of desirable public goods. In their study, participants were either given the opportunity to vote for the use of the taxes for a specific public good, or the particular use of the taxes was imposed on participants without choice. Despite the fact that the public good was not distributed directly to the participants, tax compliance was significantly higher under the voting condition than under imposition. In a further experimental study (1993), Alm, Jackson and McKee found that individuals respond positively when tax proceeds are directed towards programmes they approve of, and when they feel they have a say in the decision process. In contrast, participants' compliance suffered when they had no control over the use of their tax payments. Feld and Tyran (2002) showed that allowing participants to vote on various aspects of the laboratory tax regime affects social norms and hence compliance. Fjeldstad (2004) reported that compliance was positively related to citizens' perception that the local government acts in their interest in addition to their level of trust in the government to use revenues to provide expected services, to establish fair procedures for revenue collection and for distribution of services. Pommerehne and Weck-Hannemann (1996) provided evidence that tax non-compliance was lower in Swiss cantons in which citizens had a direct say on budgetary policy. Not only was willingness to pay taxes higher, but so also was citizen satisfaction with the efficiency of the provision of public goods. Similar findings have been reported by Feld and Kirchgässner (2000), who concluded that, compared to purely representative states, direct democracy – i.e., citizens are directly involved in political decisions – leads to a different type of communication among citizens and between citizens and representatives. Citizens have more opportunities to collect information and are better informed, while politicians have less leeway to pursue their personal interest; furthermore, public expenditures and public debt are lower, and citizens feel more responsible for their community. Overall, tax evasion is lower in direct than in representative democratic systems (Kirchgässner, Feld and Savioz, 1999). The necessity of changing the approach to citizens by tax authorities and increasing efforts in taxpayers' literacy in order to increase voluntary compliance has also been recognised by the US IRS in its mission-based strategy outlined in the document Compliance 2000. Views of people interested in tax administration and organisational goals were collected, which James (1998) summarises into various categories. The following are related to knowledge of taxpayers and tax staff: (a) simplification and fairness; simplification is necessary because continuous changes and complexity in tax law have a negative effect on compliance; (b) training, including customer service training and cross-function training of employees guaranteeing an understanding of the entire tax administration; (c) taxpayer service and education. In sum, simplification, fairness, education and training as well as adequate service appear to be essential means for improving knowledge and compliance.

3.1.2   Subjective concepts of taxation

> Fynantzer = Landbetrieger, der die Leute umbs Geld bescheisset
> [Tax inspector = Impostor who screws people for their money]
> (Basilius Faber, *Thesaurus eruditionis scholasticae* (1680))

People's attitudes, judgments and behaviour intentions are more affected by what they think than what actually is (Lewis, 1978). Since tax laws are criticised as being much too complex to be fully understood by ordinary taxpayers, and knowledge about taxes is generally limited, representations and evaluations of taxes are mainly a product of myth and misperceptions.

To some extent, people's myths – or social representations – regarding taxes are mirrored in the terms used. The term 'finances', in Latin, initially meant fines determined by a court and subsequently used for money transfers. In German, it had the negative connotation of usury, cheat and fraud. In the 1680 *Thesaurus eruditionis scholasticae* by Basilius Faber, tax collectors ('Fynantzer') were described as deceivers or impostors who sought to cheat people out of their money (Schmölders, 1960). According to Schmölders, citizens' trust and distrust of tax collectors were mirrored in the semantics of tax terminology:

> Whereas, in the Latin world, the word tax means something felt as an 'impostation' upon the citizen (impot, imposto, impuesto), the German word 'Steuer' means 'support' and the Scandinavian 'skat' the common treasure put aside for common purposes. On the basis of such different tax mentalities, closely connected with the citizens' civic or community-mindedness in general, individual tax-mindedness develops by personal experiences. Confronted with the obligation to pay, the taxpayer feels inclined to a certain degree of resistance, leading to evasion, tax-dodging, or even to open revolt.(Schmölders, 1970b, pp. 301–2)

Webley *et al.* (1991) added to these linguistic analyses in looking at the Dutch term 'belasting', meaning tax, but also carrying the connotation of a burden, a meaning also inherent to the terms 'impot', 'imposto', 'impuesto' which cognate with the English 'imposition'. They emphasise, however, that while the linguistic analyses might reveal some interesting differences between countries, their explanatory power beyond this is limited.

Yet, the linguistic connotation of 'burden' manifests itself in citizens' perceptions, as most would prefer a reduction of taxes. In Schmölders's 1960 survey, 86% of respondents in the highest income brackets pleaded for a reduction of taxes, and 75% of earners with very low income favoured tax reductions, but simultaneously supported higher welfare expenditures. Tyszka (1994) reports similar results in a study on French and Polish students' preferences regarding public finances, tax policy and welfare programmes. Both groups favoured tax reductions while at the same time asking for higher welfare expenditures. People were reluctant to pay higher taxes but appreciated public goods (e.g., Kirchler, 1997a; Van de Braak, 1983; Williamson and Wearing, 1996). Reluctance is especially high when new taxes are introduced. Even if citizens are not burdened by new taxes and would benefit from public goods financed by the higher internal revenues, they are against them. In the 1990s, the Austrian finance minister discussed taxation of the double monthly income received by Austrian employees twice a year, usually around June and December, which at the time was tax-free. Since the plan included taxation only of incomes significantly above the average income, most employees would not have felt the tax, yet would have benefited from higher state revenues and the provision of respective public goods. Rational analyses of losses and gains would, thus, have led to a profit and the majority of citizens should have opted for the new tax. Nevertheless, emotions were strongly against the plan even in the group of the non-affected. The resistance in the population led to hot disputes, culminating not only in the plan to tax the extra income of two monthly salaries being abolished, but more strikingly in the minister having to leave office (Kirchler, 1997b).

What, then, are taxpayers' ideas about taxes? Schmölders (1960) asked German citizens: 'What comes to your mind when you hear the word "taxes"?' The use of free associations to study tax mentality was an early approach to uncover social representations. The method was based on the assumption that associations which came spontaneously to people's minds would display the nucleus of their representations, which is in perfect accordance with the actual theory of social representations (e.g., Abric, 1984). Table 4 displays the aggregated results of Schmölders' (1960) study for the total sample and separately for blue-collar workers, white-collar workers, civil servants, the self-employed, farmers and retired people. While about 10% of respondents had no associations at all when they thought about 'taxes', one-third of associations were on technical concepts, such as tax laws, tax office, dates of taxes due, etc. Negative associations were observed in 29% of the cases, mainly negative feelings and claims regarding too many taxes and high tax burden. Interestingly, the most negative associations were observed in the group of self-employed (41%), while civil servants complained the least (23%). Further analyses revealed that 83% of the self-employed thought the actual tax rate was too high, while approximately 70% of blue-collar workers, white-collar workers and farmers did so. Only 63% of civil servants thought so. Almost none of the participants thought taxes should be higher (0–2%), while approximately 30%, except the self-employed, found the actual tax rate acceptable.

Differential representations of taxes were also found in more recent studies in Austria (Kirchler, 1998) and Italy (Berti and Kirchler, 2001). These studies focused on representations about taxation and differences between taxpayer groups. It was hypothesised that different groups of citizens hold distinct cognitive representations and feel differently about

Table 4: *Percentages of free associations to the stimulus word 'taxes'*
(Schmölders, 1960, p. 77)

Associations to 'taxes'	Total	Blue-collar workers	White-collar workers	Civil servants	Self-employed	Farmers	Retired people
Technical termini (e.g., tax office, types of taxes, tax law)	39	43	39	42	27	33	31
Negative aspects	29	30	31	23	41	35	26
– *unpleasant feelings*	*13*	*13*	*15*	*10*	*18*	*14*	*10*
– *too many, too high taxes*	*8*	*9*	*9*	*6*	*10*	*8*	*7*
– *'bad' tax office*	*3*	*3*	*2*	*2*	*5*	*9*	*4*
– *aggressive expressions*	*2*	*2*	*2*	*2*	*5*	*1*	*2*
– *refusal of use of taxes*	*2*	*2*	*2*	*2*	*2*	*2*	*1*
– *getting angry*	*1*	*1*	*1*	*1*	*1*	*1*	*2*
Necessity, necessary evil	23	18	23	28	26	22	28
No responses	9	9	7	7	6	10	15

taxes. While most people recognise the need for contributing to the public budget and are aware of public goods, their feelings towards taxes are often negative. Taxes are perceived either as a loss of personal freedom to decide how to invest one's own money, as contributions without a fair return, or as a repeated request by the government to fill the gaps in the state's finances caused by inefficient management by politicians. Loss, or perceived loss, of freedom are frequently responded to by reactance and the attempt to re-establish the control one has lost (Brehm, 1966; Pelzmann, 1985). Reactance and non-compliance are hypothesised to be more likely to occur if people receive their entire gross income in cash and pay taxes directly out of their pockets (as opposed to taxes being withheld). Entrepreneurs who run their own businesses or self-employed people who want to re-invest their profit may perceive taxes both as a loss of personal freedom to make choices about their finances and as a considerable loss of their own money. In the framework of prospect theory, the self-employed may therefore perceive evasion as a risky prospect in the loss domain (Kahneman and Tversky, 1979; Schepanski and Shearer, 1995).

Hence, it can be expected that self-employed people are more likely to take the risk of tax evasion and develop stronger anti-tax sentiments than employees. Anti-tax sentiments may be both the consequence of a perceived loss of money and a means to justify non-compliance.

Employees who receive only their monthly net income in cash and are aware of their gross salary and taxes only 'on paper' may be less aware of their tax payments and may consider taxes to be less of a concrete loss of their own money. Employees may conceive of contributions to the state and access to public benefits as an exchange relationship between individuals and the government. Since taxation is a means of achieving a more equal income distribution, wealthier people may perceive their contributions and benefits not to be in balance, whereas the poorer citizens should perceive exchanges to be either in their favour or in balance. White-collar workers and civil servants may think of taxes in terms of exchanges. Their arguments against taxes are hypothesised to be related to fairness and reciprocity rules.

Independent of the accuracy of such evaluations, there is a trend in many countries to blame the government for inefficient spending of taxpayers' money. Also, various scandals reported and vividly discussed in the media are often used as arguments proving that politicians are mostly interested in personal advantages rather than those for the society. Besides reactance motives and lack of fairness, individuals may blame individual politicians and governmental institutions as either incompetent decision-makers or selfish representatives rather than community-oriented political leaders.

In a study by Kirchler (1998), 171 blue-collar workers, white-collar workers, civil servants, entrepreneurs and students were asked to indicate their thoughts and feelings towards taxes and tax evaders, which produced 1,003 associations that resulted in 547 different words. The different associations were categorised, and frequencies of categories mentioned by the five employment groups were analysed using correspondence analysis, which yielded a three-dimensional space of representations, depicted in figure 3. The first dimension distinguishes between blue-collar workers and the other employment groups. The second factor separates students and entrepreneurs from white-collar workers and civil servants, and the third factor groups together entrepreneurs and civil servants on the one hand, and white-collar workers and students on the other hand. The results show that entrepreneurs think of punishment and disincentive to work, public constraint, a lack of clarity in tax law and public use of taxes, and complex bureaucratic rules. Entrepreneurs perceive taxes as a form of pressure and a hindrance to work. Moreover, they claim that bureaucratic laws and rules are too

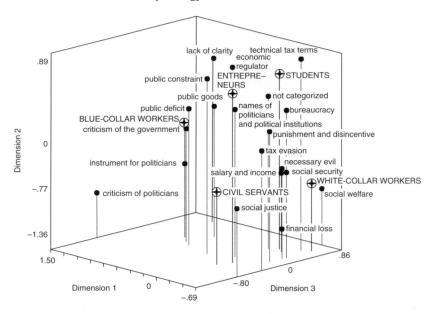

Figure 3: Semantic space of associations to 'taxes' by entrepreneurs, blue-
and white-collar workers, civil servants and students (Kirchler, 1998)

complex and that fiscal policy is unclear. Blue-collar workers most frequently criticise the government and politicians in general, claiming that
they use taxes strategically to achieve their own selfish goals and are
responsible for the huge public deficit. However, blue-collar workers
are also aware of public goods that are provided through public investments of money. White-collar workers mention that social security and
social welfare are guaranteed by taxes. They also call taxes a necessary evil
that has an effect on income and signifies a financial loss. Civil servants
indicate the usefulness of taxes in redistributing wealth and achieving
greater social justice; taxes also have a negative connotation for them
because non-cooperative people try to avoid and evade taxes and benefit
both from their individual gain by withholding their contributions and
from their access to public goods. Finally, students, the group with least
experience in paying taxes, think of theories and technical concepts,
mention names of politicians and sometimes the names of famous figures
from fiction and comics. The results are describable on the basis of
reactance theory and exchange theories: entrepreneurs appear to perceive
taxes as a loss of freedom, mentioning punishment for their work or
hindrance to work or force and constraint. Blue-collar workers, white-
collar workers, and civil servants may have exchange relationships in

Please, put yourself in the following situation:
Mr. Paul K. is owner of a successful travel agency.
Last month he has earned an extra income in the amount of 75,000 ATS for organising a
     special event.
Mr. Paul K. considers making use of legal tax loopholes in order to reduce his tax
     payments.
[Mr. Paul K. considers not declaring his extra income in his income declaration.]
[Mr. Paul K. considers relocating his headquarters to another country in order to reduce
     the tax burden in the future.]

Note: The expression in the third paragraph without parentheses describes tax avoidance;
the expressions in parentheses describe tax evasion and tax flight.

Figure 4: Scenario about tax avoidance, tax evasion and tax flight
(Kirchler, Maciejovsky and Schneider, 2003)

mind when mentioning public goods, welfare, social security and justice.
Students, on the other hand, who are not affected directly by tax payments, tend to give the most abstract answers.

A further study on representations focused on tax avoidance, tax evasion and tax flight (Kirchler, Maciejovsky and Schneider, 2003). From a
macro-economic perspective, and apart from legal considerations, tax
avoidance, tax evasion and tax flight have similar negative effects on the
national budget. Hence, economists favour analysing their effects jointly,
no longer discriminating between them (e.g., Cross and Shaw, 1982).
However, from a psychological perspective, taxpayers perceive tax avoidance, tax evasion and tax flight differently due to legal differences and
moral considerations (Etzioni, 1988). Despite identical economic consequences, people have an appreciation of the difference between legal
and illegal behaviour. In Kirchler, Maciejovsky and Schneider's (2003)
investigation into social representations of tax avoidance, tax flight and
tax evasion, fiscal officers, students of economics and business administration specialising in auditing and accounting, business lawyers and
entrepreneurs were asked to produce free associations and evaluations of
the three concepts. Figure 4 presents the descriptions of the behaviours
that were used to elicit associations.

Participants produced 880 associations overall; 507 of them were
different words. Participants clearly distinguished between tax avoidance, tax evasion, and tax flight in their spontaneous associations,
which shows that they have different concepts of each. Tax avoidance
was associated with legal acts, with an intention to save taxes, with cleverness, and was considered a good idea and also associated with taxes as
costs. Tax evasion, on the other hand, was associated with illegal aspects,
fraud, criminal prosecution, risk, tax-audit, punishment, penalty and the

risk of getting caught. Also, rather neutral associations like income declaration and tax saving as well as black money were produced. Tax flight was associated with an intention to save taxes, with an impression that taxes are substantially lower abroad, taking into account double tax agreements and costs of relocation. The core elements of tax avoidance refer to legality and cleverness, whereas tax evasion was considered to be illegal, a criminal offence, and as being risky. Interestingly, tax saving was considered to be a motive for all three tax-reduction possibilities. However, they differed with respect to the perceived importance of that motive. Tax saving was considered to be a central motive for tax flight and tax avoidance, but was only mentioned relatively late in the association process for tax evasion, indicating that the wish to save taxes is overlaid by thoughts of illegality, risk or criminal prosecution. In a further step of analysis, the 507 different associations were categorised into 35 semantic categories. A correspondence analysis on frequencies of associations to the three stimuli by the four groups of respondents yielded a two-dimensional semantic field of representations (figure 5). Tax avoidance was perceived as legal and as moral, tax evasion as illegal and immoral,

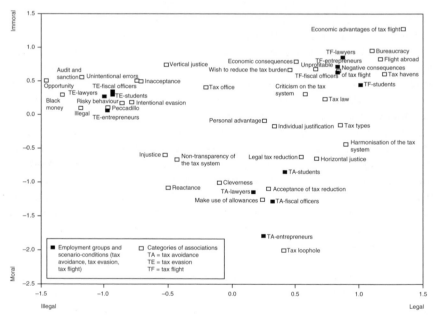

Figure 5: Two-dimensional result of correspondence analysis of associations on tax avoidance, tax evasion and tax flight with respect to employment group (Kirchler, Maciejovsky and Schneider, 2003)

and finally tax flight as legal and as immoral. More precisely, tax avoidance was associated with the acceptance of tax reduction, making use of tax allowances, legal tax reduction, horizontal justice and using tax loopholes. Tax evasion was associated with risky behaviour, peccadillo, intentional evasion, audit and sanction, opportunity, black money, unacceptance, intentional errors and vertical justice. Hence, tax evasion again was basically associated with the shadow economy and is considered as a criminal offence. Tax flight was associated with tax havens, negative consequences of tax flight, flight abroad, bureaucracy, economic advantages of tax flight, economic consequences, criticism on the tax system and the wish to reduce the tax burden. It is interesting to note that sanctions and audits – determinants of evasion considered in economic models – were associated with tax evasion. However, exchange inequity with the state and opportunity to evade were also typical associations. Opportunity and inequity considerations are frequently studied variables in psychological investigations (e.g., Dornstein, 1987; Kirchler, 1997a; Spicer and Becker, 1980; Spicer and Lundstedt, 1976). While inequity in the relationship between taxpayers and the state proved to be relevant with tax evasion, horizontal justice was associated with tax avoidance. Also reactance and injustice in general were related to tax avoidance. Tax flight, on the other hand, seemed to be considered if bureaucracy was increasing (see figure 5).

With regard to subjective constructs of tax issues, Kirchler, Niemirowski and Wearing (2006) investigated similarities between subjective views of tax officers and taxpayers, arguing that the quality of interaction between taxpayers and tax authorities depends on a mutual understanding and acceptance that is shaped by shared views. If taxpayers and tax authorities view tax issues similarly, they should be able to better understand each other (Cialdini, 1993). As a consequence, taxpayers may judge tax officials as being experts and not just accept that they have the legitimate and normative power to exert sanctions if they detect that taxpayers had made errors or violated the law (French and Raven, 1959). Shared views, mutual acceptance and facilitation of communication should affect perceived procedural fairness. The variables investigated in Kirchler, Niemirowski and Wearing's (2006) study were subjective beliefs regarding the complexity of the tax law, tax avoidance mentality and tax ethics, as well as social norms, evaluation of government activities and perceived fairness, in terms of an equitable exchange between taxpayers and the government, and an equitable tax burden of taxpayers as compared to other taxpayers. In addition, the evaluation of interaction experiences with tax officers and tax preparers was considered. It was found that taxpayers' behaviour, as it was reported by the Australian Taxation Office, was related to willingness to cooperate, which was mediating the effect of shared perceptions between taxpayers and tax officers on observed compliance. In particular, willingness to cooperate was significantly higher if there were similarities between prototypical tax officers' and taxpayers' subjective views in tax mentality, tax ethics and evaluation of support provided by tax staff. Independent of the absolute level of knowledge, tax mentality, etc., it was the level of similar subjective views which affected reported compliance. However, willingness to cooperate was related to dissimilar perceptions and evaluations of support provided by tax preparers. This latter result was interpreted as being due to in-group biases in the sample of tax staff, suggesting that Australian Taxation Office officials tend to judge their support services more positively than support provided by a competitive out-group (Turner *et al.*, 1987; Turner and Onorato, 1997). Figure 6 shows the results of regression analyses testing observed tax compliance and its relation to willingness to cooperate in terms of filing one's tax return in time and correctly, as well as the relation between willingness to cooperate and shared views of tax issues.

Thus far, subjective knowledge about taxation has been discussed and subjective concepts presented. To sum up, taxpayers' knowledge is generally poor, and survey studies reveal that taxpayers feel unqualified to file their taxes appropriately; thus, they need to seek help from tax practitioners. Despite their lack of competence and rather negative subjective concepts and evaluations of taxation, most taxpayers want tax practitioners to assist in correctly filing their taxes rather than provide advice to aggressively reduce the tax burden. Studies on subjective concepts about taxation show that perceptions and interpretations of taxation differ between employment groups: whereas the self-employed consider mainly limitation of freedom to invest 'their' money in their business, other white-collar workers and civil servants refer to fairness and norms.

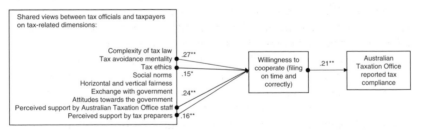

Figure 6: Observed tax behaviour, related to willingness to cooperate and shared views on tax-related dimensions (B-values and p-values; ⋆ = p < .05; ⋆⋆ = p < .01) (Kirchler, Niemirowski and Wearing, 2006)

Taxpayers in general consider tax evasion illegal, but tax avoidance and tax flight legal, and accept them as driven by motives to save one's own money. In the final part of this section, possible consequences of the similarities in taxpayers' and tax officials' views of taxation are considered. It may be concluded that similarity of views is related to the parties' mutual understanding of each other and the law, leading to a willingness to cooperate.

3.2   Attitudes

In the previous two sections, knowledge about taxation, subjective concepts of taxes and tax non-compliance were discussed as aspects of social representations of taxation. The present section focuses on evaluative aspects and their complex relationship with tax behaviour. As conceptualised by Ajzen's 1991 theory of planned behaviour, behaviour is only partly predicted by attitudes. Subjective norms and perceived control of behaviour are further variables that need to be considered as determinants of behaviour intentions, and, in turn, of actual behaviour. Therefore, after discussing attitudes, the following two sections comprise research on norms and subjective perceptions of control of behaviour.

It is assumed that a person in favour of an event or situation would act accordingly. A taxpayer evaluating tax avoidance positively is expected to be less compliant compared to a taxpayer judging tax avoidance negatively. Individuals' positive versus negative evaluation of an event is a dominant characteristic of their attitude (Ajzen, 1993; Fishbein and Ajzen, 1975). Eagly and Chaiken (1993) define 'attitude' as a psychological (behavioural) tendency that is expressed by evaluating a particular object or situation with some degree of favour or disfavour. Fishbein and Ajzen perceive attitudes as an individual's disposition to respond favourably or unfavourably to an object, person, institution or event, or to any discernible aspect of the individual's world (Ajzen, 1993; Fishbein and Ajzen, 1975). Definitions refer to cognitive, affective and conative or behavioural facets of attitudes. While cognitive responses are expressions of beliefs about characteristics or attributes of an event or situation (e.g., believing that taxes are useful for the provision of public goods, or taxes are wasted money), affective responses are feelings toward the attitude object (e.g., feelings related to taxes as expression of citizens' cooperation with the state, feelings related to taxes as loss of one's own money, evaluation of taxes as a means for income redistribution, feelings toward government spending policy). Behavioural responses are intentions and actions with respect to the attitude object (e.g., commitment to the commons, responses to loopholes in the tax law).

The literature on tax psychology offers a large number of studies on attitudes and tax compliance. However, theoretical conceptualisations and operationalisation and measurement of attitudes vary considerably, and so does the use of the terms. While some authors conceive of attitudes as (a) subjective evaluations of tax evasion (e.g., Porcano, 1988; Wärneryd and Walerud, 1982), others also include (b) evaluations of crime in general (e.g., Wahlund, 1992), and refer to (c) judgments of the government and state in general (e.g., Schmölders, 1960), and to (d) intolerance of tax evasion (e.g., Wilson and Sheffrin, 2005); some also include (e) attitudes and moral beliefs about the propriety of evasion (e.g., Weigel, Hessing and Elffers, 1987), (f) moral attitudes towards tax evasion (e.g., Orviska and Hudson, 2002), or (g) tax mentality including beliefs and evaluations of evasion and awareness of tax non-compliance in reference groups (e.g., Lewis, 1978; Schmölders, 1960).

Within the frame of the theory of planned behaviour (Fishbein and Ajzen, 1975) and the theory of reasoned action (Ajzen, 1991), attitudes are measured by presenting individuals with the attitude object, e.g., tax evasion. All aspects with which an individual associates the attitude object – i.e., his or her cognitions or beliefs and the strength of these beliefs, as well as evaluations of them – are measured. The added component products of strength of beliefs and evaluations are considered as an individual's attitude. In tax compliance studies, Likert-type scales have also been developed to measure participants' degree of favouring tax evasion; sometimes evaluations of taxpayers' behaviour are confounded with evaluations of tax authorities, the government or fiscal policy. In some studies, the resulting variable is called attitudes, whereas in other studies authors use the term tax mentality. Sometimes attitude measures also include fairness perceptions and subjective norms. The lack of clearly distinctive measures makes it difficult to aggregate results from different investigations and to draw clear conclusions. Lewis clearly addresses the many problems with attitudes:

The term 'attitude' is used loosely and often refers to replies to only a few items. Some confusion arises, as there are also measures of tax perceptions that appear at first sight to be synonymous with tax ethics. These tax perceptions refer to taxpayers' views on the use of taxes, the 'burden of taxes' and exchange (perceived benefits received compared with taxes paid). Additionally, there is a measure of tax-evasion behaviour, based on replies to the two questions 'Would you classify yourself as a person who every year has reported all of his income to the fiscal authorities?' and 'Would you classify yourself as a person who never has made a higher deduction than was justified?'(Lewis, 1982, p. 141)

Keeping in mind the heterogeneity of the direction of attitudes towards the government and fiscal policy in general or taxation in particular, as well as heterogeneity of measures, results of studies on the evaluation of the state and taxation can be summarised as follows.

In his 1960 survey, Schmölders asked respondents to indicate to what degree they are in favour of 'the state'. At the time, 56% expressed positive feelings, as compared to 13% with clearly negative feelings, whereas 31% were neutral or undecided. The perceived public goods offered by the state in exchange for tax payments were shelter and security (28%), work and pensions (17%), laws and rights (6%), freedom (4%), and education and other benefits (6%). Respondents with higher education evaluated the state more positively as compared to respondents with only primary school education, and civil servants and white-collar workers were clearly more in favour of the state than were blue-collar workers. With regard to taxation, respondents were quite sceptical, preferring taxes to be reduced, even if their income was in the lowest brackets and their respective tax burden low. Paying taxes was often perceived as a loss. Schmölders differentiated between views of taxes as a contribution to the commons, or as money that is taken away by the state. While two-thirds agreed that they had to give or contribute something, one-third clearly perceived taxes as an imposition. While almost equal percentages of men (30%) and women (33%) perceived taxes as a loss, in the younger samples, negative connotations were more frequent than in the older samples. The respective percentages for the under-30-year-old, 31–50-year-old, 51–65-year-old and over-66-year-old groups were 36%, 33%, 29% and 23%, respectively. Also, low education and lower work status were covarying with negative connotations.

Lewis found that attitudes towards taxes depend mainly on income. In his study (1979), participants were asked to indicate their agreement with sixteen Likert-type statements referring to tax avoidance, one's tax burden, adequate treatment of tax evaders, fairness of progressive tax rates and the relationship between evasion and tax rates. The most relevant discriminant variable of tax attitudes was income: people with higher incomes had higher antipathy towards taxation in general and progressive tax rates in particular; they felt that avoidance was fairer than did people with low income, and thought that those who evade should be treated leniently by the law. Wilson and Sheffrin (2005) used the US IRS Taxpayer Compliance Measurement Program data and divided the sample into moral and immoral taxpayers. Moral taxpayers were defined as those who did not tolerate evasion of low amounts, whereas immoral taxpayers were defined as those who had more favourable attitudes towards evading higher amounts. Immoral people were found to be less honest than moral taxpayers. When taxpayers considered the tax system to be 'very fair', they were 5% more likely to be honest as compared to those perceiving the tax system just 'fair'. Moreover, immoral people were more likely to cheat if they had a higher income or were self-employed.

In Kirchler's 1998 study and Berti and Kirchler's 2001 study on social representations of taxes in Austria and Italy, respondents were presented with a typical taxpayer, an honest taxpayer and a tax evader, and were asked to describe and evaluate them on a semantic differential, as developed by Peabody (1985). This allows the researcher to separate judgments that are descriptive from those that are evaluative. The most striking result was the rather positive description and evaluation of tax evaders. Whereas typical taxpayers were rated most negatively and honest taxpayers most positively, tax evaders were rated rather positively. As figure 7 shows, tax evaders were described as being the most intelligent and as being rather hard-working, whereas the typical taxpayer was

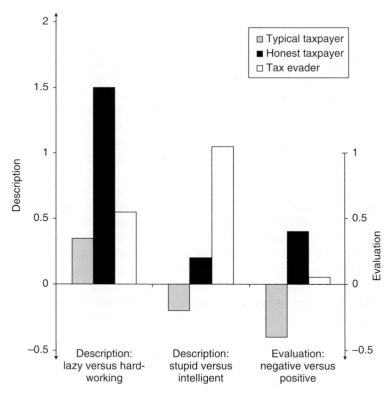

Figure 7: Description and evaluation of typical taxpayers, honest tax-payers and tax evaders (judgments range from −3 (lazy, stupid) to +3 (hard-working, intelligent); evaluations range from −1 = negative to +1 = positive evaluation) (Kirchler, 1998)

perceived as being lazy and not very intelligent. Honest people were perceived as hard-working, but not as intelligent as tax evaders.

The harshness of these results may be surprising. In fact, despite taxpayers' willingness to comply, tax evasion is not perceived as a serious crime, but rather as a clever act. In the German surveys conducted by Schmölders (1960, 1964), approximately half of the respondents compared a person deliberately evading taxes with a cunning businessman, while only one-quarter judged such a person as a thief or deceiver. Similar results are reported by Burton, Karlinsky and Blanthorne (2005), Song and Yarbrough (1978) and Vogel (1974), who found that drunk driving or stealing a car were judged more severely than tax evasion; tax evasion is perceived as somewhat worse than stealing a bicycle.

The struggle of individuals and businesses to improve their financial situation is widely accepted in society and perceived as a prerequisite of wealth. As Lamnek, Olbrich and Schaefer (2000) emphasise, work and achievement are fundamental values in societies with a Christian tradition, and wealth is perceived as a consequence of hard work. Some types of shadow work might be perceived as a virtue rather than a vice, especially if it is hard work; and keeping what one has earned may be judged less criminal than incorrectly taking advantage of public goods which one is not supposed to possess. The asymmetrical condemnation between paying a reduced amount of tax and receiving benefits which are not due is also supported by Orviska and Hudson (2002). Three-quarters of the respondents found it wrong or seriously wrong to take undue benefits; three-quarters admitted they would not engage in taking benefits. Responses to evading tax were more lax. Slightly more than half found not declaring cash payments incorrect and about 60% said they would do it (figure 8). As found in many studies on socio-demographic differences, the older and female respondents disapproved of evasion most, while the young and male respondents held more lax attitudes.

On the basis of these findings it is not surprising that ordinary taxpayers do not condemn tax avoidance and tax flight, and are quite broad-minded with regard to tax evasion. Kirchler, Maciejovsky and Schneider (2003) asked participants to produce associations towards tax avoidance, evasion and flight and to judge them as either positive, neutral or negative. From these responses, indices of evaluation were computed (de Rosa, 1996). The polarity index is calculated by taking the difference between the number of positive and negative associations relative to the total number of associations produced by a participant. It ranges from -1 (negative evaluation) to $+1$ (positive evaluation). Independent of employment group, participants produced most negative associations in the condition of tax evasion ($M = -.26$; $SD = .48$); rather neutral associations in the

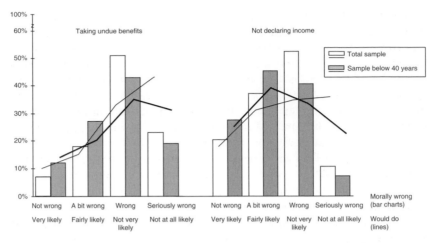

Figure 8: Attitudes towards taking undue benefits and not declaring income (bar charts indicate percentages of judgments of morally wrong behaviour, lines indicate percentages of people who might show the behaviour) (adopted from Orviska and Hudson, 2002, p. 91)

tax flight condition (M = .11; SD = .56); and relatively positive associations in the tax avoidance condition (M = .29; SD = .52). Participants were also asked to evaluate fairness of the three behaviours on a scale ranging from 1 (being unfair) to 9 (being very fair). While fiscal officers generally perceived all three tax-reduction possibilities to be relatively unfair, entrepreneurs considered tax flight much fairer in comparison to other groups of participants. In all employment groups, tax avoidance was considered to be quite fair (M = 8.17; SD = 1.84), whereas tax evasion was considered to be least fair (M = 2.92; SD = 2.27). Subjective fairness of tax flight was rated in between tax avoidance and tax evasion (M = 6.34; SD = 2.79).

Attitudes are assumed to determine behaviour. On the basis of agreement to the following statements, Wärneryd and Walerud (1982) assessed three facets of attitudes in a sample of 426 Swedish taxpayers: propensity for gambling ('If you see a chance to reduce your taxes you should take it even if it is not allowed'; 'More people would try to evade tax if they knew they would not be found out'); propriety instinct ('The taxes take away money that really should be mine'); and feelings of inequity ('Taking into consideration what the citizens get from the state, our taxes are not too high'; 'The Swedish taxation system is unjust') (p. 198). Those who had admitted to tax evasion were more likely to have high propensity for gambling and stronger feelings of inequity than others. Self-admitted tax evasion was also correlated with judgments of different crimes, such as drink driving, 'black' payments to an artisan, not reporting extra income or accepting black money. Further analyses including socio-demographic variables, opportunity to evade, tax knowledge, risk of being found out, political party sympathy, etc. revealed that age, opportunity for tax evasion and attitudes towards tax crimes were the most relevant factors for explaining self-reported tax evasion. Younger people, people with more opportunities to evade and more lenient judgments of tax crimes seem to be least compliant.

The relevance of attitudes towards the government, fiscal policy and tax non-compliance in determining tax behaviour has been recognised in empirical studies conducted in various countries from the beginning of psychological studies on taxation until the present (e.g., Chan, Troutman and O'Bryan, 2000; Dornstein, 1976; Fetchenhauer, 2004; Groenland and van Veldhoven, 1983; Niemirowski *et al.*, 2002; Orviska and Hudson, 2002; Porcano, 1988; Trivedi, Shehata and Mestelman, 2004; Vogel, 1974; Wahlund, 1992; Wallschutzky, 1984; Webley, Cole and Eidjar, 2001). Most of these studies found statistically significant, although weak, relationships between attitudes and self-reported behaviour. Thus, the proportion of explained variance of actual behaviour by attitudes is expected to be even weaker. In the literature on tax psychology there are few studies on actual tax behaviour. Since it is a delicate matter to interview people about illegal activities, and particularly about tax evasion, and simulation studies in the laboratory can be criticised as only a weak proxy for actual tax compliance, empirical studies have tended to focus on attitudes towards tax evasion rather than behaviour itself. However, the relationship between attitudes and behaviour is complex, and attitudes cannot be perceived as a convincing proxy for behaviour.

Weigel and colleagues developed a social psychological model of tax evasion behaviour that considers social and psychological conditions as antecedents of behaviour. Among other variables, attitudes and moral beliefs about the propriety of evasion are included (Weigel, Hessing and Elffers, 1987). The Dutch research group was able to collect data from taxpayers who were audited and fined for evasion as well as from a group found to have filed correctly (Elffers, Weigel and Hessing, 1987; Hessing, Elffers and Weigel, 1988). Besides these strong behavioural data, self-reports on tax compliance were collected as well as measures of psychological instigations and constraints. The findings, reported in table 5, demonstrate that attitudes explain in part self-reported tax evasion, but are insignificant predictors of actual behaviour. Also, the correlations between attitudes and self-reports, although being significant, did not explain more than 4% to 8% of variance.

Table 5: *Correlations between tax evasion and measures of psychological instigations and constraints (Elffers, Weigel and Hessing, 1987, p. 328)*

	Tax evasion measures Behavioural outcome measures:		
Psychological variables	2-year self-report	Documented status	Documented amount of tax evaded
Personal instigations			
Dissatisfactions			
1. Dissatisfactions with tax authorities	.05	.21**	.22**
2. Comprehensibility of rules and information	.10	.20**	.28***
Personality orientation			
1. Competitiveness	.05	.17*	.20**
2. Alienation	.10	.22**	.29***
3. Tolerance of deviance	−.01	.18*	.22**
Personal constraints			
Fear of punishment			
1. Perceived certainty	−.27***	−.03	−.01
2. Perceived severity	−.07	.09	.13
3. Perceived risk index	−.30***	.02	−.03
Social controls			
1. Perceived frequency	.22**	−.09	.00
2. Perceived social support	.22**	−.01	.07
Personal controls			
1. Attitude toward under-reporting	−.25***	.04	.07
2. Attitude toward false deductions	−.19**	.10	.12

Notes:
*=$p < .05$; **=$p < .01$; ***=$p < .001$

Fishbein and Ajzen's (1975) theory of reasoned action models behaviour as dependent on behavioural intentions. Behavioural intentions are, in turn, determined by attitudes toward the behaviour and subjective norms. The theory of planned behaviour, which is the successor of the theory of reasoned action, also includes perceived behavioural control as a determinant of behavioural intention (Ajzen, 1991). Behavioural intention is a mediating variable between attitudes, norms and perception of control on one hand and behaviour on the other. An individual will find a particular behaviour to be more attractive the more the behaviour is assumed to result in a highly valued outcome. Subjective norms are a function of an individual's perceived expectation that one or more relevant referents would approve of a particular behaviour and the extent to which the individual will be motivated to comply with such referent's beliefs. Behavioural control refers to the subjective perception of the extent of control one has in performing a particular behaviour. Perceived behavioural control is linked to behaviour indirectly through intentions. However, the actual control individuals have over their behaviour affects their behaviour directly.

Positive attitudes should be positively related to behaviour intentions, as are strong norms favouring a specific behaviour, and control which an individual perceives to have over his or her behaviour. With regard to tax evasion, taxpayers should be more likely to comply if they associate positive beliefs with tax compliance, if the social norms they consider important condemn tax evasion, and if they perceive to have few opportunities to evade. Bobek and Hatfield (2003) studied tax compliance using the framework of the theory of planned behaviour and found support for the theory. However, individuals' moral obligation was found to exert additional influence. Lewis (1982) adapted Fishbein and Ajzen's theory of tax evasion to include 'external variables', such as demographic characteristics (sex, age, income, social class), attitudes towards targets (e.g., fiscal authorities, government) and personality traits (e.g., risk aversion, authoritarianism). At the time of publication the theory of reasoned action was not yet developed, thus Lewis did not include perceived behaviour control or opportunities as the third determinant of behaviour intention. Figure 9 presents Lewis' model, including opportunities.

Attitudes and behaviour are not necessarily closely related, as consistency theory would assume, and as several studies on tax compliance implicitly suggest. Rather, attitudes and behaviour need to be treated as separate dimensions with some relationship to each other, writes V. Braithwaite (2003a). In a similar vein Lewis summarises evidence on the attitude–behaviour relationship: 'While the relationship between tax attitudes and tax evasion is not a simple one, we can be confident in our general prediction that if tax attitudes become worse, tax evasion will increase, although a more precise statement about which attitudes are reflected in behavioural intentions, using Fishbein's and Ajzen's (1975) terms, and in actual tax evasion is not yet within our grasp.' (Lewis, 1982, p. 177). V. Braithwaite adds:

The management of tax systems is a complex business and it is likely to become increasingly so in the 21st century as they are forced to adjust to the changes

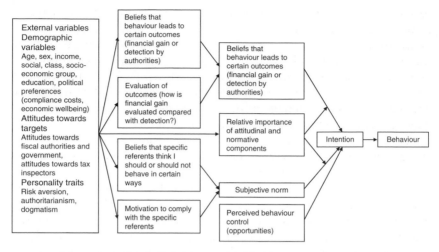

Figure 9: Attitude–behaviour model for the case of tax evasion according to Lewis, 1982, p. 172

accompanying globalisation. The popular stereotype of the 'taxman' collecting the revenue through the process of detecting non-compliance and imposing penalties provides a simplistic account of the realities of modern tax administration ... As tax systems are adjusted, the community needs to be educated, persuaded and encouraged to cooperate, long after the vote is cast at the ballot box ... Containing problems of tax avoidance, checking problems of tax evasion and convincing the public that tax reforms are for the public good require a conception of taxpayers that is multidimensional and dynamic, but at the same time leaves taxpayers in no doubt about the integrity of the tax administration as a whole. (V. Braithwaite, 2003a, p. 15)

Even if evaluations of the tax authority and taxation of an attitudinal kind are distinct from compliance as behaviour, both are important aspects of community responsiveness. We can be confident that social representations of authorities and taxes in general and attitudes in particular are important to foster an understanding and acceptance of fiscal policy that imposes a burden on citizens, but at the same time, provides public goods to enhance the wealth of the nation.

3.3   Norms

Besides attitudes as combined beliefs about an entity and evaluations of these beliefs, Fishbein and Ajzen perceive behaviour intentions as depending on norms and behaviour control (Ajzen, 1991; Fishbein and

Ajzen, 1975). Like attitudes, norms have received considerable attention in tax research. However, the conceptualisation and use of norms as predictors of tax compliance seems to be even more heterogeneous than the use of attitudes. There is considerable overlap between perceived personal norms, values and a person's tax ethics, defined as belief that there is a moral imperative that one should deliberately comply; and social norms, usually defined as prevalence or acceptance of tax evasion among a reference group (Wenzel, 2005b).

The way norms are operationalised and measured in research can at times heavily overlap with taxpayers' personality characteristics, value orientation, personal versus social norms and commitment to them, as well as societal norms, trust in institutions and cultural standards. Conceptualisations vary from internalised individual standards of what is correct behaviour, over awareness and acknowledgement of socially approved standards of correct behaviour, to societal and cultural standards resulting in imposing rules and laws. The lack of clearly distinctive measures makes it difficult to aggregate results from different investigations and to draw clear conclusions. It is, however, generally assumed that higher moral standards correlate positively with tax compliance, but the relationship is complex, as Wenzel has convincingly shown (2004a, 2004d, 2005b).

3.3.1   Personal norms

A person's tax ethic is related to personality factors, such as moral reasoning, authoritarianism and Machiavellianism, egoism, norm dependency, and values. The overlap between the terms and concepts used is not only evident in the theoretical definitions but above all in the operationalisation and in the way they are measured. For instance, a personal characteristic which is related to tax ethics and behaviour according to norms is norm dependency. Norm dependency is considered a trait factor in the big five personality model, which is related to honesty, Machiavellianism, altruism versus egoism and orientations towards cooperation versus selfish utility maximisation (Angermeier, Bednorz and Hursh, 1994; Costa and McCrae, 1992; Goldberg, 1990; McCrae and Costa, 1992). Business white-collar crime in general has been associated with low behavioural self-control, high hedonism and high narcissism (Blickle et al., 2006). Super-ego, conscience and values are also perceived as related, as are religious beliefs and political party preference. Generally, norm-dependency, altruism, strong religious beliefs and preferences for political parties favouring cooperation rather than individualism should be correlated with high personal ethics and eventually with willingness to comply.

A person's moral conscience, according to Kohlberg's (1969) stage theory, develops as he or she matures. Six sequential stages of moral reasoning are distinguished: at stages 1 and 2, individuals take an individual perspective in the stages of pre-conventional thinking, characterised by obedience and instrumental egoism and simple exchange. In these stages, individuals do what they are told primarily to avoid punishment and consider mainly the costs and benefits of exchanges. At stage 3, interpersonal concordance, people are considerate and are keen to get along and cooperate with others. At stage 4, behaviour is determined by laws and duties, which everyone in the society is obligated to follow. At stage 5, societal consensus, people feel obligated by the arrangements they agreed to and focus on fairness of rules and processes as determined by equity and equality. In the last stage, non-arbitrary social cooperation matures, and personal fairness concepts and behaviour rules derive from general principles of what is just. The highest level of moral reasoning is post-conventional thinking, in which individuals develop their own personal principles. On the basis of one's moral conscience, tax ethics develop and are shaped by interpersonal communication, and by values and standards discussed, approved and communicated in the society and eventually imposed by authorities. The importance of moral feelings and moral costs when cheating was emphasised by Baldry (1987), who later called for a new agenda in tax policy and in the economic analysis of tax evasion (1994). Trivedi, Shehata and Lynn (2003) also provide evidence for the relevance of moral reasoning and tax compliance behaviour in an experimental setting (see also Jackson and Milliron, 1986; Trivedi, Shehata and Mestelman, 2004). Moreover, Reckers, Sanders and Roark (1994) specifically tested whether an individual's ethical beliefs about tax compliance moderated withholding effects (in the experiment, taxes were either over-withheld or due) and whether tax rate affected tax evasion decisions. Tax ethics were found relevant in tax compliance decisions.

Kirchler and Berger (1998) investigated the reported compliance of finance officers, self-employed people and entrepreneurial taxpayers in a study conducted in Austria as dependent on socio-demographic characteristics, justice perceptions and moral standards. Ethical orientation was measured as Machiavellianism. The concept of Machiavellianism was introduced by Christie and Geis in their 1970 publication. Machiavellianism is named after the Italian political writer Niccolò Machiavelli (1469–1527), who argued that a political sovereign considered the goals of the state to be higher than moral norms. Generally, Machiavellianism defines an orientation towards one's own interests that stretches beyond the limits of ethical standards. Individuals considered to have Machiavellian characteristics have relatively low affective connections to others, are characterised by emotional distance, are loosely bound to conventional moral standards and ideologies, and have strong utilitarian preferences. Both finance officers and self-employed taxpayers who demonstrated high levels of Machiavellianism were found to have low tax ethics and were more likely to report non-compliance. Similar evidence stems from Webley, Cole and Eidjar's 2001 study on egoism measured as Machiavellianism, attitudes towards the law and alienation. Hypothetical and self-reported evaders had higher loadings than non-evaders. Also, Trivedi and colleagues found that value orientation in terms of egoism and altruism, that is on the extreme of wanting the best for others, determined compliance (Trivedi, Shehuta and Lynn, 2003). Egoism was found to be significantly different in groups of Value Added Tax evaders and non-evaders (Adams and Webley, 2001). Elffers and his team found that tolerance of deviance, competitiveness orientation, a sense of alienation from others together with feelings of dissatisfaction with life and pessimism about the future increased the probability of observed evasion, but were not significantly related to self-reported compliance measures (Elffers, Weigel and Hessing, 1987).

Values held by individuals concern the social goals of the society they want to live in, the organisation of that society and the method of distribution of resources. According to Blamey and V. Braithwaite, the two value orientations, derived from Rokeach's 1973 work, that were found to underlie the ways in which people respond to social and political issues and policies and interventions, are the security and harmony value orientations (Blamey and Braithwaite, 1997; V. Braithwaite, 1994, 1998). Security value orientation describes principles for allocating resources and regulating human conduct. At the societal level, security values regard the virtue of the rule of law, the wish for national greatness, national economic development and security, and the role of reward for individual effort as a principle of good governance. Harmony value orientation describes principles about the ways in which people should be connecting and engaging with others. They regard the desirability of a peaceful world, where human dignity is valued and respected, and equal opportunity, economic equality and cooperation is pursued. Both value orientations are expected to increase tax morale and were indeed found to have positive effects on tax morale and internalised obligation to repay an educational loan as provided by the Australian Higher Education Contribution Scheme (V. Braithwaite, 2003a). V. Braithwaite and Ahmed (2005) showed that tax morale is built on values and fairness perceptions, and is also interconnected with experiences in related domains. In their study on Australian graduates' tax morale and willingness to repay student loans in the frame of the Higher Education Contribution Scheme, they found that the willingness to pay back loans depended on both graduates' shared vision of what constitutes a desirable society and their satisfaction with their university courses. In cases where university courses were dis-satisfying, graduates were more opposed to the Higher Education Contribution Scheme and were less willing to meet their payment obliga-tions. From an exchange perspective, obtained benefits and requested contributions were likely to be perceived as unbalanced, and morale to pay eroded. Not only did the authors find morale to pay back student loans as dependent on values and fairness perceptions, but also that there existed 'spill over effects' from graduates' morale to repay their student loans to their tax morale. The authors also argue that tax morale is based on values, and since values are fairly stable over time, they give tax morale a certain kind of robustness against controversy and upheaval. However, personal circumstances and opposition to particular government policies, in con-trast, exert a destabilising influence, causing tax morale to fluctuate. The authors conclude, therefore, that tax morale is not only a relevant deter-minant of compliance, but also a useful barometer for judging how the tax system is represented in citizens' minds, and it may reveal much about the functional moral legitimacy of governments and their activities (V. Braithwaite and Ahmed, 2005). Legitimacy refers to people's belief that an authority or institution acts appropriately, reasonably and fairly and leads people to feel personally obligated to defer to those authorities (Tyler, 2006).

Studies on a person's honesty and tax compliance found that honesty is significantly related to all compliance variables, hypothetical evasion, previous underreporting of income and previous evasion (Erard and Feinstein, 1994a; Porcano, 1988).

Also, strong religious beliefs and a strong moral conscience are related to compliance. Torgler (2003d) analysed Canadian data from the World Values Survey and found evidence that trust in government and religio-sity have a systematic positive influence on tax morale. Schwartz and Orleans (1967) conducted a field experiment in which a sub-sample of the participants were informed about possible sanctions of evasion one month before tax returns were due, another group was exposed to a moral appeal to comply, and two remaining groups received either information not related to taxes or no information. The moral appeal was found to have the highest impact on income tax declaration, while sanctions were far less effective and unrelated, while the group that received no informa-tion had the lowest income declarations. A survey in the United States found that religious salience correlated with intentions to comply, with shame and embarrassment having strong inverse relations with intentions to cheat and acting as intervening variables (Grasmick, Bursik and Cochran, 1991).

With regard to political party preference, Wahlund (1992) argues that one's political affiliation is related to attitudes towards taxes. People affiliated to parties favouring social democratic values might be more inclined to comply than people voting for liberal parties favouring 'less state' and more market regulations.

Tax mentality is sometimes conceptualised as a combination of attitudes and approval of tax non-compliance, and perceived as a norm that individuals develop over time. An individual with a tax mentality disapproving of deviant behaviour should be less inclined to evade taxes himself or herself than an individual with a lax mentality (Lewis, 1982; Wahlund, 1992).

Finally, personal norms may be strengthened if taxpayers anticipate guilt and shame in situations where norms are violated (Grasmick and Bursik Jr, 1990; Grasmick, Bursik and Cochran, 1991; see also Thurman, St John and Riggs, 1984; Tibbetts, Joulfaian and Rider, 1997). Erard and Feinstein (1994b) adapted guilt and shame to the context of tax compliance, arguing that taxpayers who fill in their returns are likely to anticipate guilt when contemplating under-reporting and escaping detection. When contemplating under-reporting and subsequently being caught, they are likely to anticipate shame. In their review on tax evasion, Andreoni, Erard and Feinstein (1998) refer to anticipated guilt and shame as a moral norm. King and Sheffrin (2002) write about emotions individuals consider in decision-making, such as choosing to be truthful about one's income to avoid feelings of guilt, regret or shame, which arise if caught; and Orviska and Hudson (2002) emphasise the importance of sentiments in relation to social stigma. In an experiment by Bosco and Mittone, participants were informed about the damage their non-compliance caused to others, and were, thus, blamed for their non-cooperative behaviour (Bosco and Mittone, 1997). Feelings of guilt and shame may have been the driving mechanisms not to evade taxes. Ahmed and Braithwaite dedicated much attention to shame as an emotion felt by individuals when they breached a social and/or moral standard, and concluded that certain responses to shame increase compliance (Ahmed and Braithwaite, 2004; Ahmed, 2004). The process of shame management, referring to acceptance or denial of norm violations when an individual's ethical identity is threatened, seems to be of high importance in regulating taxpayers' behaviour. While shame avoidance (i.e., pretending that nothing was happening or making a joke of it) and shame displacement processes (i.e., attributing causes of wrongdoing externally and feeling angry with the tax office) were found to be negatively related to personal norms of tax honesty, shame acknowledgement in terms of feelings of guilt, humiliation and embarrassment was positively related and found to have a deterring effect on tax non-compliance (Ahmed, 2004). According to shame management theory, a person's ethical identity is likely to become jeopardised by following deviant behaviour. A person feels not only shame and guilt but also discomfort in the form of embarrassment or awareness of rejection by others. Shame management is assumed to be adaptive if a person can handle shame and shame-related feelings constructively by acknowledging wrongdoing, and if a person uses those feelings to change the future behaviour. Shame management can also be maladaptive if shame is avoided or displaced. Experiences of shame related to norm violating behaviour and acknowledgment is likely to lead to anticipated shame in situations in which a person has the choice to comply or not. Anticipated shame becomes, thus, a cost factor in evaluating one's likely advantages and disadvantages of tax evasion.

With reference to Vogel's (1974) and Torgler's (2003c) typologies of taxpayers, strong personal norms relate to the concepts of honest and intrinsic taxpayers. According to Torgler, 'honest taxpayers' constantly cooperate. They are not searching for ways to reduce their taxes, but behave honestly on the basis of their absolute ethical norms. As found in many experimental studies, there is indeed a high percentage of participants who constantly behave honestly (e.g., Baldry, 1994; James and Alley, 2002). According to Torgler, the 'motivation of the "intrinsic taxpayers" includes among other, the feeling of obligation, which motivates a person without being forced' (Torgler, 2003c, p. 125). Intrinsic taxpayers are sensitive to the behaviour of institutions, the government and tax administrators. Their willingness to cooperate depends on institutional conditions rather than on the other taxpayers' behaviour. 'Social taxpayers" behaviour is determined by social norms and their anticipated emotions if they violate norms, such as embarrassment. If they know relevant others who evade taxes, they will evade as well; conversely, if their reference group disapproves of evasion, they will comply. In short, social taxpayers are motivated by social norms.

3.3.2   Social norms

Wenzel (2005b) refers to social norms as perceived frequency or acceptance of tax evasion among a reference group. Similarly, Fehr and colleagues define social norms as 'behaviour regularity that is based on a socially shared belief how one ought to behave which triggers the enforcement of the prescribed behaviour by informal social sanctions' (Fehr and

Gächter, 1998, p. 854; see also Fehr, Fischbacher and Gächter, 2002). They stress the social aspect of cooperation and convincingly use market simulation experiments and ultimatum games to demonstrate that reciprocity is a strong norm that individuals obey (Gintis *et al.*, 2003). With regard to reciprocity they also emphasise the importance of social exchange, which is relevant in participants' judgments of fairness and justice. The aspect of reciprocity is recognised also by Güth and Sausgruber (2004) in a tax experiment.

Social norms are a function of an individual's perceived expectation that one or more relevant referents would approve of a particular behaviour and the extent to which the individual will be motivated to comply with such a referent's beliefs (Ajzen, 1991). Alm, McClelland and Schulze (1999) define a social norm as representing a pattern of behaviour that is judged in a similar way by relevant others and therefore is sustained by social approval or disapproval. Taxpayers who perceive others as behaving according to socially accepted rules and who communicate with others about appropriate behaviour will adopt the socially shared norms and behave appropriately. If the reference group signals that non-compliance will be tolerated, then compliance will decrease.

Alm and his colleagues conducted an experiment with participants being endowed with an income and required to pay taxes on the income they declared. Several rounds were played with tax rates, audit rates and fine rates varying. In cases of undeclared income and audits, participants had to pay the omitted tax and a fine. After each round, when taxes and fines were collected, the 'group tax fund' was calculated and multiplied by a 'group surplus multiplier'. The resulting fund was then divided equally among the participants. After several rounds, participants voted via majority rule on the fiscal parameters which they wished to face in the next rounds. Whereas in the early rounds, participants were not allowed to communicate with each other, in the final rounds they were allowed to discuss the vote before voting for the future rules. In all rounds without discussion, the participants rejected stricter enforcement, and this rejection led to substantial post-vote decline in compliance relative to earlier rounds with identical parameters. In contrast, when participants were allowed to discuss, they voted for greater enforcement, and post-vote compliance exceeded pre-vote compliance under identical audit and fine rates, approaching approximately 100%. The authors attribute this finding to jointly developed and binding social norms (Alm, McClelland and Schulze, 1999). Also, clearly imposed regulations as a form of social norms determine behaviour: Hume, Larkins and Iyer (1999) showed that 'The Statements on Responsibilities in Tax Practice', issued in the USA as a regulatory directive for correct tax filing, which is recommended for licensed tax preparers, is perceived as a demand for ethical behaviour and has an effect on licensed tax preparers as they follow the statements more often than unlicensed preparers.

The relevance of social norms is generally supported in empirical studies on tax evasion. In 1982, Wärneryd and Walerud published their findings that black economy payments within vocational groups are related to non-compliance; and in 1988, Porcano reported that perception of existing evasion is significantly related to hypothetical evasion, previous under-reporting of income and previous evasion. Several additional studies also found significant differences between non-evaders and hypothetical and self-reported evaders with regard to perceived social support from friends, and the perceived prevalence of evasion among friends and colleagues (Bergman and Nevarez, 2005; Cullis and Lewis, 1997; Liebig and Mau, 2005; Sigala, Burgoyne and Webley, 1999; Webley, Robben and Morris, 1988; Webley, Cole and Eidjar, 2001). Torgler (2005b) reports that tax morale in Latin America is lower if people know others who evade or have heard about practised tax avoidance. Welch et al. (2005) also found that the more prevalent an individual perceives tax evasion to be within the community, the less likely the individual will be to judge the act of non-compliance harshly, the less likely the individual will fear informal sanctions directed against it, and the more inclined he or she will be to commit tax evasion in the future.

In an in-depth, semi-structured interview study with British employed and self-employed taxpayers in various occupations, Sigala, Burgoyne and Webley (1999) found that social norms as perception of usual behaviour in one's reference group were among the most important factors related to tax compliance. The authors conclude that, when people are uncertain of what an objectively appropriate and correct behaviour is, they tend to be influenced by social norms of a salient group to which they belong and with whose members they identify. A 2003 publication by Trivedi, Shehata and Lynn reports that peer reports influenced participants' compliance in an experiment. Weigel, Hessing and Elffers (1987) integrated social norms in their tax evasion model, terming them 'social control', which is defined as the number of evaders in one's reference group. Elffers's research team tested Weigel, Hessing and Elffers's (1987) model and found perceived frequency of tax evasion in one's reference group and anticipated social disapproval to be significantly correlated with self-reported evasion, but not with observed tax evasion, which was determined by personal norms (i.e., tolerance of deviance, competitiveness orientation, a sense of alienation from others; Elffers, Weigel and Hessing, 1987). Schwartz and Orleans (1967) and Spicer and Lundstedt (1976) maintain that taxpayer norms are important factors underlying their behaviour and normative appeals may be more effective than sanctions in inducing compliance. For example, in field experimental research undertaken by Spicer and Lundstedt in the US, taxpayers' norms were found to be an important factor underlying taxpayers' behaviour and normative appeals more effective than sanctions in inducing compliance. If taxpayers know many people in groups important to them who evade taxes, then their commitment to the social norm of tax compliance will be weaker. Finally, Lewis (1982) concludes in his review on 'The Psychology of Taxation' that illegal opportunities as well as contact with tax evaders and possible learning from their non-compliant behaviour are among the most important determinants of tax evasion.

If a taxpayer believes that non-compliance is widespread and a socially accepted behaviour, then this taxpayer is more likely not to comply. However, the relationship between social norms and tax compliance is more complex. While research has consistently found evidence for the relevance of taxpayers' personal norms determining their tax compliance, the influence of social norms on tax compliance is less clear. Wenzel (2004a) refers to self-categorisation theory (Turner *et al.*, 1987; Turner and Onorato, 1997) and shows that the impact of social norms is shaped by individuals' attachment to their reference group. Self-categorisation theory offers a refined analysis of the relationship between social norms and social influence. As Wenzel explains, the analysis differs from traditional dual-process accounts of social influence, which distinguish between informational and normative influence. The traditional approach assumes that the informational value of social influence leads to change of attitudes, whereas normative influence leads to mere outward compliance without being reflected in a change of one's personal beliefs. Norms are regarded as external pressure to behave accordingly. In contrast, self-categorisation theory argues for a unified social influence process with normative and informational influence functioning as interactive processes. Normative influence is true influence based on the internalisation of the views of relevant others. As members of the same social group, members are expected to hold similar views as the group. With regard to tax compliance and social norms, Wenzel concludes that taxpayers are more likely to be influenced by other taxpayers who are considered members of one's relevant self-category; that is, members of the group with which a taxpayer identifies. If, however, others are not perceived as part of one's self-category and identification is low, there is no expectation to hold similar views and to behave accordingly, and individuals may distance themselves from such groups.

Wenzel's conclusions and assumptions were tested in an Australian survey involving more than 2,000 taxpayers, which assessed tax non-compliance (i.e., non-lodgement, tax debts, not declaring all or part of pay income, exaggerating deductions), identification of respondents with Australia, social norms in terms of perceived injunctive norms of what most people think and do, and personal norms in terms of what a person thinks should be done. It was shown that one's personal norm exerted a consistent impact on reported tax compliance. Also, the interaction between identification with Australia and perceived social norms exerted a significant influence on reported non-compliance, confirming Wenzel's argument that the higher the identification with Australia and the stricter social norms are perceived to be, the more likely it is that a person complies. While social norms can indeed influence people's tax-paying behaviour, it is, however, necessary to clarify whether the group holding specific norms is one with which a taxpayer highly identifies or whether a taxpayer perceives himself or herself to be different and wants to keep his or her distance.

The strong effect of social norms in situations of high identification with the reference group's position on tax compliance, and additionally, the effect of social norms on personal norms, was demonstrated by Wenzel (2005b) in a study testing whether social norms are true motivations or mere rationalisations of compliant behaviour. It could be argued that social norms, rather than influencing tax compliance or non-compliance, are used as justifications in cases of non-compliance. In the case where a taxpayer is accused of evasion, he or she may argue that 'everyone' evades or refer to unfair exchange with the state or unfair treatment by the government (Falkinger, 1988). In the study, Wenzel applied cross-lagged panel analyses to data from a two-wave survey in Australia. Again, it was confirmed that tax ethics as an individual norm causally affects tax compliance. Social norms causally affected personally held tax ethics if respondents identified strongly with Australia, as shown in figure 10. In situations of high identification with Australia, perceived social norms at time 1 had an impact on a taxpayer's personal norm at time 2; and personal norms were found to be important predictors of tax compliance. Regarding social norms as either motivating compliance or providing rationalisations of non-compliance, tax compliance was found both to be affected by social norms, and, in turn, to affect the perception of social norms.

Having demonstrated the importance of identification with one's reference group and social norms and their impact on personal norms and tax compliance, Wenzel has identified practical applications for these findings by demonstrating how they might be useful to tax authorities (Wenzel, 2005a). He points out that there is a distinction between injunctive norms, i.e., what most people think one should do, and descriptive

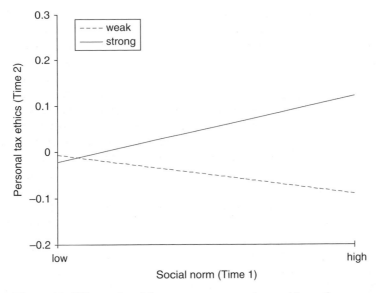

Figure 10: Effects of social norms on personal tax ethics at low versus high levels of identification (Wenzel, 2005b, p. 501)

norms, the perception of what most people actually do. While most studies on social norms have focused on the perceived prevalence of tax evasion among others, i.e., the descriptive social norm, fewer studies have examined the perceived level of acceptance of tax evasion, i.e., the injunctive social norm. Survey evidence suggests that taxpayers suspect that many people evade tax and think it is appropriate behaviour, but they also disapprove of such behaviour. This suggests that there might be a misperception of social norms, assuming that other people accept tax cheating to a greater degree than one does individually. Wenzel conducted his field experiment on a random sample of Australian taxpayers, who received a questionnaire about their own views as well as the suspected views of most other taxpayers concerning honesty in deduction claims. A few weeks later, one group of these taxpayers received feedback on the findings, namely about a self–other discrepancy in injunctive taxpaying norms. Two other groups did not receive this intervention and served as control groups: one group participated in the survey but did not receive any feedback, while another group neither took part in the survey nor received any feedback. After the lodgement deadline, tax return details were accessed by the Australian Taxation Office and deduction claims were compared between the three groups. The manipulations had an impact on actual taxpaying behaviour. It was predicted that feedback about self–other discrepancies in injunctive taxpaying norms would increase tax compliance and this would be reflected in lower deductions claimed in the feedback condition compared to survey-only and control groups. Indeed, there was a significant reduction in claims for non-work-related expenses among those in the injunctive norm feedback condition. These results suggest not only that social norms play an important role in tax non-compliance, but also that an accurate understanding of the behaviour of other taxpayers is important (Wenzel, 2005a). Tax authorities could ensure that taxpayers do not exaggerate their perceptions and interpretations of others' tax non-compliance behaviour by communicating the actual compliance rate, and thus, contribute to taxpayers' corrections of their perceived social norms. Similar results were obtained by Alm, Jackson and McKee (2005) in a laboratory experiment in which information about audit frequency and audit results were disseminated 'unofficially' by other participants assuming the role of taxpayers or 'officially' by the experimenters.

In her analysis of taxpayer attitudes and fairness judgments, Taylor (2003) makes a similar point as Wenzel (2005a), arguing that social identity is an important factor and that attitudes and fairness perceptions depend on the group with which a person identifies (e.g., friends, occupational group or the nation). Taylor demonstrates that identification at the superordinate level (e.g., the nation) is more relevant than identification at the subgroup level (e.g., occupational group). Therefore, it can be concluded that communication of behaviour and, thus, social norms, should focus on the superordinate level of identification. In other words, if a taxpayer believes that tax compliance in her or his country is perceived as a virtue and the majority of people comply and condemn evasion, than she or he is more likely to comply as compared to a taxpayer who considers her or his occupational group one which is also against evasion. Combining Taylor's and Wenzel's arguments, tax authorities should communicate social norms on the collective level, which may enhance a feeling of civic duty as a societal norm which is likely to enforce compliance. Taylor states that 'the appeal to civic virtue is associated with a qualitative shift in self-perception from "me" to "us", a corresponding shift in who is included in the frame of reference, and a corresponding decrease in personal self-interest and more concern about outcomes for all' (Taylor, 2003, p. 75).

3.3.3   Societal norms

Norms are conceived as behaviour standards on three levels: the individual, social reference group and collective level. On the individual level, norms define internalised standards of how to behave; on the social level, norms determine the behaviour of a social group (e.g., friends, acquaintances and vocational group) based on shared standards. Finally, on the collective or national level, norms become cultural standards, often mirrored in the actual law. Research on tax compliance has focused on personal ethics and subjective perception of behavioural habits in taxpayers' reference groups. On the cultural level, norms have been addressed mainly under the terms tax morale and civic duty, and also under the term cultural norms.

Cultural norms and societal institutions are perceived as important in determining tax compliance. As Schmölders (1970b) emphasises, tax compliance is a 'behavioural problem', and the success of taxes depends on cooperation. For example, Alm, Sanchez and deJuan (1995) found that compliance is higher in experiments conducted in the United States than in an identical setting in Spain. They attribute the difference to distinct social norms. Similarly, recent studies attribute national differences in tax compliance to different norms and to different stages in the development of institutions and citizens' varying trust in the government (Alm, Martinez-Vazquez and Schneider, 2004; Alm and Torgler, 2006; Chan, Troutman and O'Bryan, 2000; Torgler, 2003b; Gërxhani, 2004; Schneider and Klinglmair, 2004). Lending further evidence to this line of thinking, Torgler (2003a), using the World Values Survey data for the years 1990 and 1997, found that in the post-reunification period in Germany, inhabitants of East Germany had stronger norms to comply than those of West Germany, but also that the norms and tax morale in the East seemed to erode over time.

The recognition of the importance of societal norms goes hand in hand with the demand for a revision of the relationship between citizens, government and institutions in order to reduce the social distance between citizens and authorities and establish trust in political leadership and administration, which leads to cooperation (e.g., Bergman, 2002; Fjeldstad, 2004; Feld and Frey, 2005a; Frey, 2004; Frey and Eichenberger, 2002; Kirchgässner, Feld and Savioz, 1999; Pommerehne and Frey, 1992; Torgler, 2005a, 2005b; Tyler, 2001a, 2001b). Rather than responding to non-compliance by intrusive audits and severe punishment, supportive communication and interaction inspiring trust as well as appeals to cooperation will encourage compliance. Stainer, Stainer and Segal (1997) demand: 'Tax planning must be exercised in an atmosphere of integrity, mutual trust and, above all, a good ethical climate,' and continue by quoting the *Financial Times*, which observes, 'it is part of a civilised society that people, inside and outside business, act morally. No more and no less' (p. 218).

3.4   Behaviour control: perceived opportunities of non-compliance

Perceived behaviour control relates to self-efficacy (Bandura, 1977). In the current context, perceived behaviour control refers to one's self-confidence to be able to file taxes in a self-advantageous way. As tax laws are complex, and ordinary taxpayers have limited understanding of them, and because a majority seeks advice from tax practitioners to correctly prepare a tax return, it can be expected that self-confidence in engineering one's tax files in an advantageous way is generally rather low. Perception of opportunities depends on subjective tax knowledge and actual opportunities. Taxpayers taxed at source have objectively almost no opportunity to engage in income non-compliance. It is to be expected that they feel like they do not have many opportunities regarding their tax behaviour. In many European countries, employees receive net salary, with taxes and social security contributions delivered by the employer. While in most European countries employees with income subject to withholding taxes have little opportunity to claim unwarranted deductions, they could still engage in shadow work and conceal black economy income. On the other hand, in Australia, for instance, every income earner is requested to file a tax return. In these countries people have more opportunities to 'design' their tax returns.

Opportunity in terms of probability of cash receipts and non-withholding at source is conceived as an important situational constraint in Weigel, Hessing and Elffer's 1987 model on tax evasion. Generally, greater opportunity – or, more precisely, perceived greater opportunity – to under-declare taxes is associated with self-employment and with moonlighting. Self-employed people not only have to declare their gross income but collect gross income as 'their earned money' and need to pay 'out of pocket'. Besides higher opportunities to conceal income and to declare unwarranted deductions, paying 'out of pocket' is more likely to be perceived as a loss than receiving income with taxes already deducted.

Research has consistently shown that the opportunity not to comply is one of the most important determinants of tax evasion or avoidance (e.g., Antonides and Robben, 1995; Groenland and van Veldhoven, 1983; Lewis, 1982; Robben, 1990; Webley et al., 1991). As reported by Slemrod, Blumenthal and Christian (2001) and King and Sheffrin (2002), according to the US IRS, in 1988, voluntary reporting in the US was slightly below 100% for wages and salaries, but only 40% to 70% for self-employed income. Wallschutzky (1984) reports data on documented evidence of tax evasion in Australia showing that 43% of the sample of convicted tax evaders were self-employed as opposed to 13% of non-evaders.

Self-employed taxpayers are also more likely to admit non-compliance. In an early study in Sweden, Vogel (1974) found that 39% of taxpayers who received income not taxed at source admitted non-compliance, as compared to 21% of taxpayers with income taxed at source.

In simulation studies in England and in the Netherlands, Webley, Cole and Eidjar (2001) tested, among other variables, opportunity to evade. Participants imagined being landscape-gardeners who had to file tax returns. Under the condition of high opportunity to evade, they had agreed to earn some extra money by weekend work, or they had the possibility to overstate deductions. The effect of opportunity was not clear. In experiments simply manipulating opportunity as possibility not to declare extra income, no effects were found. However, if opportunity was handled by manipulating cheating possibilities and possibility to escape detection, significant effects were found. The authors argued that in experimental simulations it might be necessary to manipulate opportunity as detectability. Detectability is mainly related to perceived opportunity rather than to the actual opportunity to evade.

Actual opportunity to evade and perceived opportunity are highly correlated in survey studies. In his 1992 model, Wahlund not only found a high correlation between both variables, but also that both determine admitted tax avoidance and tax evasion, with actual opportunities having slightly higher influence than perceived opportunity. Wärneryd and Walerud (1982) found perceived opportunity for tax evasion to be significantly related to paying and receiving black economy money and to tax evasion. Webley, Cole and Eidjar (2001) found perceived opportunity to be one of the most important predictors of self-reported tax evasion in England, France and Norway. Porcano studied the influence of eighteen variables on hypothetical tax evasion, previous under-reporting of income and previous overstating of deductions. Opportunity was the most important predictor for under-reporting and overstating deductions and one of the most relevant predictors of admitted tax evasion. Evaders tended to be males who had income sources that were not traceable (Porcano, 1988; see also, e.g., Clotfelter, 1983; Witte and Woodbury, 1985). With one noticeable exception (see Mason and Calvin, 1978), research has convincingly supported the relevance of opportunity as a situational constraint. Perceived opportunity, defined as the perceived possibility to control one's own behaviour, is a strong predictor of tax non-compliance.

3.5   Fairness

Fairness concerns are the most frequently mentioned topics when citizens are asked what they think about the tax system (e.g., V. Braithwaite,

2003c; Rawlings, 2003; Taylor, 2003). In their review of tax compliance research, Andreoni, Erard and Feinstein (1998) recognise the importance of incorporating morals and social dynamics in economic theory. Besides moral principles and sentiments, the social dynamics that have received much attention are issues of fairness, either of the tax code or its enforcement, and taxpayers' evaluation of government expenditures. The authors conclude: 'There seems to be little dispute about whether these factors are important in individual compliance decisions', however, they add, 'little is known or agreed upon about how best to include these effects in a theoretical or empirical analysis of tax compliance' (p. 852).

The relevance of fairness issues was already recognised by Schmölders (1960), who maintained that beliefs about unfair treatment relative to others and unfair treatment relative to the benefits a taxpayer draws from public goods are relevant components of tax morale. In his study, approximately three-quarters of German taxpayers thought that their tax burden was too high, while one-quarter found it appropriate. In particular, the self-employed complained about too high a burden (83%); whereas civil servants complained the least (63%); blue-collar workers, white-collar workers and farmers were in the middle range (70–72%).

Schmölders (1975) holds that tax rates of 50% are the maximum that people seem to accept (see also Lévy-Garboua, Masclet and Montmarquette, 2005). According to a 2002 experimental study by Porschke and Witte, people are not completely against taxes, but find taxes around 30% just. However, if people do not focus on achievement principles but on cooperation, willingness to accept higher rates is higher. Most respondents in Schmölders' work believed that taxes are not only an excessive burden, but also unfairly distributed across occupational groups; furthermore, they felt that the government did not provide an equitable recompense in terms of public goods. A majority of people felt cheated.

Since Schmölders' classic study, the body of knowledge on equity considerations has grown significantly, but findings are inconsistent (e.g., Antonides and Robben, 1995; Brooks and Doob, 1990; Jackson and Milliron, 1986; Mason and Calvin, 1978; Thorndike and Ventry, 2002). The inconsistency of findings is not surprising, given that research has addressed mostly heterogeneous aspects of fairness considerations without carefully distinguishing between fairness perceptions deriving from comparisons between one's own tax burden and the taxes paid by others, or from an unbalanced exchange relationship between taxpayers and the state, or whether procedural issues are evaluated. Not only were fairness perceptions often defined without differentiating between these different aspects, but operationalisations and measurements were often vague. Either a global judgment was assessed, or isolated aspects of fairness were measured. The most frequent differentiation in tax compliance research referred to exchange equity with the government and equity of one's contributions relative to the contributions of other taxpayers (Adams, 1965). However, even this differentiation is not consistently made in the literature. While some authors term equity of one's contributions relative to the contributions of taxpayers in similar income groups 'horizontal fairness', and name exchange equity with the government 'vertical fairness' (e.g., Kirchler, Maciejovsky and Schneider, 2003; Webley, 2004), others distinguish between exchange equity (i.e., the balance between taxes paid and benefits derived from public goods), horizontal equity (i.e., the relative burden of taxes for a member of an income group compared to other members of the same income group), and vertical equity (i.e., the burden of taxes for certain income groups relative to the tax burden of other income groups or the progressivity of income tax; e.g., Kinsey and Grasmick, 1993; Wenzel, 2003).

Wenzel (2003) provides a conceptual framework for justice and fairness considerations which are based on conceptual distinctions made in social psychological justice research. His conceptual framework maps the field of justice research in tax compliance and allows for a systematic integration of empirical findings. In the following, Wenzel's concept is presented in detail.

In social psychology, three areas of justice are differentiated: (a) distributive justice, (b) procedural justice, and (c) retributive justice.

(a) Distributive justice refers to the exchange of resources, both benefits and costs. Equity theories draw attention to the fair distribution of the results of exchanges between partners (Adams, 1965; Homans, 1961; Walster, Walster and Berscheid, 1978). If rewards and costs are borne equally and distributed fairly between partners, exchange is balanced, and the relationship is judged to be satisfactory. According to the equity rule, which is most likely applied in business relationships, partners are compensated in proportion to their contributions. In the field of tax compliance, distributive justice refers to taxpayers' perception of the balance of their share to the commons relative to the benefits they are entitled to receive, and to the contributions others make relative to their share of public goods.

(b) Procedural justice refers to the processes of resource distribution. In other words, if people perceive the formula used to distribute resources (benefits and costs) as fair, then procedural fairness is high. Procedures of allocation of resources are regarded as fair if the partners involved are treated in a way they think is appropriate (Thibaut and Walker, 1978; Tyler, 1990; Tyler and Degoey, 1996). According to

Leventhal (1980), treatments are considered fair if decisions about resource allocation are perceived as being consistent, accurate and free of errors, representative and ethical, and correctable in case of errors. In discussing public trust and confidence in institutions, Tyler (2001a) has argued that the key issue that shapes public views is a process-based evaluation of the fairness of procedures that are used to exercise authority. Central to this process is the communication of respect for the individual.

(c) Retributive justice is concerned with the perceived appropriateness of sanctions in cases of norm breaking (Tyler, 1990). The central questions refer to attributions of responsibility to those guilty of wrong-doing, the restoration of damages to the wronged party and the punishment a norm-breaker deserves.

Justice considerations are in contrast to the neoclassical model of rational decision-making, as they assume that taxpayers evaluate their expected outcome in a given situation and take the best alternative (Allingham and Sandmo, 1972; Becker, 1968). Justice considerations imply that taxpayers compare their contributions and benefits as well as their treatment with others, and judgments of fairness depend on the perspective a person takes. Judgments of fairness may regard individual treatment and outcomes relative to other individuals, or focus on group and societal outcomes. At an individual level, taxpayers are concerned with their individual tax burden and with their share of public goods. Wenzel (2003) developed a framework that relied on two dimensions: the first dimension classified justice and fairness perceptions at an individual, group or societal level, while the second dimension distinguished between the distribution of resources, procedures and retributive justice.

At the individual level, the perceived recipient unit is the individual. Taxpayers are concerned about fairness of their outcomes as well as being treated in a way they are entitled to in relation to their merits, efforts and needs. At the group level, the perceived recipient unit is a social group, e.g., occupational group, income group, a minority group in the country. Taxpayers are concerned about fairness of the outcomes as well as of the treatment of their group. Group members judge entitlements and treatments that they receive as members of a specific group, and resource allocation and procedures directed towards their group. Concerns regard specific constraints, tax rates, benefits, audits; and sanction practices are made with reference to a specific group. On the group level, dynamics of social categorisation and identification with a category come into play. At the societal level, the category to which taxpayers refer is the whole nation. Fairness judgments regard taxation in the country, fairness of progressive, regressive or flat tax, and procedures applied by the tax office. Table 6

Table 6: *Distributive justice, procedural justice and retributive justice by level of analysis (Wenzel, 2003, pp. 49–58)*

Level of analysis	Individual level	Group level	Societal level
Distributive justice in tax research			
Tax burdens	personal tax burden; compared to others; other times; one's relative income	In-group's tax burden; compared to other groups; other times; its relative income	tax level; distribution; progressivity
Tax-based benefits	personal benefits compared to others; other times; one's relative taxes	In-group's benefits; compared to other groups; other times; its relative income	level of spending; efficiency; distribution over different policies
Avoidance/evasion opportunities	personal options compared to others; other times	In-group's options relative to other groups	level; distribution of opportunities
Procedural justice in tax research			
Interactional treatment	respect for the individual; consistency relative to other individuals	respect for the in-group; consistency relative to other groups	rights for taxpayers and service standards
Process and decision control	voice; control; consultation of individual	voice; control, consultation and representation of in-group	consultation of taxpayers in general; democratic structures
Information and explanation	explanations and justifications for decisions affecting the individual	explanation and justifications for decisions affecting the in-group	transparency; presentation in media
Compliance costs	efficiency; service versus costs for the individual	efficiency; service versus costs for the group	administration and compliance costs; complexity of the tax system
Retributive justice in tax research			
Penalties	appropriateness of penalty for individual (relative to the offence, others)	appropriateness of penalty for in-group (relative to the offence, others)	severity of penalties; distribution penalties for different offences; quality of penalties
Audits	rigidity or inconsiderateness of audit for individual case	rigidity or inconsiderateness of audit for in-group case	rigidity or inconsiderateness of audits in general

summarises fairness issues regarding resource distribution, procedures and treatment on individual, group and societal levels.

3.5.1   Distributive justice

Taxes serve the aim of creating and providing public goods and redistributing income such that low-income earners profit more, while high-income earners contribute more to the provision of public goods. The Gini-coefficient is an economic index expressing the effect of taxes on the redistribution of resources in favour of the poor. As Lea, Tarpy and Webley reported in 1987, the Gini-coefficient showed that Great Britain did succeed in redistributing income towards a more equal level during the period prior to publication. However, the majority of citizens still believe that taxes are unfairly distributed and the rich are advantaged.

Research on fairness judgments and tax compliance has mainly focused on distributive justice, without always clearly differentiating between the three reference levels. According to Wenzel, distributive fairness research considers tax burdens and tax-funded public benefits. He also considers perceived opportunities of tax avoidance as a resource that can be perceived as unequally available to taxpayers.

Research on horizontal fairness has examined the distribution of resources between taxpayers of comparable income groups. Dean, Keenan and Kenney (1980) found that horizontal fairness is indeed a major concern, as a considerable percentage of taxpayers believe that their tax burden is much higher as compared to the tax burden of individuals with similar income. Kinsey and Grasmick report evidence for horizontal equity playing a major role with regard to tax compliance. If an individual's tax burden is of the same magnitude as that of comparable others, tax compliance increases. The results by Spicer and Becker (1980) and de Juan, Lasheras and Mayo (1994) point in the same direction. Spicer and Becker found that individuals who perceive themselves in a disadvantageous tax situation are more likely to evade taxes, whereas an advantageous situation is related to higher compliance. In their experiment each subject faced the same tax rate; however, one-third was told that the average tax rate was higher; one-third was told that it was lower, and one-third was told that their tax rate was average. The results suggested that perceived inequity has a strong influence on evasion. A similar study with different tax-free allowances available to different groups of participants did not confirm any effect on tax evasion (Webley, Robben and Morris, 1988).

Besides horizontal fairness, there are vertical fairness and exchange fairness, which are also of major concern to taxpayers. Rawlings (2003) explored the relationship between culturally mediated narratives of fairness, conceptions of the state, group and individual identities, and citizenship and debates about globalisation in Australian perspectives on tax administration. About two-thirds of the respondents to a survey stated at some point that the tax system should be fair and related fairness to trust in the government. Here are some of the observations made by the respondents with regard to the tax system and vertical fairness:

it [the tax system] is unfair to the community as a whole. There are too many loopholes for creative accounting and the top end of town is able to exploit these deficiencies. I wish the Government would scrap the lot and start again. (p. 286)

Stop very wealthy people from using schemes to pay little tax . . . They have clever lawyers who know all the loopholes. (p. 291)

There are too many loopholes that big business and rich people use. Kerry Packer pays less personal income tax than I do. How can they say that is fair?
(p. 291; the late Kerry Packer was one of the wealthiest people in Australia)

V. Braithwaite (2003c) found that a majority of Australians (76.9%) think that chief executives of large national corporations pay much less or a bit less than their fair share of tax; 70.1% think that owner-managers of large companies do not pay their fair share, and still more than half of the respondents thought that senior judges, barristers, surgeons, doctors and families earning more than 100,000 Australian dollars per year do not pay their fair share, while only 4.9% of respondents admitted not paying their own fair share. In order to increase compliance, respondents voted for more transparency to ensure that large corporations and wealthier people pay more tax, and also for containment and efficiency in terms of minimising the regulations and paperwork for taxpayers, lowering taxes and providing incentives to contribute honestly as well as keeping costs of administrating a tax system down.

Spicer and Lundstedt (1976) argued that taxpayers are involved in an exchange relationship with the government. Taxpayers may be seen as exchanging purchasing power in the market in return for government service. If this is the case, then it seems reasonable to suppose that taxpayers' behaviour may be affected by their satisfaction or lack of satisfaction with their terms of trade with the government. Even if taxpayers are not able to assess the exact value of what they pay and what they receive from the government, they will have a general impression and attitudes concerning their own and others' terms of trade with the government. In their survey, tax resistance scores were found to be positively related to scores on the index of inequity items and to the number of tax evaders known personally by the respondent, and related to the perceived probability of detection. Age was the most important background variable, explaining 29% of the total variance in scores on the tax resistance scale. Increasing age was related to lower tax resistance.

Taxpayers hold beliefs about what the government is spending on various public goods and what the government should spend, and they hold beliefs about what they receive from the government and what they should receive. Kirchler (1997a) asked Austrian taxpayers about their beliefs and found that the government is, on average, perceived as correctly spending its funds. In particular, it should spend slightly more on education, science and research, public health, public security, transport and housing, and slightly less on defence, arts and cultural events, economic development and social security, as well as construction of streets. With regard to personal participation in the use of public goods, the respondents thought that they should have more access than actually was the case to all kinds of public goods (see table 7). Exchange fairness seems to be quite imbalanced.

Moser, Evans III and Kim (1995) conducted an experiment to examine whether taxpayers' responses to a tax rate change depended on both economic factors and perceptions of horizontal and exchange inequity. Exchange inequity was manipulated by varying tax rates while holding public goods and services constant. Tax rates were either increasing from 20% in the first rounds in the experiment up to 30% and 45%, or decreasing from 45% or 30% to 20%. Horizontal inequity was manipulated by informing participants at the start of each experimental period that the tax rate they faced in that period was higher (namely 20%, 30% or 45%) than the tax rate faced by other taxpayers (7%, 10% or 15%, respectively). Under the condition of equity, participants were informed that all taxpayers faced the same tax rate. It was found that horizontal equity interacts with exchange equity. Taxpayers' responses to a tax rate change depended on both economic effects and perceptions of horizontal and exchange inequity. When taxpayers' tax rate was higher than others' tax rate and exchange was disadvantageous, then non-compliance increased. When tax rates decreased, participants reported more income when they were inequitably treated relative to others. Calderwood and Webley (1992) and Wartick (1994) also investigated taxpayers' responses to changes of tax rates. Changing tax rates are likely to direct taxpayers towards comparing actual burdens with their previous burdens. Again, tax compliance decreased when comparisons yielded disadvantageous results, unless justifications for the change were provided.

In a game-theoretic approach, Pommerehne, Hart and Frey (1994) modelled the interaction between individuals and the government as a dynamic process to analyse the relationship between government's public

Table 7: *Average perceived public expenditures and desired expenditures for various public goods, and perceived subjective utility and desired utility of public goods (1 = very low, 5 = very high) (Kirchler, 1997a)*

Public goods	Perceived amount of public expenditure		Desired amount of public expenditure		Perceived individual utility of public goods		Desired individual utility of public expenditure	
	M	SD	M	SD	M	SD	M	SD
Education	2.99	1.10	4.16	0.77	2.62	1.31	3.54	1.36
Science and research	2.38	1.03	3.87	1.00	2.08	1.16	3.27	1.18
Public health	3.74	1.25	4.08	0.89	3.17	1.24	3.99	0.92
Economic development	3.21	1.07	2.89	0.99	2.11	1.13	2.75	1.20
Art and culture	3.37	1.12	2.67	0.94	2.47	1.25	3.10	1.18
Agriculture	2.85	1.04	3.23	0.99	2.12	1.12	2.61	1.32
Military defence	3.26	1.43	2.42	1.15	1.74	1.00	2.23	1.25
Social security	3.90	1.10	3.67	0.93	2.31	1.14	3.29	1.10
Public security	3.06	0.90	3.65	0.89	2.81	1.07	3.53	1.03
Construction of streets	3.46	1.27	3.13	0.96	3.17	1.14	3.33	1.04
Public transport	3.14	1.04	3.38	0.90	2.72	1.14	3.35	1.09
Housing construction	3.20	1.10	3.68	1.10	2.05	1.27	3.26	1.32
Total	3.21	0.38	3.43	0.41	2.45	0.65	3.19	0.63

Note:
M = arithmetic mean; SD = standard deviation.

good provision, government waste, fairness considerations and taxpayer compliance. After each period of interaction, participants reflected on the experience of the previous period and decided how much tax to pay. Willingness to pay taxes was found to depend on provision of public goods and government waste in the previous periods. It seems that taxpayers follow a tit-for-tat strategy, seeking to balance their share to the government with their participation in public goods provided by the government. Thus, tax evasion may be a strategy to restore equity in the tax system (e.g., Mittone, 2006; Robben *et al.* 1989; Thibaut, Fredland and Walker, 1974).

Falkinger's 1995 work showed that the impact of equity on tax evasion depended on how taxpayers' risk aversion was affected by perceived equity. He presented an economic as well as psychological argument to explain a positive relationship between risk aversion and equity, and thus, between evasion and inequity. The economic argument considers cases where the valuation of public output increases with income. The psychological argument is based on the hypothesis that people find evasion more blameworthy in a system that is considered to be just than in an unfair system. With such a norm, an increase in equity increases the bad reputation or bad conscience of evaders and leads to a reduction in evasion.

Wallschutzky compared convicted tax evaders with a control group in Australia and found that while men, the self-employed, higher-income strata taxpayers and people born outside Australia had a higher non-compliance rate, no significant differences in evaluations of income tax relative to government services existed (Wallschutzky, 1984). However, interviews revealed that evaders mentioned the exchange relationship as the most important factor in their evading decisions. In a similar study in the United States, Mason and Calvin (1978) asked taxpayers to evaluate their tax levels compared to the public goods they received, and the number of benefits compared to the benefits of the average person in the country. Neither rating was related to self-reported evasion. However, the assumption that perceived exchange injustice lowered compliance was confirmed in Porcano's 1988 study, and in an experiment by Alm, McClelland and Schulze (1992), who manipulated the magnitude of returns relative to the taxes paid and found that compliance increased with the favourability of that ratio. Alm, Jackson and McKee (1993) found evidence for an exchange relationship in a laboratory simulation, where the amount of taxes paid was greater if public goods were provided. Furthermore, cross-national survey research carried out in Europe by Strümpel (1966) indicates that positive attitudes towards the tax system, including perceptions of equity or fairness, can exert a significant influence on the level of tax compliance within a country.

There is increasing empirical evidence supporting the existence of a positive relationship between perceived public spending and tax compliance. Tax cheating decreases the more taxpayers feel that their taxes are paid back in the form of public services (Pommerehne and Frey, 1992). This relationship between give and take corresponds to the social psychological notion of a basic 'norm of reciprocity' (Gouldner, 1960) and to equity and social exchange theories as postulated by Adams (1965), Blau (1964), Homans (1961) and Walster, Walster and Berscheid (1978).

Taxpayers may evaluate fairness of tax burdens, tax-funded benefits, and tax avoidance opportunities not only at the individual level but also for their reference group (Wenzel, 2003). Comparisons can be made to previous outcomes, to imagined referents and also to other groups. Vertical justice research focused on comparisons to other groups' burdens, benefits and opportunities. Roberts and Hite (1994) report that vertical unfairness of the tax schedule leads to increased tax evasion. Kinsey and Grasmick (1993) found that American taxpayers' belief that the tax system benefited the rich had a significant effect on respondents' expressed acceptability of tax evasion. In their 1976 survey, Spicer and Lundstedt collected open-ended responses to questions regarding the fairness or unfairness of the distribution of the burden of taxes. The answers revealed the importance of vertical justice perceptions: of those who thought the distribution to be unfair, 75% stated that a major reason was extensive tax avoidance by affluent taxpayers or corporations.

Finally, at the societal level, taxpayers may evaluate the fairness of the tax system. There is evidence that suggests that the structure of taxes has an influence on people's willingness to evade (Baldry, 1987; Cowell, 1992). The perception that the government may be using tax proceeds for inappropriate purposes also plays a role in predisposing people to evade taxes (Vogel, 1974), as does the disagreement with the provision of public goods. Brosio and colleagues (2002) argue that the higher non-compliance in the poorer Italian south as compared to the richer northern regions can be an expression of disagreement with state provision of public goods. Additionally, Myles (2000) concludes that tax evasion can emerge as a response to disagreement with government policy.

On the societal level, the existence of progressive, regressive or flat taxes is a particularly important topic. Acceptance of flat tax rates rather than progressive tax rates has been widely discussed. However, due to the complexity of the issues and limited interest and understanding, the expressed preferences of taxpayers often lack validity. As Roberts, Hite and Bradley (1994) demonstrated, preferences depend highly on the format of the questions in a survey. Nevertheless, it is perhaps not citizens' objective knowledge and preferences that count most in relation to tax behaviour, but their subjective representations and evaluations of tax issues.

Another reason for non-compliance on the societal level may be the inequitable tax system as it is established by tax shelters. Hite's 1990 study on the effect of tax shelters provides data on this issue. Participants read scenarios and imagined either being able to use tax shelters or not. The scenarios had no effect on perceived inequity; however respondents with previous tax shelters reported the hypothetical tax shelter as equitable, whereas those without a previous tax shelter reported the hypothetical one as inequitable.

3.5.2 Procedural justice

In tax research, procedural justice has received considerably less attention than distributive justice, although it is well known that citizens do care about procedural aspects, such as voice, dignity and respect for relational and symbolic reasons, in their relations with political institutions. According to Tyler and Lind (1992), neutrality of the procedure, the trustworthiness of the third party, and polite, dignified and respectful treatment are essential for perceiving procedures as fair. Willingness to comply with laws is determined predominantly by the perceived fairness of procedures. Procedural fairness plays a key role in shaping the legitimacy that citizens grant to government authority, which in turn supports the system that is essential to govern effectively without coercion (Tyler, 1990, 2006). Thus, procedural justice research has important implications for governance and social cooperation (MacCoun, 2005).

On the individual level, procedural justice refers to the quality of treatment in interactions between taxpayers and authorities, the quality of information provided by tax authorities and the compliance and administration costs as well as dynamics of allocation of revenues. Access to, and provision of, information related to the tax law and explanations for a tax law change can increase fairness perceptions (Wartick, 1994). Information that reduces tax law complexity and increases transparency leads to perceptions of greater fairness (Carnes and Cuccia, 1996). Efficiency of interactions between taxpayers and tax authorities, length of queues at information desks, satisfaction with audit treatment, etc. determine perceptions of procedural justice (Wallschutzky, 1984). At the individual level, fair treatment of individual taxpayers and the culture of interaction are relevant aspects of fairness and justice perceptions and the building of trust (Job and Reinhart, 2003; Job, Stout and Smith, 2007; Tyler, 2001a). Following Tyler's 1990 work, Smith and Stalans (1991) regard respectful and responsive treatment by tax authorities and officers as well as respectfulness, neutrality and trustworthiness as positive incentives related to procedural justice perceptions. Furthermore, taxpayers who blame tax auditors for being unresponsive to their views and comments are likely to think that auditors try less hard to be fair (Stalans and Lind, 1997).

On the group and societal levels, procedural fairness concerns the neutrality of tax officers regarding groups such as occupational or income groupings. The perception that certain constituencies have more liberty leads to the perception of unfair treatment (Murphy, 2003c, 2004b). If tax authorities and officers treat taxpayers fairly, in a respectful and responsible way, trust in the institution and cooperation are likely to increase on the individual, group and societal level. This implies that tax officers need to be responsive to taxpayers and not hand out 'standard treatment' (e.g., V. Braithwaite, 2003d; James, 1998). Moreover, if taxpayers are heard and agree with decisions on how to spend tax revenues, their fairness evaluations are more favourable. Direct democracy has significant positive effects on tax morale in Switzerland, a country where participation rights vary substantially across different cantons. The more taxpayers are able to participate in political decision-making by popular rights, the more the government respects taxpayers' preferences in spending tax revenue, and the more the 'tax contract' is based on trust, the higher the level of tax morale (Frey, 2003; Torgler, 2005a). In addition, tax morale is affected by direct participation in general. Tax morale is especially strong if participation concerns political decisions closely related to financial issues. Trust in the government and in governmental institutions has a systematic positive influence on tax morale (Fjeldstad, 2004; Pommerehne and Frey, 1992; Torgler, 2003d, 2005b; Tyler and Degoey, 1996).

Aspects of procedural justice were found to be related to compliance intentions. Perceived supportiveness of advice by tax officers correlates with self-reported compliance, which in turn determines compliance behaviour (Kirchler, Niemirowski and Wearing, 2006). Also, having a say with regard to spending tax revenues increases compliance. Conversely, compliance is lower if spending decisions are imposed on taxpayers. Alm, Jackson and McKee (1993) conducted an experiment on participants' compliance under the conditions of imposed revenue spending or spending according to majority votes. Procedural qualities of the decision affected tax compliance. Smith and Stalans (1991) found that material and non-material incentives may encourage compliance in laboratory conditions. However, Porcano (1988) did not find a significant effect of procedural justice on compliance intent. The study was on the effect of procedural justice, operationalised as having some say in formulating tax laws and in enforcement procedures applied by the tax authorities, and on taxpayers' wishes to be heard more. Given the number of additional variables investigated by this study, possible justice effects on self-reported tax evasion may have been masked by other related variables.

A common assumption of the economics of tax evasion, extending beyond the basis of neoclassical economic assumptions, is that the choice of a taxpayer to evade taxes depends upon the perceived fairness of the tax system. According to Vihanto (2003), taxpayers are more compliant with tax laws to which they can in principle give their full consent. People tend to adhere to a conceptual social or psychological contract similar in nature to a typical contract. A contractual relationship implies duties and rights for each contract partner, in this case, taxpayers and the government. The contractual relationship has implications both for the level of contributions and benefits and at the procedural level, namely the way tax authorities and officers treat taxpayers. If tax administrations treat taxpayers disrespectfully, as inferiors in an authoritarian relationship, the psychological tax contract is violated and citizens have good reason not to comply with their part of the contract and thus, evade taxes. If distribution of burdens and access to public goods is perceived to be fair and procedural justice is high, taxpayers feel an obligation and willingness to comply, spurred by their psychological contract with the community in general and the government in particular. People have a natural tendency to follow the same rules as the members of groups with which they share common affinities. Social norms and herd behaviour, as well as an implicit psychological contract between taxpayers and the government, enhance cooperation and loyalty. Equity and fair treatment build trust and lead to the development of a psychological contract and eventually to compliance due to binding social norms regulating interaction. Perceived justice in tax systems is brought about by unambiguous tax laws that reduce opportunities for arbitrary interpretation, transparent criteria of taxation that enable taxpayers to perceive their total tax burden and thereby monitor the doings of the government, comprehensive tax laws, the decentralising of taxing power from the government to local levels with unambiguous rules, the acceptability of the tax laws, and governmental efforts to prevent cheating for revenue sharing, as well as government prevention of tax cheating (Vihanto, 2003). Moreover, these factors lead to trust, which is defined as the 'expectation which arises within a community of regular, honest and cooperative behaviour, based on commonly shared norms, on the part of other members of the community' (Fukuyama, 1995, p. 26).

Tax non-compliance can also result from disapproval of government policy: Erard and Feinstein have reported a famous example of how disapproval of a government policy may trigger non-compliance, as seen in 'the story of Henry David Thoreau, who in 1837 refused to pay his taxes to the federal government as a protest against its unwillingness to combat slavery more actively; he spent one night in jail' (Erard and Feinstein, 1994a, p. 17). Crush (1985) has reported a study of overt and covert forms of African resistance to colonial policies in their refusal to pay taxes. The study provides insight into the diversity and creativity of African reactions to enforced proletarianisation, the differentiated character of rural society and the nature and role of the colonial state. The role of the state in creating the conditions for capital accumulation constantly undermined its supplementary role as the guarantor of social order. Colonial taxation often proved to be a blunt instrument in achieving stated ends. The imperatives behind heavy colonial taxation, its variable impact on a stratified agrarian society and the innovative responses of Swazi households culminated in a widespread campaign of tax evasion.

3.5.3 Retributive justice

Like procedural justice, retributive justice has rarely been investigated in the field of tax compliance. Moreover, retributive justice is closely related to the interaction between tax authorities and taxpayers as well as to procedural justice. Retributive justice regards the rigidity of audits and the responsibility of wrongdoing, the restoration process and appropriateness of penalties in cases of norm breaking.

Unreasonable and intrusive audits and unfair penalties lead to negative attitudes toward the tax office and taxes (e.g., Strümpel, 1969; Spicer and Lundstedt, 1976). Hasseldine and Kaplan (1992) conducted a study in New Zealand on the role of communication as a means of encouraging compliance and the relative effects of economic sanctions, informal sanctions and positive conscience appeals. Four groups of participants read hypothetical tax-related scenarios containing details of legal sanctions, informal sanctions, an appeal to conscience or no information about sanctions and no appeal to conscience. They found that informal communication was most effective in enhancing compliance. However, it should be kept in mind that penalties for wrongdoing are widely accepted if measures are perceived as appropriate. Especially in countries with high tax morale, cheating taxes challenges societal cooperation and is therefore perceived as a major offence which should be strictly punished. In 1992, Pommerehne and Frey reported that in Swiss referendum cantons, people have greater trust in the government than in non-referendum cantons and their cooperation with the government and tax morale are higher; additionally, in order to keep the high cooperative standards, people favour severe punishment for wrongdoing. With regard to the perception of just sanctions, it might be expected that citizens do not hold a general attitude about what is appropriate punishment, but rather consider the causes of evasion when deciding on the punishment. The impact of causal attributions on tax evasion judgments was also investigated, and findings indicated that personal need and the degree of societal consensus affect penalty judgments (Kaplan, Reckers and Reynolds, 1986).

Falkinger and Walther (1991) have been critical of the way in which tax law applies only punishment for wrongdoing, while providing no positive reinforcement for honest behaviour. Taking the economic analysis and moral and practical doubts together, they propose to introduce into the existing penalty system at least some pecuniary reward for controlled honesty. This would open up the possibility that compliance could become an alternative of rational choice, being not only morally correct, but also economically suboptimal, without displaying the negative features of prohibitive punishment (see also Hite, 1989; Paternoster and Simpson, 1996).

The government needs to apply consistent rules to sanction evasion and apply appropriate measures against it. While for several years, the Australian Taxation Office tolerated the practices of tax minimisation schemes and enjoyment of generous tax breaks, in 1998 it announced that a number of initiatives would be implemented to combat aggressive tax planning and crack down on tax minimisation schemes. The tax office declared them illegal and amended previous tax assessments. Taxpayers involved in the schemes faced large bills, penalties and interest charges. There was not merely a perceived inconsistency over time; more significantly, middle- and working-class people resented the decision because they thought it reflected discriminatory treatment towards them and favoured the rich, who went unpunished (Wenzel, 2003). Murphy (2003a) has reported that the majority of scheme investors, however, resisted the tax office's attempts to recover scheme-related tax debts. The widespread resistance exhibited by scheme investors was due partly to the manner in which the tax office dealt with the schemes issue. Using survey data collected from tax scheme investors and general taxpayers, Murphy showed that those who invested in tax schemes were more disillusioned with the tax system, were more hostile and resistant towards the tax office, and were also more likely to resent paying tax as a result. In-depth interviews with twenty-nine scheme investors revealed that many of them had defied the tax office's demands because they perceived the procedures used to handle the situation to be unfair (Murphy, 2003b). Given these findings, Murphy has argued that to effectively shape desired behaviour, regulators will need to move towards strategies that aim to emphasise the procedural and retributive justice aspects. In further studies (2004a, 2004b), she has discussed the use of threats and legal coercion as regulatory tools and their ineffectiveness in gaining compliance. She demonstrated the need for variables such as trust to be considered when managing non-compliance. If regulators are seen to be acting fairly, people will trust the motives of that authority and will defer to their decisions voluntarily.

Also, tax amnesties raise the question of whether they are perceived as fair treatment of tax avoidance and evasion. In tax policy, tax amnesties have frequently been justified as politically popular ways to generate increases in government revenue. Malik and Schwab (1991) have argued that amnesties are irrelevant in the standard economic tax evasion model. In that model, consumers would never take advantage of an opportunity to report additional income during an amnesty because the amount of income reported initially would still be optimal. However, other models predict that taxpayers are not certain about the disutility from tax evasion when they file their tax returns, and if they would like to be more honest than they have been, an amnesty gives them an opportunity to report additional income. Thus, everyone gains from an amnesty, in the sense that those who participate are made better off, and the government collects additional revenue. However, amnesties also have costs. Andreoni (1991) underlines the possibility of a tax amnesty actually decreasing, rather than increasing, the efficiency and equity of the tax system. As the probability of an amnesty rises, and thus the future opportunity to declare any dishonesty free of penalty, people report less income. For this reason, there are valid concerns about tax amnesty. First, if anticipated, an amnesty may increase cheating and reduce the efficiency of the tax system. Second, an amnesty may be inequitable by letting cheaters 'off the hook'. Furthermore, Alm, McKee and Beck (1990) found in an experimental setting that the introduction of a tax amnesty in which participants can pay previously unpaid taxes without penalty lowers post-amnesty compliance. Stella (1991) examined the circumstances under which amnesties are likely to have a beneficial impact on revenue collections. He concluded that, while in general it may be correct to impose a reduced penalty on individuals who voluntarily disclose tax evasion, short-lived amnesties of the type most frequently observed in practice are unlikely to generate genuinely additional revenue, particularly when judged against the potential danger of reducing future tax compliance due to expectations of future amnesties or unfairness perceptions. Amnesties have the advantage of bringing taxpayers who previously evaded tax but have changed their attitude back into the system. Taxpayers who are already honest may, however, consider a tax amnesty unfair, because it does not acknowledge their integrity, disadvantages them materially and rewards tax evasion (Hasseldine, 1998b). Tax amnesties bear the risk that honest taxpayers perceive them as rewarding non-compliant behaviour, being an inappropriate retributive justice measure and, as such, being unfair to those who paid taxes honestly.

3.5.4   Individual and situational differences in justice concerns

Although it seems reasonable to assume that willingness to pay one's taxes rises if the distribution of tax burdens across citizens and groups is perceived as fair, if the exchange relationship with the government is balanced, and if procedural justice is high, the results of empirical studies do not unequivocally confirm this assumption. Lack of congruent findings in tax compliance research is not limited to justice perceptions. Jackson and Milliron (1986) reviewed forty-three studies dealing with fourteen variables supposedly influencing compliance. None of these variables was unequivocally found to have either a consistently positive or negative impact on compliance. In some of the studies, ten variables were found to have a positive impact, while other studies reported a negative influence, or the variables had no effect on compliance.

To the best of our knowledge, no study has revealed negative effects of perceived distributive justice; however, the positive impact on tax compliance was not always confirmed, and if the impact reached statistical significance, the effects were rather small. While it can be argued that tax behaviour is complex, with many variables influencing tax compliance, making it unlikely that one isolated determinant might explain a large proportion of variance, it should also be noted that there are probably inter-individual and situational differences with regard to the relevance of fairness and justice issues that might not be important to all taxpayers to an equal extent or relevant in all circumstances.

For instance, experimental results have shown that taxpayers who received no public transfer generally perceived their exchange equity with the government to be less equitable than taxpayers who received a public transfer. However, as Kim (2002) shows, the effect of the public transfer on reported income depends on the extent to which taxpayers refer to their perception of equity in their tax-reporting decisions. Participants who perceived equity to be important in their tax-reporting decisions reported more income when they received a public transfer, but reported less income when they received no public transfer, as predicted by equity theory. In contrast, participants who perceived equity to be less important in their tax-reporting decisions acted directionally consistent

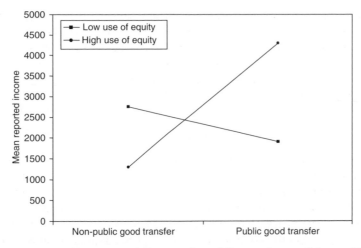

Figure 11: Mean reported income by public transfer condition and high and low use of equity considerations in tax reports (Kim, 2002, p. 778)

with the predictions of the neoclassical economic model (see figure 11). Kirchler's 1998 analysis of social representations of taxes yielded differences in the core representations of self-employed and employed people. As figure 13 details, the semantic space of associations to 'taxes', issues related to justice and exchange (e.g., social welfare, public goods and social justice) are central to white-collar workers, civil servants and, to some extent, blue-collar workers, but less to the self-employed, who associate taxation with loss of personal freedom and punishment. If the self-employed do not evaluate taxes from the perspective of distributive justice, then it is unsurprising that a survey conducted with the self-employed would not confirm that justice issues are related to compliance.

Another bias that might reduce the effect of justice on compliance is the unclear cause-effect relationship between justice perceptions and tax behaviour. Rather than being the cause for non-compliance, perceptions of injustice may be an ex-post rationalisation of otherwise caused tax non-compliance. Falkinger (1988) investigated the impact on tax evasion of perceived equity in the taxpayer–government relationship. While the common argument is that taxpayers may view their relationship to the government as one of exchange, where taxes are paid in return for benefits and tax evasion is a means to adjust the corresponding terms of trade with the government if they are perceived to be unfair, Falkinger has argued that, rather than being the cause of compliance, justice perceptions might be a justification of non-compliance in hindsight. His analysis showed that taxpayers who were at all aware of the fact that they received some benefits in exchange for the taxes evaded comparatively less than tax-payers who were not. But the main hypothesis of the equity argument – that the proportion by which a taxpayer evades his taxes decreases if the share of public expenditures from which he benefits increases – was not unambiguously confirmed on theoretical grounds. If the taxpayers' demand for public goods is satiated to a certain degree, a higher share in public expenditures will induce them to evade even more. The inter-pretation is that, in this case, taxpayers feel the taxes are relatively useless. Taxpayers who are less satiated with respect to public goods will react in accordance with the equity hypothesis. They will reduce tax evasion if a higher share in public expenditures is to their benefit. There is also some theoretical support for the supposition that the equity argument is an ex post facto rationalisation of tax evasion. This is especially likely in a large, anonymous society with affluent public provision whereas, at a local level and in the face of unsatisfied public needs, the inequity argument that tax evasion is a rational adjustment to unequal benefits from public activities becomes more credible.

Besides inter-individual differences, situational differences may lower the predicted effect of justice issues. Kinsey, Grasmick and Smith (1991) claim that existing research on distributive justice provides little guidance for understanding how people select and process justice-related informa-tion in a stimulus-rich environment. Because individuals' information-processing capacities are limited, most individuals base their distributive justice perceptions on very few – one or two – salient dimensions of the situation. Prospect theory (Kahneman and Tversky, 1979) emphasises the initial editing stage that 'frames' a situation and defines the reference points against which behavioural alternatives will be evaluated. Kinsey and her colleagues examined how taxpayers evaluate the distributive justice of personal income tax burdens, suggesting that taxpayers employ either an outcome-processing or a norm-processing frame of tax fairness evaluations. Framing is affected by substantive tax policies and the tax situations of individuals. Taxpayers who qualify for tax deductions and other tax preferences employ an outcome-processing frame and focus on perceived abuse of government power when evaluating fairness. Those unable to claim tax breaks employ a norm-processing frame and focus on vertical social comparisons and their inability to qualify for valued tax breaks. Fairness perceptions and evaluations vary with the activated framing.

Depending on the actual social situation, taxpayers may perceive them-selves as individuals or as members of a social group, such as a particular occupational group, or as members of the nation and interpret and evaluate fairness issues differently. Torgler (2003d) has argued that individuals who are proud of their country behave differently than those who are not proud. Pride produces a sense of group identification, and according to Wenzel (2000, 2001, 2004b, 2004c), social identification has a relevant impact on justice concerns and tax behaviour.

3.5.5   Justice and social identification

Justice research has yielded inconsistent evidence for the impact of justice perceptions on tax compliance due to three main causes: different aspects of justice and fairness were investigated, the operationalisation and measurement of justice varies considerably, and inter-individual and situational differences were largely neglected. Moreover, as Taylor and Wenzel have shown, fairness judgments are not stable but depend on the object of comparison and on taxpayers' identification with a social group or category to which justice refers (Taylor, 2003; Wenzel, 2002; see also Wenzel, 2001, 2004b, 2004c).

According to social categorisation theory (Turner et al., 1987; Turner and Onorato, 1997) and the group value model (Lind and Tyler, 1988; Tyler, 1994), taxpayers are more concerned about fairness and less about personal outcomes and egoistic advantages when they identify strongly with the group to which procedures and distributions apply. Wenzel (2002) has argued that on the basis of social identity theory and the group value model, taxpayers want to be treated fairly as members of the group, as fair treatment acknowledges their membership and status in the group and maintains the values of the group. Taxpayers seek procedural justice in terms of neutrality, trustworthiness and respect. Since fairness issues are especially important if individuals identify strongly with their group, Wenzel has hypothesised that tax compliance will increase if taxpayers identify strongly with their relevant social category, and if they perceive high procedural and distributive justice.

Wenzel (2002) tested effects of social identification on justice percep-tions and tax compliance on an Australian sample of more than 2,000 taxpayers who responded to questions on tax compliance (under-declaration of various forms of income, exaggerated claims for deduc-tions, and rebates, general engagement in tax planning and use of specific forms of tax minimisation); their inclusive identification by indicating their feelings of pride in being a member of the Australian community; outcome considerations in terms of favourable decisions by the tax authorities; procedural justice (respect, trustworthiness, neutrality); and distributive justice (perception of similar tax burdens for taxpayers with similar income). Besides the frequently reported age and sex differences in the tax compliance literature (older respondents and women reported that they were more compliant and more likely to report their income), he found that respondents who identified more strongly with Australia reported being more compliant. Respondents who identified less with Australia were more outcome oriented; they were more compliant when tax decisions were in their favour. Perceived procedural justice was related to greater tax compliance only for respondents who identified strongly with Australia, whereas it was somewhat positively related to non-compliance for the less identified. This result may have wide-reaching implications with regard to tax research and practical implications: if taxpayers who identify weakly with their nation and its political institutions are outcome oriented, they may consider taxes from an individual profit maximisation perspective, consider what they have to pay and what they get in return, and take (rational) decisions on how to profit most. If, on the other hand, highly identifying taxpayers consider procedural justice aspects more than distribution of resources, their willingness to cooperate with the government in general, and with tax authorities in particular, may be more immediate than the result of a profit maximisation reflection. If procedural justice is perceived as high and the authorities are perceived as legitimate, cooperation may be more normative and voluntary. With regard to tax research, social and national identification may prove to be a crucial dimension, able to differentiate between circumstances under which taxpayers comply voluntarily or are making (rational) decisions, aiming to increase individual profit, and cooperating only if they are forced to do so by the applications of audits and fines. Identification may be a relevant differential variable explaining under what conditions tax mentality, personal and social norms, and fairness matter with regard to tax compliance and under what conditions audits and fines are more effective in enforcing tax compliance. According to social and national identification and justice considerations it is relevant that government and tax authorities follow the rules of behaviour that lead to perceived procedural fairness, if voluntary compliance is desired.

Wenzel (2004c) further investigated social identification, justice perception and tax compliance in a study on individual- and group-level identification and justice perceptions. Individual-level justice refers to people's evaluations and concerns about the realisation of their individual entitlements. Group-level justice denotes people's evaluations and concerns about the realisation of their group's entitlement. Finally, inclusive level justice refers to people's views about the appropriate distribution of outcomes across all individuals or groups considered 'potential recipients'. Depending on social identification, he has argued that taxpayers compare their benefits and burdens and the treatment they get and evaluate justice on different levels. In his study he found no justice concerns when both group and national identification were weak, individual-level concerns were confirmed when group identification was strong, and group-level concerns were found when both subgroup and national identification were strong. People were concerned that they or their reference groups received appropriate treatment and resources, and, depending on the level of identification, justice evaluations fluctuated.

From a social identity perspective, compliance is an outcome of self-categorisation processes and identification with a social group (Taylor, 2003; Wenzel, 2004c). Taylor argues that compliance with tax laws is more likely to occur when a superordinate identity (e.g., one's nation) is salient rather than when a subgroup identity (e.g., one's occupation groups) is salient, and when the authority in question (e.g., tax authorities) is included in that superordinate identity. The degree to which authorities are perceived to be representative of those over whom they have power has important implications for tax behaviour. When authorities are perceived to behave fairly and respectfully, greater compliance results; and when they are perceived as representative, their decisions are seen as legitimate because they are acting in the collective interest (Taylor, 2001). On the other hand, unrepresentative authorities are perceived as illegitimate because they do not represent 'us' appropriately (Haslam, 2001). Taylor argues further that legitimacy leads to acceptance of decisions and obedience to rules, regardless of whether people agree with them or like the outcomes. Representative authorities also confer a sense of pride in being a member of groups over which those authorities reign (Taylor, 2003). She analysed unsolicited, spontaneous written comments made by taxpayers at the end of a tax survey conducted in Australia and found that almost all the comments referred to injustice. The most common complaint was that the tax system was inequitable (51%). Perceptions of justice, fairness and equity varied with self-categorisations. Those at the subgroup level were more concerned about unfair procedures and outcomes than those identifying at the superordinate level. Those who perceived the Australian Taxation Office as exhibiting high representativeness regarded being an honest taxpayer as more important, felt less resentment about paying tax and more obligated to obey the rules than did those who perceived low representativeness. Moreover, identification and varying salience of superordinate groups were related to motivational postures (V. Braithwaite, 2003a), conceived as condensed knowledge, attitudes, norms and perceived opportunities as well as fairness perceptions establishing the bridge to, and catalyst of, behaviour. In her 2003 publication, Taylor explicitly acknowledges that motivational postures are not stable individual traits but reflect the dynamic context in which taxpayers are situated. This means that the motivational postures are fluid, and taxpayers can shift between them, depending on the levels of inclusiveness of self-categorisation and the perceived representativeness of authorities. As her study shows, participants who were more capitulating and committed were more likely to see the government and the tax office as representatives of the Australian people as compared to the disengaged and resistant participants.

3.6   Motivation to comply

3.6.1   Motivational postures

The motivation to comply depends on subjective constructs of tax phenomena and collective sense-making of subjective tax knowledge, on myths and legends about taxation and others' tax behaviour, on subjective constructs and evaluations of perceived and internalised norms, perceived opportunities not to comply and fairness perceptions. The condensation of these variables results in the motivation and drive of taxpayers to behave honestly. The aggregation of subjective constructs and socially shared beliefs and evaluations is related to 'motivational postures' as described by V. Braithwaite (2003a). V. Braithwaite, however, uses motivational postures to describe the aggregation of subjective constructs in a more narrow way. Motivational postures are conceived as surrounding a particular authority, expressing social distance from that authority. The concept of motivational postures as 'interconnected beliefs and attitudes that are consciously held and openly shared with others' includes individuals' attitudes towards the tax system, and the tax office, how authority is used and what the authority is trying to achieve.

On the level of the society and nation, the aggregate of citizens' beliefs and evaluations of the state, taxation and non-compliance yield tax morale (Schmölders, 1960) and civic duty (Frey, 1997). On the individual level, motivational postures are the driving factor of compliance and non-compliance, whereas at the national level, tax morale and civic duty are the motivational forces leading to or deterring from engagement in the shadow economy, tax evasion and avoidance.

Motivational postures are an integrative concept of taxpayers' beliefs, evaluations and expectations relative to their tax authority, as well as their actions in response to their beliefs, evaluations and expectations. Thus, motivational postures integrate the concepts described above: subjective knowledge of tax law, subjective concepts, attitudes, norms and fairness perceptions, as well as intended behaviour. Motivational postures determine how taxpayers position themselves in relation to tax authorities. They determine cooperation and non-compliance and justification processes. V. Braithwaite (2003a) refers to Bogardus's 1928 psychological concept of 'social distance', which is central to citizens' position towards authorities, describing the degree to which individuals or groups have positive feelings and ascribe status to the regulatory authority. Tax authorities may have formal power and legal legitimacy to constrain taxpayers to fulfil their duties, but this does not guarantee psychological legitimacy, which is mainly based on ascribed expert status, leading to taxpayers' willingness to cooperate due to their conviction that the tax authorities are engaging in relevant and accepted behaviour (French and Raven, 1959). V. Braithwaite offers a definition of motivational postures and the origin of motivational postures that is similar to the definition of social representations, which are also conceived as determinants of behaviour (see also Moscovici, 2001). She states:

Individuals and groups articulate their beliefs, develop rationalisations for their feelings, and use values and ideologies to justify the ways they position themselves in relation to legally sanctioned authorities . . . These interconnected sets of beliefs and attitudes are shared, borrowed, challenged, and elaborated upon even further as part of the social life of a community. The interconnected sets of beliefs and attitudes that are consciously held and openly shared with others are called motivational postures. (V. Braithwaite, 2003a, p. 18)

V. Braithwaite and her colleagues have identified five motivational postures (V. Braithwaite, 2003a; V. Braithwaite *et al.*, 1994). Commitment and capitulation reflect an overall positive orientation towards tax authorities, whereas resistance, disengagement and game-playing reflect a negative orientation. Table 8 represents definitions of the five postures accompanied by statements representing them.

In 2000, V. Braithwaite (2003a) conducted a survey of more than 2,000 Australian taxpayers and found (a) that different motivational postures can be held simultaneously and do not represent stable individual characteristics, but rather ones that taxpayers can shift between (Taylor, 2003), and (b) that commitment and capitulation were the most frequent motivational postures. Resistance, game-playing and disengagement were found less frequently. Moreover, commitment and capitulation were negatively related to evasion and tax avoidance, whereas the other three postures were positively related (see table 9).

V. Braithwaite has emphasised that community responsiveness to the tax system and tax authority is multidimensional, changeable and has as much to do with social relationships as with technical and administrative procedures. Motivational postures describe the stance of taxpayers that must be managed when a tax authority seeks to change or wants explanations for taxpaying behaviour. The Australian Taxation Office has

Table 8: *Motivational postures and statements representing them (V. Braithwaite, 2003a, p. 20)*

Motivational posture	Description	Statements representing motivational postures
Commitment	Commitment combines a positive orientation towards tax authorities and deference. The tax system is perceived as desirable, tax law and tax collection are perceived as fair. Committed taxpayers feel a moral obligation to pay their share and to act in the interest of the collective.	a) Paying tax is the right thing to do. b) I feel a moral obligation to pay my tax. c) Overall, I pay my tax with goodwill.
Capitulation	Capitulation reflects a positive orientation in terms of acceptance of the tax authorities which hold legitimate power to pursue the collective's goals. As long as citizens act according to the law, authorities are perceived to act in a supportive way.	d) If you cooperate with the Tax Office, they are likely to be cooperative with you. e) The tax system may not be perfect, but it works well enough for most of us. f) No matter how cooperative or uncooperative the Tax Office is, the best policy is to always be cooperative with them.
Resistance	Resistance reflects a negative orientation and defiance. The authority of tax officers may be doubted and their acts may be perceived as controlling and dominating rather than as supportive.	g) If you don't cooperate with the Tax Office, they will get tough with you. h) It's important not to let the Tax Office push you around. i) It's impossible to satisfy the Tax Office completely.
Disengagement	Disengagement also reflects a negative orientation and correlates with resistance. Individuals and groups keep socially distant and blocked from view and have moved beyond seeing any point in challenging tax authorities.	j) If I find out that I am not doing what the Tax Office wants, I'm not going to lose any sleep over it. k) I don't care if I am not doing the right thing by the Tax Office. l) If the Tax Office gets tough with me, I will become uncooperative with them.
Game-playing	Game-playing expresses a view of law as something that can be moulded to suit one's purposes rather than as a set of regulations that should be respected as guideline of one's actions. In the field of tax behaviour, game-playing refers to 'cops-and-robbers' games with taxpayers detecting loopholes for their advantages and perceiving tax officers as cops who engage in catching cunning taxpayers.	m) I enjoy spending time working out how changes in the tax system will affect me. n) I enjoy talking to friends about loopholes in the tax system. o) I like the game of finding the grey area of tax law.

Table 9: *Frequency of motivational postures and correlations with tax evasion and avoidance (V. Braithwaite, 2003a, pp. 33–4)*

Motivational postures	Frequency (%)	Evasion-related actions (r)	Avoidance-related actions (r)
Commitment	92	−.05	.11
Capitulation	73	−.04	−.06
Resistance	55	.12	.12
Disengagement	7	.14	.07
Game-playing	13	.07	.17

developed a model which links motivating factors in taxpayers' compliance behaviour to the appropriate tax office response. A description of the model was provided by V. Braithwaite and Job (2003) and is available on line, at http://ctsi.anu.edu.au/publications/research%20notes/RN5.pdf. The model shows a continuum of taxpayer motivational postures at four levels varying from commitment over capitulation and resistance to disengagement, together with the appropriate compliance strategy.

As figure 12 shows, depending on the motivational posture of taxpayers, enforcement strategies should vary from self-regulation to enforced self-regulation, and from discretionary and non-discretionary command regulation to prosecution. When taxpayers admit wrongdoing, correct their mistakes and begin meeting the law's expectations, the tax official's task is to educate, keep records and deliver service and advice. When taxpayers behave in an adversarial fashion, show resistance and disengagement, tax officials should respond with much harder measures, command regulation and finally respond with prosecution (V. Braithwaite, 2003b; see also James *et al.*, 2003, who have summarised examples of reforms in various countries, paying special attention to the Australian Compliance Model).

3.6.2   Tax morale

On the aggregate societal level, the concept of tax morale implies the collective (intrinsic) motivation to comply. Tax morale, coined in 1960 by Schmölders, is defined as the 'attitude of a group or the whole population of taxpayers regarding the question of accomplishment or neglect of their tax duties; it is anchored in citizens' tax mentality and in their consciousness to be citizens, which is the base of their inner acceptance of tax duties and acknowledgment of the sovereignty of the state' (pp. 97–8). V. Braithwaite and Ahmed (2005) refer to tax morale as

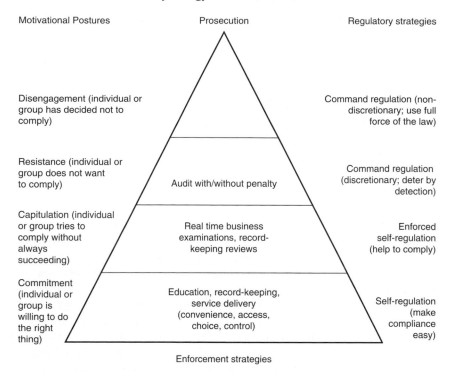

Figure 12: Australian Taxation Office Compliance Model (adapted from V. Braithwaite, 2003b, p. 3, and from James *et al.*, 2003)

'internalised obligation to pay tax' (see also Frey and Feld, 2002). Similarly, Frey (1997) and Alm and Torgler (2006) define tax morale as an 'intrinsic motivation' to pay one's taxes, which Orviska and Hudson (2002) link to the concept of civic duty. Civic duty proposes that people are motivated not just by a concern to maximise their own well-being, but by a sense of responsibility and loyalty to the society and nation. Responsible citizens with high levels of civic duty are collaborative even if the system allows non-compliance. Their behaviour is not regulated externally by audits and sanctions but by their concern for the society. Willingness to comply derives from a strong sense of civic duty.

In the tax literature, the concept of tax morale is frequently not explicitly defined, and operationalisations and measurement in empirical work are rather heterogeneous. Feld and Frey have addressed this shortcoming in 2002, claiming that most studies treat tax morale as a black box. Neither the concept itself nor how morale might arise or be maintained

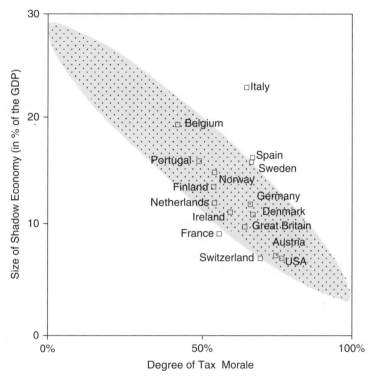

Figure 13: Tax morale and the size of shadow economy (Alm and Torgler, 2006, p. 243)

is discussed. It is usually perceived as being part of the meta-preferences of citizens. They go on to criticise the way in which the concept is often used as the residuum in the analysis capturing unknown influences on tax evasion. Indeed, most studies on shadow economy and tax evasion, comparing indices across nations, refer to cultural differences and attribute them to varying government–citizen relationships and tax morale.

According to Schmölders (1960), tax morale becomes most visible in citizens' moral evaluation of tax evasion (see also Schmölders, 1970a). It is not always clear in Schmölders's work whether tax morale is conceived as a concept on the national or individual level. The way in which the German survey was conducted suggests that the concept of morale is conceived on the national level, while measurements of the concept are focused on citizens' tax mentality, and, on the individual level, integrate knowledge, attitudes towards the government and taxation, condemnation of tax evasion and subjective experiences of fair treatment by the government. Although Schmölders was not able to refer to the concept of social representations in his 1960 publication, his approach to tax morale has much in common with what Moscovici (1961, 2001) and other colleagues developed in later decades in social psychology. From the perspective of social representations theory, tax morale can be perceived as socially shared knowledge, beliefs and evaluation of tax issues, as well as behavioural intentions and anticipated social approval and disapproval. While the concept relates to the social and national level, it is measured by assessing knowledge and attitudes borne by individuals, however, developed through social communication processes rather than by the individual in a social vacuum. Considering tax morale as a social representation that guides taxpayers' behaviour, the concept has also much in common with V. Braithwaite's concept of motivational postures (2003a), which places an even greater emphasis on the relationship with the tax authority. The concept of tax morale was first studied by Strümpel (1966, 1969) and later by Vogel (1974), Lewis (1982), Frey (1997), Eichenberger and Frey (2002), Torgler (2002) and, in the context of Australian higher education policy, by V. Braithwaite and Ahmed (2005). Generally, higher morale was found to be positively related to tax compliance, and on the aggregate level, high tax morale in a country was found to be negatively related to shadow economy. Alm and Torgler (2006) have referred to Schmölders's (1970b) work on tax morale, defined as intrinsic motivation to pay one's taxes, as an important determinant of economic activities and economic development. Using Schneider and Klinglmair's 2004 estimates of the shadow economy, they analysed the linear relationship between morale and size of shadow economy and found an impressive covariation, as shown in figure 13. Indeed, these findings and V. Braithwaite's work on motivational postures demonstrate the importance of subjective and socially shared representations of tax phenomena with regard to citizens' engagement in the shadow economy and tax evasion and avoidance.

4　Tax compliance decisions

A taxpayer may voluntarily decide to pay taxes or make an explicit decision to avoid paying the full share. A single person's contribution does not really make much difference in the overall contributions to public goods. Therefore, not paying one's taxes is advantageous as the amount of public goods and one's participation in them remains almost unchanged, while at the same time one saves on taxes. If few taxpayers evade taxes, public goods will not disappear or be reduced significantly; however, if a considerable number of taxpayers evade, the provision of public goods is not guaranteed and ultimately everyone will suffer from a suboptimal choice.

The tax system represents a social dilemma with individual interests being in conflict with collective interests: two or more people are interdependent on obtaining outcomes; if few people try to maximise their own outcomes, defection is the rational choice. However, if a large number or all people maximise their outcome, the effect is that, sooner or later, everyone gets less than if they had chosen to cooperate (Dawes, 1980; Messick and Brewer, 1983; Mérö, 1996; Stroebe and Frey, 1982; Van Lange *et al.* 1992). In other words, the tax system represents an n-player social dilemma, often referred to as tragedy of the commons (Hardin, 1968), with defection as each taxpayer's rational strategy, independent of how other taxpayers decide to behave. If single taxpayers choose to pay their full share of taxes, they will be worse off because they support the free-riding, parasitic others (Torgler, 2003d).

In everyday life, social dilemmas are frequent: friends who dine together at a restaurant and share the bill can choose the rational alternative and order an expensive dish, paying only part as all others share the bill, or cooperate by choosing a less expensive meal. If all go for the expensive meal, single shares of the bill are likely to be higher than in case of separate payments; if some choose the expensive alternatives, the others will co-finance their parasitic but rational behaviour. Other examples regard public transport and free riding, environmental issues and nature preservation, energy and water saving, overpopulation, insurance fraud, participation at political elections, heroic behaviour in war, etc.

Defection and cooperation in social dilemmas are studied in various disciplines such as mathematics, economics, sociology and psychology. Social dilemmas can be created easily in laboratory settings to study participants' cooperation or defection. For instance, several participants could be endowed with a specific amount of money at the beginning of an experiment and informed that they can contribute to a common good by anonymously handing over either all, part, or none of their money. The sum of contributions will then be doubled, and every participant receives an equal share of the doubled contributions. The conditions could be more rigid by informing the participants that the collected amount will be doubled only if a certain percentage of the overall endowments is handed over; if the joint amount is lower, the common good will not be redistributed. The experiment resembles everyday life dilemmas more if the initial endowment, contributions and redistribution are embedded in a familiar context, e.g., using public transport and free riding, running a business and investing or not investing in environmental and nature protection techniques, or paying or avoiding payment of taxes. Webley *et al.* (1991) studied behaviour in social dilemma situations in the laboratory by simulating business firms that participants manage over several periods, with taxes due after each period.

From a mathematical and economic perspective, the optimal strategy for rational individuals is not to cooperate. On the aggregate level, this strategy leads to the worst outcome for the commons and ultimately for each individual. Therefore, participants need to be forced to cooperate by control mechanisms and severe sanctions in case of defection. A psychological perspective raises two considerations. First, individuals are not necessarily egoistic utility maximisers but frequently behave altruistically; they even donate to charity if there are no constraints and their donations remain anonymous. Second, control and sanctions are not necessarily the best strategies to ensure cooperation. In the case where one's own rational behaviour harms others, people are often considerate. The content and context of the situation are important determinants of cooperation, even if the structure of the social dilemma remains invariant and the rational strategy is defection (Poppe, 2005). Also, ethical standards, individual and social norms, fairness considerations, etc. prevent inconsiderate, egoistic utility maximisation. In social dilemma experiments, participants' cooperative behaviour also increases if their behaviour is publicly known, if they are allowed to communicate with each other and if mutual sympathy is established (Dawes, 1980; Mérö, 1996; Stroebe and Frey, 1982; Van Lange *et al.*, 1992).

The neoclassical economic approach to tax behaviour starts from the assumption that individuals and groups are rational agents trying to maximise their outcome by avoiding taxes. Audits and sanctions to detect evasion are perceived as the dominant instruments to ensure cooperative behaviour. The likelihood of audits and sanctions allows a taxpayer to conceive of the tax system as a game in which they choose between (a) a sure loss, namely the taxes due, or (b) a probable gain via evasion and non-detection, or (c) a probable major loss resulting from evasion, detection and punishment. Paraphrasing Bernasconi (1998), evading taxes is like gambling: there are gains to be made if the evasion is successful and costs in terms of penalties if not.

Since the introduction of Becker's (1968) influential economic approach to criminal activities, which treats criminal activity as a rational individual decision, decisions whether or not to pay taxes are predominantly considered choices regarding optimal portfolio allocation between a safe and a risky option. Becker assumes that individuals maximise the expected utility of the criminal behaviour by weighting the uncertain benefits of successful deviance against the risk of detection and punishment. With regard to taxes, individuals are assumed to maximise their expected utility of the evasion by weighting the uncertain benefits of successful evasion against the risk of audits, detection and sanctions. In the early 1970s, Allingham and Sandmo (1972) and Srinivasan (1973) formulated independently of each other a model of tax evasion along these lines of reasoning which has since dominated the academic research in economics and in part also in psychology.

In their seminal works, Allingham and Sandmo and Srinivasan start with the assumption that taxpayers have the choice between two main strategies: a taxpayer may (a) declare the actual income, or (b) declare less than the actual income. When selecting the latter strategy, the payoff will depend on whether or not the taxpayer is investigated by the tax authorities. If the taxpayer is not investigated, he or she is clearly better off than under strategy (a). If the taxpayer is investigated and evasion is detected, he or she is worse off. Taxpayers are assumed to engage in maximising income by taking a decision under uncertainty. The economic model is based on the assumption that taxpayers are self-interested and generally engage in tax evasion if it pays. The theory states that taxpayers will evaluate the expected outcomes of the choice to evade and the choice not to evade taxes. They will compare the outcomes and prefer the option with the highest expected profit. Since taxes represent costs, a rational taxpayer chooses the option that costs less. Elffers describes the economic considerations made by Allingham and Sandmo (1972) and Srinivasan (1973) as follows:

The expected cost of the honest choice is simple: you have to pay the amount of tax T corresponding to your taxable income I, where the relation between T and I is formulated in the tax law. Let us denote T as $T = T(I)$, an increasing function of I. In a so-called flat tax system, $T = rI$ for some rate r between 0 and 1; in the common bracket-type tax system $T(I)$ is a stepwise linear function of I, with steps corresponding with rates applicable to the successive brackets. Notice that the outcome of the honest choice is deterministic, given an income level I: the cost is fixed, no probabilities whatsoever play a role in the outcome. The expected result of the dishonest choice is slightly more complex, as it is dependent on whether the tax inspector finds out that a taxpayer tries to cheat or not. Suppose that the taxpayer contemplates not declaring his or her real taxable income I, but instead conceals an amount C, thus filing an income $I - C$. If the tax inspector finds out, at least the same amount of taxes $T(I)$ will be collected as in the honest case; in addition a fine, F, may be applied. In a number of tax administrations, the fine F is related to either the amount concealed C, or to the tax evaded $T(I) - T(I - C)$. In general, we denote the fine $F = F(I, C)$. If, however, the tax inspector fails to detect the underdeclared income altogether, the taxpayer pays only the amount $T(I–C)$ after all. If we assume that the probability of detection of the intended evasion is p (independent of the other parameters in the model), we see the expected costs of the choice of evading to be:

$$p^*[T(I) + F(I, C)] + (1 - p)^*[T(I - C)]$$

which amounts to

$$T(I) + p^*F(I, C) + (1 - p)^*[T(I - C) - T(I)].$$

According to rational choice theory, these expected costs must be compared with the (fixed) costs of the honest choice, $T(I)$. A rational taxpayer chooses to be honest if the difference D between those two costs,

$$D = p^*F(I, C) + (1 - p)^*[T(I - C) - T(I)]$$

is positive . . .

It is clear that D is an increasing function of p and of F, so a higher chance of detection and more severe punishment will increase the likelihood of an honest choice. (Elffers, 1999, pp. 556–7)

The standard economic model assumes that taxpayers make decisions on the basis of four parameters: the probability of evasion detection, punishment of evasion, tax rates and income level. Theoretical analyses of tax evasion conclude that the probability of detection and sanctions negatively affects evasion tendencies because these variables reduce the expected value of evasion. Besides conclusions about audit probability and fines, the model offers some conclusions about tax non-compliance with increasing income. These conclusions are, however, less clear. Analyses of tax rate also revealed inconclusive results (Allingham and Sandmo, 1972; Weck-Hannemann and Pommerehne, 1989).

Since its publication, the vast majority of economic studies on tax behaviour refer to the Allingham and Sandmo model. Different variables have been included in the model and refinements were made. James and Alley (2002) summarise the basic questions that have been addressed as referring to the relative effectiveness of a higher level of auditing and auditing schemes, the level of resources that should be devoted to enforcement and their costs, the effect of more severe penalties or rewards in the case of honest tax reporting, and to the form the penalties should take. Moreover, uncertainty and risk aversion were considered, along with issues of optimal taxation, social welfare and the government budget constraint, and the connection between tax evasion and labour supply. Ambiguities in the model and discrepancies between theoretical predictions and observations in empirical studies led to changes in the model, such as the consideration of penalty on evaded tax rather than on undeclared income. If the penalty is proportional to the evaded tax rather than to the undeclared income, as assumed by Allingham and Sandmo in their model, then an increase in the income tax rate must increase declared income (Yitzhaki, 1974). This counterintuitive prediction and contradictory empirical data have led to renewed refinements (e.g., Lin and Yang, 2001; Yaniv, 1994). The running repair of the neoclassical model resembles a continual management of crisis without much hope for attaining a model that effectively describes and predicts tax behaviour.

If the model worked, it would be easy for finance ministers to increase tax compliance just by increasing the frequency of audits and severity of fines. If audits were too expensive, increasing fines alone would also help. However, there are several constraints that need to be considered. Sandmo (2003) remarks on policy lessons deriving from the model:

If one wishes to achieve a given degree of deterrence, this may be achieved by low probabilities and high penalties or by low penalties and high probabilities. The concern for low costs of tax administration leads one to favour the second alternative; this was Becker's (1968) argument in his general analysis of the economics of crime. However, such a policy might lead to unacceptable high penalties for a few violations committed by many, a horizontal equity argument neglected by Becker. (p. 23)

Another political strategy to combat evasion might consider changing the marginal tax rate. However, the model does not offer clear conclusions as to whether reducing or increasing the marginal tax rate reduces evasion.

4.1   Audit probabilities, fines, tax rate and income effects

Empirical research consistently shows that the rational model is not working as neoclassical economics had intended. In 1992, Fischer, Wartick and Mark reviewed a bulk of studies directed at learning more about the relationship between probability of detection and compliance behaviour. It appears that the reviewed studies, which employed different methods, generally point in the same direction and strengthen the confidence that increasing the probability of detection will result in less non-compliant behaviour. However, the effect is, if anything, very small. Similarly, while the effect of fines is significant in many studies, their impact on tax compliance in general is small, if not negligible (Andreoni, Erard and Feinstein, 1998). The effects of tax rate and income are also disputable. In the following section, results of studies using different methodological approaches to understand effects of audit rates, fines, tax rate and income are summarised.

4.1.1   Audit rates

The effect of audit probabilities on compliance has been studied most frequently as effect of the objective probability of audit occurrences. Fischer, Wartick and Mark (1992) conducted a comprehensive review of the literature on detection probability and concluded that studies using different methods to study the probability of audits, detection or perceived detection strengthen the hypothesis that increasing the probability of detection will result in more compliant behaviour.

A simulation study using Swiss data from 1970 and 1979 found a significant but small deterring effect of the audit and detection probabilities on evasion (Weck-Hannemann and Pommerehne, 1989). In a later study, audit probability was slightly related to compliance, whereas penalty rate was not (Pommerehne and Weck-Hannemann, 1996). A further analysis of Swiss data on tax morale by Torgler (2005a) yielded neither a significant audit probability effect nor significant effects of fine and tax rates, whereas trust in the legal system and direct democratic rights proved to be highly significant determinants of tax morale. These findings prove that perceived procedural justice as described above is a crucial determinant of citizens' voluntary cooperation, whereas in a system perceived as treating citizens unfairly, cooperation must be enforced by coercion.

Slemrod, Blumenthal and Christian (2001) conducted a field experiment in 1995, in which more than 1,700 randomly selected taxpayers in the United States were informed by letter that the returns they were about to file would be 'closely examined'. A control group did not receive this letter. The taxpayers were informed that they had been selected at random to be part of a study, that they would be contacted about any discrepancies, and that if any irregularities were found, their current and past returns filed might be reviewed. It was found that low- and middle-income taxpayers in the experimental condition, with more opportunities to evade, on average increased tax payments compared to the previous year. The researchers interpreted this as evidence of increased compliance as the result of the increased probability of an expected audit. Surprisingly, in the group of high-income taxpayers the reverse was found. In an experimental approach in the laboratory, Spicer and Thomas (1982) varied audit probabilities over twenty-four periods played, from 5% in the first eight rounds to 25% in the next eight rounds to 15% in the final eight rounds. A second sample participated in the same experiment with information about low, high and medium audit probabilities in the three sets of periods, and a third sample was not informed at all about audit rates. Fines for evasion were set seven times above the evaded amount. As expected, the higher the audit probability, the lower evasion was. Moreover – and in opposition to the results reported in an experiment by Friedland (1982) – precise information had a stronger effect than verbal descriptions of audit probabilities or no information. However, the effects were generally low: the correlations between audit probabilities and percentages of taxes evaded amounted to $r = -0.25, -0.18$ and 0.01 in the three samples with precise information, verbal information and no information, respectively. With regard to the likelihood of evasion, the respective correlations were $r = -0.32, -0.38$ and -0.14. Considering that the results are based on only fifty-four participants, and that correlations indicate that at best audit probabilities explain 10% of evasion, it is risky to draw any conclusions regarding the effect of audit probabilities. Alm, Cronshaw and McKee (1993) investigated random audits, the application of a cut-off rule which implies that taxpayers reporting less than a designated amount will automatically be investigated, and audits implying control of the past or future tax files in case of detection of irregularities. First, higher audit rates had a significant impact on compliance rates: under the condition of random audits with probabilities varying from 5% over 30% to 50%, the compliance rates amounted to 27.7%, 34.3% and 49.2%, respectively. Second, conditional future or past audits in case of detection of irregularities increased compliance to 51.6% and 55.9%. The highest compliance rate with 80.8% was found under the condition of the cut-off rule. The dominance of cut-off rules over standard random audit policies was also confirmed by Reinganum and Wilde (1985). Moreover, surveys were conducted to study the effect of perceived audit probability on self-reported tax compliance. Generally these studies found the predicted effect of audit probability was low and often did not reach statistical significance (e.g., Mason and Calvin, 1978; Song and Yarbrough, 1978; Spicer and Lundstedt, 1976; Wärneryd and Walerud, 1982). Scholz and Pinney

(1995) found that the subjective risk of getting caught is more closely related to feelings of duty than to objective risk factors. Objective audit probabilities affected only taxpayers with greater temptation to cheat, but duty to be honest influenced tempted taxpayers as much as ordinary taxpayers. Finally, audits and fines are included in economic and psychological models of tax behaviour. For instance, Weigel, Hessing and Elffers (1987) integrate probability of apprehension and punishment as well as perceived risk and severity of punishment as situational and personal constraints into their model of tax evasion behaviour, and Orviska and Hudson (2002) include probability of being caught and fines in their model as determinants of evasion.

It can be argued that it is not the actual audit probability which influences tax compliance, but the probability of detection of tax fraud. From the perspective of behavioural economics, it should be expected that, rather than the actual audit risk, it is the subjective estimation which determines behaviour. Indeed, the actual audit probability in the USA has fallen below 1% (Alm, 1991; Hamilton, 1999). Relative to the low probability of investigation, compliance is surprisingly high, which has partially been attributed to subjective overweighting of low probabilities (Alm, McClelland and Schulze, 1992). Fischer, Wartick and Mark (1992) reviewed several studies showing that actual and perceived audit rates differ. Moreover, the relationship between perceived audit and detection probabilities and compliance is much more complex than assumed by the neoclassical economic model. Complexity is even higher, considering that sequences of audits are inconsistent. Worsham (1996) found that inconsistent audit rates actually increased the level of compliance. Mason and Calvin (1978) detected a significant relation between perceived detection probability and compliance. On the other hand, Wärneryd and Walerud (1982) found no significant relationship in a Swiss study in which taxpayers were interviewed by telephone. A significant relation was found between perceived probability of detection and attitudes towards tax resistance, but not a significant negative correlation between perceived probability of detection and self-reported evasion (Spicer and Lundstedt, 1976). Similarly, Elffers, Weigel and Hessing (1987) report significant correlations between perceived risk and self-reported compliance, but no significant relationship between perceived risk and observed behaviour. Hessing et al. (1993) studied fraudulent claims of unemployment benefits using their tax evasion model (Weigel, Hessing and Elffers, 1987) and found that both the perceived likelihood of being caught and the estimated severity of punishment if caught can explain self-reported and officially reported honest versus fraudulent behaviour. Finally, Trivedi and his colleagues (Trivedi, Shehata and

Lynn, 2003; Trivedi, Shehata and Mestelman, 2004) studied effects of tax equity, social norms and employment status in an experiment with audit rates either being 0% or 25%. Under the condition of no audits, participants' behaviour followed the rational model, and evasion was significantly higher as compared to the audit condition.

Perceived detection probability is related to attitudes regarding tax resistance but not strongly related to self-reported tax evasion or compliance behaviour (Spicer and Lundstedt, 1976). With regard to objective audit probabilities and subjectively perceived probabilities, Andreoni, Erard and Feinstein conclude their 1998 review by stating that audit probabilities have little effect on compliance and perhaps the effect of subjective audit and detection probabilities is mediated via psychological variables, such as moral obligations. They end with the following thoughts:

The studies discussed here indicate that individuals generally make poor predictions of the probability of audit and magnitude of fines from tax evasion. Moreover, there is consistency between their sense of a moral obligation to be honest and the tendency to overestimate the chance of being caught. Perhaps as a consequence, a high subjective probability of detection is associated with significantly more compliant behaviour. (Andreoni, Erard and Feinstein, 1998, p. 846)

4.1.2   Fines

Penalties are frequently assumed to be useful measures to prohibit undesired behaviour; consequently economic scholars have focused on penalty schemes and their effectiveness (Landsberger and Meilijson, 1982). Audit probability and sanctions were investigated successfully in econometric modelling, survey studies and in laboratory experiments. Friedland, Maital and Rutenberg (1978) conducted a pioneering experiment in which, framed as a game rather than a real-life tax situation, fifteen participants were instructed to try to earn as much money as possible. Tax rates amounted to either 25% or 50%, audit probabilities were either 6.67% with sanctions fifteen times the evaded amount, or 33.33%, and sanctions three times the evaded amount. In every round of the experiment, participants were allocated imaginary monthly income of approximately the average monthly income in Israel prior to filing their taxes. Incomes rose by approximately 3% from round to round, until the experiment ended after round ten, and participants were paid for participation depending on their performance. Table 10 shows the average percentage of declared income by experimental conditions. The expectancy values of evasion or compliance were invariant under the experimental conditions: multiplying audit probabilities with punishment rates

Table 10: *Average percentage of declared income by audit probability, punishment and tax rate (Friedland, Maital and Rutenberg, 1978)*

		Tax rate	
Audit probability	Punishment rate	25%	50%
0.067%	15 times evaded amount	87.4%	66.4%
0.333%	3 times evaded amount	79.6%	56.5%

yielded products of 1, which indicates that, in the long run, evasion led to the same results as compliance. Nevertheless, the results show that, first, a higher tax rate leads to less declared income, and second, higher punishment seems to be slightly more efficient in preventing evasion than higher audit rates. In an experiment in South Korea, Park and Hyun (2003) found similar results: compliance increased both with audit rate and fines. Moreover, elasticity of fines was much higher than elasticity of audit rates. However, in a follow-up experiment, Friedland (1982) did not find the stronger effect of punishment over audit rates.

Similar experiments with more face-validity were conducted by Webley *et al.* (1991). In one experiment, audit probability was either 16.67% or 50%, whereas severity of fine was twice or six times the evaded amount. Income was more often under-declared if audit probability was low. In the twelve rounds, income was under-declared 3.8 times in the case of one audit in six rounds versus 2.9 times in the case of three audits in six rounds. Severity of fine had no influence on the frequency of under-reporting. With regard to mean percentages of income not declared, both audit probability (21% under the condition of low audit probability versus 14% in the case of high audit probability) and severity of fine (22% versus 13% in low versus high fine conditions, respectively) had some influence. The highest percentage of declared income was observed under the condition of high audit probability and high sanctions (90%), and the lowest under the condition of low audit probability and low sanctions (73%). In the case of either low audit probability and high sanctions, or high audit probability and low sanctions, the declared income amounted to 84% or 82%, respectively. Compared with the results reported by Friedland, Maital and Rutenberg in 1978, this experiment did not confirm the higher effect of punishment compared with audit probability; in fact the opposite was shown. Considering the number of times that income was under-declared, audit probability was more effective than severity of fines. The significant impact of fines and audit

Table 11: *Average compliance rate by fine rate and audit probability (standard deviations in parentheses; Alm, Sanchez and deJuan, 1995, p. 11)*

Audit probability	Fine rate		
	1	2	4
0.05	9.0 (4.0)	6.9 (3.2)	12.2 (4.2)
0.30	10.9 (6.0)	21.4 (4.4)	39.8 (7.4)
0.60	9.8 (8.0)	54.8 (10.6)	70.3 (7.5)

rates was also found in the United States and Spain (Alm, Sanchez and deJuan, 1995). At the beginning of their experiment, Alm and his colleagues randomly gave participants an income that they had to declare. Over several rounds, the fine rate changed from 1 to 2 and 4; the audit rate was 5%, 30% or 60%. Moreover, the tax rate amounted to 10%, 30% or 50%, and public goods were assigned. Compliance varied both with fine rate and audit rate, with fine rate having a dominant impact. Table 11 shows the average compliance rate by fine rate and audit probability.

Schwartz and Orleans (1967) tested the effects of threat of fines versus moral appeals as well as no information on taxpayer compliance. While threat of fines had more effect on compliance than no information, moral appeals by far outweighed the effect of menacing punishment. In a simulation study using Swiss data, Weck-Hannemann and Pommerehne (1989) found no significant effect of punishment. The authors argue that the lack of significance could be due to specific Swiss regulations according to which sanctions are set by the parliament rather than by the tax authorities. Das-Gupta, Lahiri and Mookherjee (1995) studied determinants of taxpayer compliance in India and analysed aggregate data from 1965/1966 to 1992/1993. The estimates show that both revenues collected and compliance were significantly affected by marginal tax rates and exemption limits. In addition, inflation and declining assessment intensity had a significant negative effect, while traditional enforcement tools, such as searches, penalties and prosecution, had only a limited effect. Rather than applying prosecutions to improve compliance and revenue, the authors emphasise that assessment efficiency was much more important. Doubts on the positive effect of fines are also brought forward by Fjeldstad and Semboja (2001) in a study on tax behaviour in Tanzania. The study lends support to the hypothesis that tax compliance is positively related to ability to pay, the perceived probability of being prosecuted and the number of tax evaders known personally to the participants. Severity of sanctions appeared, however, to fuel tax resistance.

Oppressive tax enforcement and harassment of taxpayers seem to increase tax resistance, as does discontent with the delivery of public service.

Although theoretical economic analyses of the effect of audits and fines unequivocally suggest a negative relationship between audit probability and evasion fines, empirical research did not yield results. In 1992, Pommerehne and Weck-Hannemann summarised the results of eight studies conducted in the United States and one in Switzerland, concluding that the deterring effect of control and punishment is, if at all present, very low. Fischer, Wartick and Mark (1992) conclude their review of the experimental literature on the relationship between audit and detection probabilities and taxpayer compliance by emphasising the inconsistency of findings: some experiments failed to detect a significant positive relationship, other studies, attempting to determine the relative effectiveness of increased detection probability versus fines, provide weak evidence that fines are more effective, but other studies conclude that detection probability is more effective. With respect to precision of information about audit probability, Spicer and Thomas (1982) found clear information to increase compliance, whereas Friedland (1982) found the opposite result. Also, survey studies provided mixed evidence, with some suggesting that detection probability and compliance are positively related, and others failing to detect a significant relationship. Gërxhani and Schram (2006) report mixed results in different cultures: whereas in the Netherlands audit probability was related to compliance, in Albania no significant relationship was found. Also, analyses of data available from the US IRS provide conflicting evidence. Finally, Varma and Doob (1998) suggest that perceived penalties are not as important to decisions about evading tax as are perceptions of the possibility of being apprehended. Despite these mixed results, 'the most common result would seem to suggest a positive relationship between detection probability and compliance', but the effect is low (Fischer, Wartick and Mark, 1992, p. 19; see also Blackwell, 2002).

4.1.3   Marginal tax rate

Economic models of rational compliance decisions either fail to clearly predict an effect of marginal tax rate on compliance or hypothesise that higher tax rates lead to higher compliance. Most empirical research shows, however, that higher tax rates lead to less compliance. Weck-Hannemann and Pommerehne (1989; Pommerehne and Weck-Hannemann, 1996) demonstrate that evasion increases with increasing marginal tax rates. Also, Clotfelter (1983) and Slemrod (1985) found that the marginal tax rate has a significant effect on underreporting. In

Porcano's (1988) study, the tax rate had no effect on previous evasion and under-reporting, nor was the income related to tax compliance data. Baldry (1987) reports an experimental investigation on the relationship between income, tax rates and tax evasion, designed in particular to test predictions of the conventional expected-utility-maximisation analysis of evasion behaviour. Tax rate was insignificant in his study, but income was positively related to evasion. In an experiment on horizontal and exchange equity, D. V. Moser, Evans III and Kim (1995) considered tax rates and found that participants reported less income as tax rates increased. In sum, laboratory experiments which varied tax rates frequently found higher evasion covarying with increasing tax rates (e.g., Alm, Jackson and McKee, 1992b; J. H. Collins and Plumlee, 1991; Friedland, Maital and Rutenberg, 1978; Park and Hyun, 2003); however, Alm, Sanchez and deJuan (1995) found the opposite in a Spanish sample, and Baldry (1987) did not find a significant effect at all.

It can be argued that high tax rates, rather than influencing tax honesty, may serve as a disincentive to work. The argument goes as follows: increasing the tax rates for the more affluent will induce them to work less, which will generate less wealth for them and also negatively affect the economy as a whole. According to the 'substitution hypothesis', higher tax rates lower the costs of leisure, and consequently people will reduce their work engagement. According to the 'income effect hypothesis', the opposite should be true: higher rates of taxation reduce real income, and, thus, people will work more in order to keep their living standards. Although both hypotheses are theoretically interesting, there does not seem to be a clear and strong effect of tax rate changes on work engagement. A 1983 study by Leuthold reports that men may increase and women decrease work effort for increases in the marginal tax rate, whereas Calderwood and Webley (1992) hold that most people are not at all responsive to tax rate changes. Overall, 58% of the participants they interviewed said they would not change the hours they worked in response to a tax change (5% decrease or 5% increase). The remaining 35% would work more (independent of increase or decrease), and 7% less. Specifically, if taxes increased, people said they would work more (22%).

4.1.4   Income

The rational decision-making approach also does not provide clear predictions with regard to income effects. Anderhub et al. (2001) conducted an experiment in which participants earned their income by solving intertemporal allocation tasks. The resulting income was to be declared in a tax return that was randomly verified. If tax evasion was detected, participants were punished by a fixed penalty. The experiment consisted of four tax periods, the final two involving an increased tax rate. Higher income levels encouraged tax evasion; surprisingly, an increased tax rate did not. Similarly, Weck-Hannemann and Pommerehne (1989) found evidence for higher evasion with increasing income in their analysis of Swiss taxpayer data. Park and Hyun (2003) conducted an experiment in South Korea and found no evidence for changes in compliance across income levels. Alm, Jackson and McKee (1992b) found the opposite: in their experiment participants faced tax rates varying from 10% to 30%, and 50%, audit rates of 2%, 4% and 6%, and fines amounting to the double and triple amount of evaded income. Moreover, participants earned different incomes, and a public good was either provided or not. Income and tax rate were the most important determinants of evasion. The higher the tax rate and the lower the income were, the more participants evaded. Fine rate and audit rate were also significantly related to evasion, but the effect was small. Fishlow and Friedman (1994) also show in a theoretical model of intertemporal consumption that tax compliance declines when current income declines or inflation rises; but compliance declines also if expectations about future income improve.

Andreoni, Erard and Feinstein (1998) summarise studies on tax rates and income effects and conclude that the results of analyses of US IRS data, surveys and laboratory experiments are inconclusive. The relationship between income and evasion needs to be investigated further and is perhaps not linear as many studies implicitly assume. The authors quote Slemrod (1985), who examined tax rates, income and evasion by taking into consideration that tax liability is a step function of taxable income for most income earners. Tax evaders should have an incentive to report at the top of a tax bracket rather than at the beginning or in the middle range, whereas honest taxpayers should report their income, independent of where it falls within a tax bracket. Indeed, Slemrod found that a disproportionate share of all tax reports fall within the top quartile of a reporting bracket.

4.1.5   Reasons for weak effects of audits and fines

There are many explanations of why probability of audits and fines does not have the predicted high effect on tax compliance. First of all, the assumption that taxpayers are trying to avoid taxes if it is in their benefit must be doubted. Various studies in different countries use different methodological approaches to show that a vast majority of citizens are willing to pay taxes and do not seem to undertake economic decisions under uncertainty in order to maximise income. Most taxpayers seem to take for granted the legitimacy of the tax system and its overarching objectives. In fact, the majority of people believe themselves to be honest in their tax dealings. Indeed, the majority are honest in the gross individual income tax gap. This point is further exemplified by the structuring of the compliance model pyramid (V. Braithwaite, 2003a; see figure 12, table 9), in which the majority of taxpayers are located at the bottom and middle of the pyramid, in the fields of committed and capitulated taxpayers, rather than the top, and also in a study by Erard and Feinstein (1994a), who demonstrate that including honest taxpayers in a purely economic game-theoretic model on tax compliance leads to much improved empirical predictions. A political system perceived as treating citizens fairly evokes voluntary compliance, which may actually be corrupted by audits and fines.

Moreover, taxpayers usually do not know exact audit probabilities or the amount of fines. Objective rates hardly impact subjective behaviour, which is based on subjective perceptions of audit probabilities and fines. Subjective probabilities may vary considerably from objective probabilities, and also the weight of low probabilities (probability of income audits are lower than 1% in the United States) is subjectively much higher than objectively justified (e.g., Kahneman and Tversky, 1979). Another reason for the low effect of audits is in the possibility of non-detection of undeclared income or unwarranted deductions. Taxpayers may learn to escape taxes after unsuccessful audits, or if audited and fined they may try to get the money back in future tax filings. In his 1966 work, Strümpel noted how stringent assessment and punishment may lower compliance and willingness to comply. Interaction with fiscal authorities could lead to perceptions of stringency in assessment with increased tax resistance. It is also possible that increased tax resistance may simply increase a taxpayer's chances of being audited, which would result in a positive correlation between non-compliance and audit rate.

While most studies refer to audit rates and penalties as determinants of compliance, Halperin and Tzur (1990) take an opposite perspective, discussing audit and penalty rates as political consequences of evasion. Their research shows that the proportion of evaders is not a sufficient reason to explain the low penalty and low audit rate. In fact, both penalties and audit rates increase as the number of evaders increases. Their study suggests that the low penalty-low audit rate policy can be explained by the weight the government puts on the evader group. This weight is explained in terms of the political influence of evader groups and politicians wanting to please the evader group, which might support them in their endeavours to keep themselves in political office.

The financial self-interest model assumes that tax compliance and evasion are outcomes of rational decisions based on audit probability, detection probability and sanctions in case of evasion. On the other hand, the behavioural model of tax evasion includes economic, psychological and sociological variables such as demographic characteristics (e.g., age, sex), variables related to non-compliance opportunity (e.g., education, income level, income source, occupation), social representations and attitudes (e.g., tax ethics and social norms, fairness perceptions), and structural characteristics (e.g., complexity of the system, audit probability and detection probability, sanctions, and tax rates). Based on the rather small effects of variables considered in the neoclassical economic approach (i.e., audit probability, fines, marginal tax rate and income), several studies conclude that it is important to consider also citizens' acceptance of political and administrative actions and attitudinal, moral and justice issues as they are central to psychological and sociological approaches (Lind and Tyler, 1988; Pommerehne and Frey, 1992; Pommerehne and Weck-Hannemann, 1992; Tyler and Lind, 1992; Weck-Hannemann and Pommerehne, 1989). Andreoni, Erard and Feinstein (1998) consider the development of purely economic models of tax compliance from a perspective of game theory and principal agent theory. However, they add, these models are rather poor descriptions of real-world tax systems. With regard to tax policy, Alm, Sanchez and deJuan (1995) state:

[A] government compliance strategy based only on detection and punishment may be a reasonable starting point but not a good ending point. Instead, what is needed is a multi-faceted approach that emphasises enforcement, as well as positive rewards from greater tax compliance, the wise use of the taxpayer dollars, and the social obligation of paying one's taxes. (p. 15)

4.2   Repeated audits

Previous experimental studies on tax behaviour have been particularly concerned with determining the absolute effect of detection rates and punishment on tax filing. Most studies on audit probabilities and tax compliance assume that the probability of audit is constant and few studies investigated effects of past audits on future behaviour as well as the sequential effects of repeated audits. The experience of being audited in one year and the consequences of an audit may change taxpayers' perceptions of future audits and the perceived success in detecting irregularities. On the one hand, prior audits could increase subjective salience of audits and punishments, which lead to more compliance in the future due to an 'availability heuristic'-effect (Tversky and Kahneman, 1974). On the other hand, if audits are not successful in detecting irregularities, taxpayers may come to the conclusion that auditors have only limited capacities to detect evasion, and clever techniques will not be uncovered. Subjectively, risks of evasion may be estimated low, and evasion may be more likely in upcoming years. Moreover, taxpayers audited in one year may assume that the chance of being audited in the near future is low. In such cases, evasion rates in the near future should increase.

Experimental studies found that compliance improves in the latter rounds if participants had been audited in the earlier rounds (e.g., Spicer and Hero, 1985; Webley, 1987). As Spicer and Hero (1985, p. 266) put it, 'taxpayers do not engage in optimising strategies in making tax evasion decisions. Instead, they apparently use heuristics or ' "rules of thumb" '. In particular, the experience of being audited appears to lower levels of tax evasion even where the likelihood of an audit is completely random.' This result is, however, not supported by actual audit data. Andreoni, Erard and Feinstein (1998) quote a 1987 study by Long and Schwartz who examined data of the US IRS involving a group of tax-payers who were audited in 1969 and in 1971. The earlier audit was only marginally effective in reducing the frequency of subsequent non-compliance. The average magnitude of non-compliance among those who continued to evade in 1971 remained unchanged.

Andreoni and his team conclude their short review on prior audits by emphasising the importance of considering why audits have very little specific deterrent value. They state:

One possible explanation is that audits may not turn out as badly as taxpayers initially fear. For example, if an audit fails to uncover non-compliance that is present or if a substantial penalty is not applied to discovered non-compliance, a taxpayer may conclude that it pays to cheat. Alternatively, perhaps taxpayers do find audits to be a negative experience, but the impact of this experience is to make them want to evade more in the future in an attempt to 'get back' at the tax agency. Clearly, more research is needed both to confirm whether there is any specific deterrent effect of an audit and to uncover the reasons for the presence or absence of such an effect. This is an important area, because the econometric results to date suggest that the use of the 'stick' to enforce compliance with tax laws may not have any long-run impact. (Andreoni, Erard and Feinstein, 1998, p. 844)

Indeed, the effect of prior audits has not been frequently investigated and if it was investigated, no clear distinctions were made between effects of audits *per se* and the impact of effective detection of evasion, fines and treatment of taxpayers by tax officials. If no clear distinctions are made, it remains unclear whether audits lead to (a) overweighting of audit prob-ability in the future and therefore to higher compliance; (b) subjective concepts of specific patterns of audit probabilities and speculation of audits happening or not happening in future years, and thus to strategic compli-ance behaviour; (c) learning how to cleverly evade in order to escape the auditors, and thus to non-compliance; or (d) feelings of revenge for audits and punishments and the endeavour to get back in upcoming years what the tax office took.

The effect of audits and learning is acknowledged in few publications on tax compliance, and assumptions about the effect of audits, detection of irregularities and eventually of fines are at least twofold: it can be hypothesised that – if changes occur at all – compliance could increase or decrease after audits. Antonides and Robben (1995) briefly mention learning effects related to the low frequency of audits which could have led to the undesired opposite. 'Besides a deterring effect of auditing, a learning effect might take place since undesirable behaviour is punished. On the contrary, if audit probability is low, successful attempts at tax evasion are positively reinforced' (pp. 624–5). Taxpayers may exert considerable effort to understand their experiences with tax authorities; they may try to predict audits and understand tax auditors' strategies and consequently learn how to deal with tax authorities effectively. Beck, Davis and Jung (1991) conducted several experiments on tax compliance and found that the behaviour of the participants changed over the experimental rounds. Unfortunately, the authors did not further analyse these changes but concluded: 'The trial effect pattern suggests that learning may have occurred during the first half of each treatment condition' (p. 550). Mittone (2002) too conducted a tax experiment as a repeated choice problem, and reports that traditional treatment of uncertainty and risk cannot provide a satisfactory explanation of the behaviour of the participants, who developed a learning strategy using a trial and error process to explore the space of alternatives and produced largely different personal styles in solving uncertainty problems.

Taxpayers who are unwilling to pay their whole share and simultaneously try to escape audits and fines may endeavour to understand audit selection processes and, even if completely random, they may try to predict when the next audit might happen. The dynamic process of audits, fines and compliance remains largely unexplored. However, Kirchler, Maciejovsky and Schwarzenberger (2005) conducted an experiment with the aim of shedding some light on the effects of audit probability and sanctions on compliance in a dynamic setting with particular focus on the time lag between audits. The authors assume that the effect of audits crucially depends on the time lag between past audits and the naive expectations of taxpayers as to when the next audit is likely to occur. It may well be that naive reasoning predicts that the probability of consecutive, yet independent, audits is low, which is a violation of independence according to probability theory. If individuals are prone to this misconception of chance (see the 'gambler's fallacy', e.g., Rabin, 1998), it is expected that the more time that passes without audits, the higher the perceived probability of an audit might be. When fines are high, taxpayers endeavour to accurately predict if audits should increase; when fines are low, learning from the past may be perceived as less necessary. Kirchler, Maciejovsky and Schwarzenberger (2005) predicted that tax compliance depends on audit probability, sanctions and the time lag between past audits. In the case of frequent audits, compliance was expected to be low immediately after an audit and was assumed to increase rapidly in the course of subsequent tax filings; in the case of less frequent audits, compliance should be low after an audit and was expected to increase slowly. This pattern was assumed to be particularly pronounced under high sanction conditions. These assumptions were tested in a laboratory experiment, where participants earned their income endogenously in a competitive market. Contrary to most previous experimental studies, compliance was not investigated based on 'windfall' money distributed to participants by experimenters. Instead, participants earned their income in an asset market experiment. They were asked to declare their earnings, separately for sales revenues, resulting from selling assets, and for dividends received after each of the trading periods. Audit probabilities and fines were varied in a between-participants design. After instructing participants about the market and trading procedures, they participated in a computerised continuous double auction. Participants were informed that a total of 16–20 trading periods would be performed and that after each trading period they would be asked to declare their income (subject to a 50% tax rate), separately for sales revenues and dividends. Finally, participants were told that audit probability would either be 15% in one experimental treatment, or 30% in the other treatment. Penalties were either 50% or 100% of the evaded income. Taxable sales revenues were defined as the positive difference between the selling price of an asset and its purchase price. The analysis of data yielded a significant interaction effect between audit probability and period, and an interaction effect between fine and period. Figures 14 and 15 show that, in the high-audit condition, tax compliance was generally higher compared with the low-audit condition. Moreover, compliance decreased sharply after an audit and increased slowly in the next three consecutive trading periods. This dynamic is especially pronounced in the high-audit condition where tax behaviour seems to be quite strategic from a subjective perspective, suggesting that participants did not expect to be audited repeatedly in consecutive periods. Conversely, high and low fines had no moderating effect in the present study. Participants may have employed a strategy which emanates from a misconception of chance: they showed less compliance immediately after an audit, possibly assuming that audits are

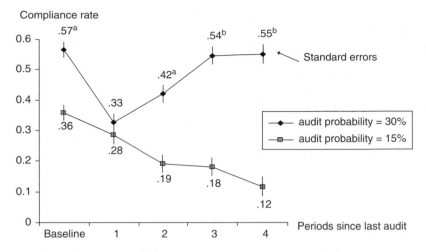

Note: [a] denotes significance at the 5% level, and [b] denotes significance at the 1% level.

Figure 14: Compliance rate by audit probability and periods since last audit (Kirchler, Maciejovsky and Schwarzenberger, 2005)

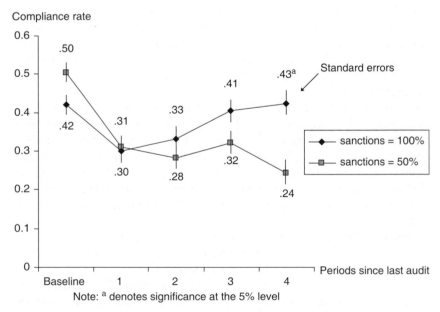

Note: [a] denotes significance at the 5% level

Figure 15: Compliance rate by sanctions and periods since last audit (Kirchler, Maciejovsky and Schwarzenberger, 2005)

interspersed uniformly across time; being audited twice in a row was perceived as rather unlikely. There was also some evidence suggesting that, rather than misperception of probability leading to less compliance immediately after an audit, sanctions led participants to repair their loss due to fines in the period following an audit and fine.

Similar results are reported by Mittone in 1999. As expected, the adjustment process of returning to the baseline compliance-rate was expedited in the high-audit condition. A less clear picture emerged in the sanctions condition. However, it seems that participants showed a tendency to be more responsive to fines in the high-sanction condition than in the low one. In addition to reparing losses due to fines, the sharp decrease in compliance after an audit could also be due to increased risk taking.

Immediately after the occurrence of an audit, compliance decreases. Mittone (2006) found similar results in a series of laboratory experiments on the dynamics of tax evasion behaviour. He reports specific behaviour patterns which support the assumption that taxpayers try to understand when audits happen and learn when it pays to be honest and when cheating is less risky. Participants were initially endowed with an income that they had to declare. The income was 1,000 Liras at the beginning, and decreased to 700 Liras after round 48. Participants played 60 business periods and had to file tax returns after each period. The number of periods corresponds to approximately the typical number of times a taxpayer has to pay taxes in life. Tax rates amounted to 20%, 30% and, in the last periods, to 40%, respectively. Audit probability was 6%, 10%, 40%, or, towards the end of the experiment, 15%; fines were 4.5 times the evaded tax. Besides other phenomena, Guala and Mittone (2005) and Mittone (2006) studied responses to different audit schemes. Tax declarations of one part of the sample were checked randomly in the first 30 periods only, whereas the other part of the sample was audited predominantly in the last 30 periods. Generally, it was found that, after an audit, evasion remained high for a few rounds and then decreased. The authors term this the 'bomb crater' effect. In war, troops under heavy enemy fire hide in the craters of recent explosions, believing it to be highly unlikely that the next bombs would fall exactly in the same spot in a short time span. Something similar seems to happen in the context of tax audits. A taxpayer who has recently been audited seems to believe that the likelihood of a subsequent audit is very remote; therefore, the risk of evasion appears to be low. After several periods, however, the assumed likelihood of audits increases again, and compliance increases. The finding that participants comply after several periods without audit could also be due to the gambler's fallacy effect described in behavioural economics literature, which describes common misconceptions of probabilities,

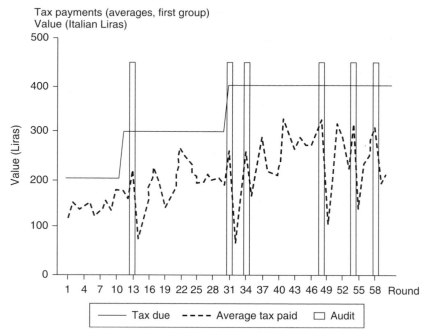

Figure 16: 'Bomb crater' effects immediately after an audit (Guala and Mittone, 2005, p. 9)

including individuals' assumption that a random event, such as an audit, is more likely to occur because it has not happened for a period of time or a random event is less likely to occur because it recently happened (for a description of the gambler's fallacy see Nationmaster-Encyclopedia, 2005). The 'bomb crater' effect is represented in figure 16, which shows that during the 60 periods, average tax payments in one of Mittone's experimental groups decreased sharply, and increased in some periods after the audit.

Second, Mittone (2006) found that redistribution of taxes increased compliance. This result corresponds to the findings on exchange fairness and was discussed in the previous section.

Third, in the sub-sample with audits in the first half of the 60 periods, evasion was significantly lower and remained lower over the whole 60 periods than in the sub-sample that was audited predominantly in the second half of the experimental periods. He termed this the 'echo' effect. Repeated auditing seems to have a strong effect on inhibiting evasion when auditing occurs at the beginning of business periods. In contrast, if no audits and fines are applied at the beginning, even a series of audits in later business periods is not enough to 'educate' taxpayers to comply. Participants seemed to become risk-seeking and did not change their risk attitude throughout the remaining periods. Figures 17a and 17b show average tax payments in two sub-samples with audits and fines applied in either the first or second half of the experiment.

Both 'bomb crater' and 'echo' effects are important in theory and practice. If taxpayers become risk inclined immediately after an audit, then auditing repeatedly may cause a robust reduction of evasion, and auditing self-employed taxpayers at the beginning of their business may lead to more compliance throughout taxpayers' business cycles than random audits or audits at a later stage of their business life. Since tax non-compliance was consistently found to be higher in younger taxpayer samples than in older samples, inspections at the beginning of a business serve additionally as controls of the younger samples, as they are likely to be over-represented in the groups of people starting a business.

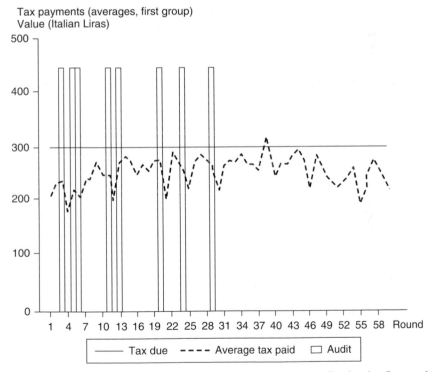

Figure 17a: 'Echo' effect in experiments with audits in the first and second half of sixty business periods, respectively (Guala and Mittone, 2005, p. 12)

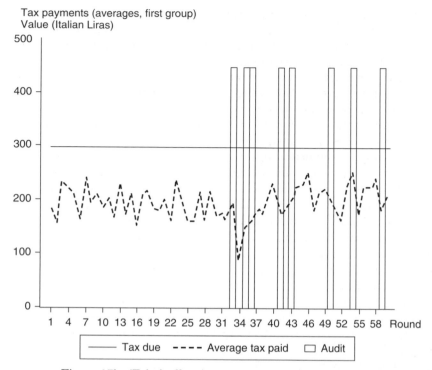

Figure 17b: 'Echo' effect in experiments with audits in the first and second half of sixty business periods, respectively (Guala and Mittone, 2005, p. 13)

The 'bomb crater' effect, describing taxpayers' decreasing compliance after an audit, leads to the assumptions that taxpayers try to understand when audits are most likely and when evasion is too risky. They seem to behave like 'robbers' in a 'cops and robbers' game, trying to detect chances to escape. Both 'bomb crater' and 'echo' effects lead to the assumption that taxpayers undergo learning processes.

Tax compliance behaviour could follow rules described in operant conditioning theory, which explains basic learning principles (Skinner, 1938). To the best of our knowledge, learning theories have never been applied to tax behaviour, although they may provide useful explanations of tax compliance after repeated auditing.

Starting with the classical experiments by Skinner, psychologists have investigated learning processes and conducted manifold studies which prove that the probability that an individual shows a specific behaviour can be influenced through reinforcement of that specific behaviour (e.g., Angermeier, Bednorz and Hursch, 1994). Skinner broadened Thorndike's 1898 law of effect, which assumes that behaviour is developed through spontaneous trials of different actions and experiencing their consequences. By manipulating the consequences, the behaviour of animals and humans can be influenced such that desired behaviour is more likely to be shown, while undesired behaviour is inhibited.

Manipulation of the likelihood of behaviour is possible either by providing positive reinforcement, that is, positive consequences to a particular behaviour, or by providing negative reinforcement, that is, removing negative effects; or by punishment of an undesired behaviour or withdrawal of positive effects. Positive reinforcement increases the probability of a desired behaviour, whereas negative reinforcement decreases the likelihood of undesired behaviour. While positive reinforcement has consistently proved to be effective, effects of punishment seem to be less robust. Behaviour that is punished often appears to be suppressed rather than extinguished, and when punishments stop, undesired behaviour may occur with higher frequency (Estes, 1944; see also Angermeier, Bednorz and Hursch, 1994). Furthermore, an undesired behaviour is often suppressed only when the punishing authorities are present, and punishment may result in hatred towards the particular institution and in revenge-seeking actions (Bongiovanni, 1977; Hyman, McDowell and Raines, 1977). Alternatively, it is suggested that extinction of unwanted behaviour is more likely by consistently ignoring that behaviour or by minimising all forms of response and attention (Herbert, 1989).

After a specific behaviour is learned by operant conditioning and no further reinforcement is provided, extinction of the conditioned behaviour is likely. Due to the absence of reinforcement, the probability of the specific behaviour decreases over time. Skinner accidentally discovered that intermittent rather than continuous reinforcement improves robustness of operant learning. Partial reinforcement results in more durable and more resistant behaviour (Bitterman, 1975; see also Angermeier, Bednorz and Hursch, 1994).

Skinner's operant conditioning theory stimulated research on reinforcement schedules. Even when the quality and quantity of reinforcement are held constant, different reinforcement schedules seem to have highly different effects on learning processes (Angermeier, Bednorz and Hursch, 1994; Ferster, Culbertson and Perron Boren, 1975). Several basic types of reinforcement schedules were investigated: fixed-ratio schedules, variable-ratio schedules, fixed-interval schedules and variable-interval schedules (Angermeier, Bednorz and Hursch, 1994; Zimbardo and Gerrig, 2004). Whereas a fixed-ratio schedule foresees reinforcement after a fixed frequency of the desired behaviours, variable-ratio schedules foresee rewarding desired behaviour at a constant ratio on average. Rapid learning most likely occurs if rewards are provided any time the individual behaves in the desired way. However, extinction processes are most likely once the rewards are absent. Fixed-interval schedules provide rewards when a determined time period has passed between the past rewards and the next performance of the desired behaviour, whereas variable-interval schedules foresee reinforcements at constant time periods in the average.

If tax compliance is perceived as determined by numerous variables and learned behaviour, then the question arises as to how often and when audits should be made and fines executed, or when audits should be made and rewards provided in cases of proven honesty. If tax authorities chose not to audit taxpayers randomly but followed reinforcement schedules to improve cooperation and rewarded honest taxpayers rather than punishing evaders, inspections might be more effective. Based on the findings by Mittone (2006), it can be assumed that tax compliance behaviour results in part from learning processes. Whether this is indeed the case needs still to be investigated, as do the effects of positive reinforcement, which has been shown to be more effective than punishment in non-tax-related contexts (see Falkinger and Walther, 1991). If a tax file is checked and considered correct, providing rewards, such as publishing names of honest taxpayers (cf. Feld and Frey, 2005b), might have stronger effects on consequential compliance than imposing fines when evasion is detected in randomly applied audits. Second, a differentiated reinforcement schedule results in higher resistance to extinction of previously learned compliance behaviour than purely random audits. In the first years, when self-employed taxpayers have to pay their taxes and do not have much experience, it may be effective to reinforce compliant behaviour to evoke a learning process. A continuous reinforcement schedule could ensure fast learning and may be applied at the beginning. Later, the schedule may be changed to a variable-ratio plan, since this seems to guarantee the highest resistance to extinction. Finally, the audit strategy may be changed again to a purely random selection of files, relying on compliance being established through learning processes and being robust.

At present, these assumptions are purely speculative as research on learning processes and tax compliance is missing. Although operant conditioning theory and reinforcement schedules may not be applicable to taxpayers in the same way as to participants in laboratory studies, it may inspire the development and effectiveness testing of plans for audit sequences. Finally, it should be mentioned that operant conditioning theory may successfully be applied not only to tax policy and strategies of repeated audits, but also to laws of classical conditioning. For instance,

Smith and Kinsey (1987) introduce celerity as a relevant determinant of tax behaviour (see Webley *et al.*, 1991, p. 16). Celerity refers to the promptness with which consequences occur, thus, to the delay between evasion and punishment and behaviour consequences. In classical conditioning experiments it has been shown that the longer the delay of punishment, the less likely behaviour will be shaped. It can be hypothesised that taxpayers who experience a long delay between incorrect tax filing and tax authorities' actions will be less likely to associate these actions with their behaviour, and thus, will be less likely to view the consequences in regard to their future filing behaviour.

4.3   Heuristics, biases and framing effects

Economic approaches to tax behaviour are predominantly focusing on decision-making processes. In economics, the concept of rationality underlying the metaphor of 'homo oeconomicus' is based on the assumption that people maximise their utility in choices and decision-making. It is assumed that the option chosen from a set of alternatives, such as paying one's taxes fully, in part, or not at all, is the best for the person concerned. Moreover, people's decisions and behaviour are governed by the rules of logic. A small number of axioms form the basis for complex models of optimal decision-making on the part of individuals and groups engaged in managing their economic affairs: when the best of a bundle of alternatives is to be chosen, an individual must clarify the characteristics of the various alternatives (Gravelle and Rees, 1981; Kirchler and Hölzl, 2003). These characteristics must be assessed, and all the apparently available options compared with each other. According to the principle of completeness, individuals are able to place alternatives in order of preference. In other words, they establish relationships between the alternatives, such as alternative A is better than or equal to alternative B, or B is as good as or preferred to A, or that the individual is indifferent between A and B. According to the principle of transitivity, individuals create consistent orders of preference and do not change their preferences arbitrarily. If, for example, an individual believes alternative A to be better than or as good as alternative B, which is in turn better than or as good as alternative C, this individual must also believe that A is better than or as good as C. If alternative A is as good as B and B as good as C, then the individual must also be indifferent between A and C. Non-satiation is another basic assumption. According to this principle, one bundle of alternatives will be preferred to another bundle if it contains at least one more comparable good, and has the same quantity of other goods as the other bundle. The axiom of continuity states that it is possible to compensate for the loss of a certain quantity of good A by a certain quantity of good B, so that a person is indifferent to the quantity of combinations. Lastly, the assumption is made that, when individuals possess a small quantity of good A and a large quantity of good B, they will only be indifferent to the loss of the part of good A if they receive in addition a comparatively large quantity of good B. This is the axiom of convexity, and conforms to the law of satiation, according to which the relative increase in utility by one additional unit of a good diminishes with the availability of that good.

Utility maximisation (frequently for egoistic goals, but sometimes for altruistic ones) and rationality are the fundamental assumptions of economics on which economic modelling of tax behaviour is also based. The question that unsettles the very foundations of economics is whether human beings actually pursue their goals in an economically logical way. What is it that people wish to maximise? Is it egoistic profit, for themselves and others, or do they strive to act in accordance with society's moral demands? In fact, even in situations of little complexity, the basic assumptions of economics are seen to be contravened. For instance, it is not certain whether individuals generally do try to maximise their own profit. Frijters (2000) found only limited support for the hypothesis that people try to maximise general satisfaction with life. Pingle (1997) found that people often choose the option prescribed by the authorities rather than the one optimal to themselves. Critics have also pointed out that in economic theory, individuals are detached from their social context, and observed in isolation from other people, as if they operated in a social vacuum according to the principles of utility maximisation and rationality. However, there are differences between isolated individuals who wish to act rationally, and the members of collective groups acting within the limits of rules and norms, as has been shown with regard to tax compliance and in many other different areas of human behaviour. The occurrence of reciprocity and cooperation is confirmed in game theory and experimental markets.

Humans are limited information processors. The more complex and the less transparent a situation is, the more participants deviate from what the rational model predicts. People often fail to grasp the full range of alternatives in order to select the best, especially in decision-making situations involving risk. In his concept of 'bounded rationality', Simon (1955) has described how people violate, often systematically, the axioms of rationality and hardly have the capacity, nor are they motivated or have the time, to consider all relevant information in a complex decision situation. Perhaps the most basic assumption in the classical model is consistency, that is, people should not change their preferences based on irrelevant matters such as the purely formal labelling of a decision topic or framing of outcomes (Kahneman and Tversky, 1984).

In reality, however, people are vulnerable to a wide range of heuristics and biases in decision-making situations, which lead to inconsistent judgments and evaluations. Cognitive heuristics are defined as processes to resolve problems or to take decisions without considering the complexity of all the information, all alternatives and opportunities, in order to abbreviate the problem-solving or decision process and reach a timely solution. Heuristics are 'rules of thumb' in complex situations in which decisions need to be made or problems resolved (e.g., Baron, 2000; Kahneman, Slovic and Tversky, 1982; Spicer and Hero, 1985; Traub, 1999; Tversky and Kahneman, 1974; Zimbardo and Gerrig, 2004).

McCaffery and Baron (2003) mention some heuristics and biases that were investigated in the tax context as well as in various areas of financial behaviour. For instance, the endowment effect, status quo bias or reference-dependent utility refer to the observation that losses from the status quo are weighted more heavily than otherwise equivalent gains. Distortion of probabilities refers to phenomena in which individuals make incoherent decisions about low, medium or high probabilities and overweighting of low probabilities. Judgment biases due to the salience and overemphasis of particular characteristics in a decision-making situation, and framing effects refer to different answers depending on the differently described, but essentially invariant, sets of questions or choices. For instance, according to the peak-end rule (Kahneman, 1994) people do not judge an event on the basis of all experiences, but select particularly salient events for their evaluation and put particular weight on the end of a sequence to form a judgment regarding the whole sequence of events. Due to limited understanding of tax issues in general and probabilities in particular, individuals were found to be inconsistent with regard to their preferences for progressive or flat tax. Depending on the metric, individuals seem to prefer progressive tax if their judgments are based on probabilities, but they like flat tax in cases where tax is presented in absolute amounts of money (McCaffery and Baron, 2003, 2004; Roberts, Hite and Bradley, 1994). Preferences for funding public goods were found to vary depending on whether individuals' contributions are coined as taxes or as contributions. Formally invariant decision problems evoke different behaviour if presented in a different frame, such as in the tax frame or as a gamble (Baldry, 1987). Moreover, people respond inconsistently in essentially invariant, but differently described, tax scenarios because they are against 'penalties' but like 'bonuses' (McCaffery and Baron, 2003, 2004). In Germany, Traub (1998) studied fairness judgments of tax rebates for married couples and families with children, and tax surcharges for singles and childless households. Essentially, the problem remained invariant: the question was whether couples with children should pay less tax than couples without children. However, it was framed either as an increase in taxes for childless couples or as tax deduction for couples with children. The results clearly showed that respondents were much more generous when the problem was presented as a tax deduction rather than a tax increase. The importance of wording and framing taxes as gain or loss is well illustrated by Traub's work. He referred to the German Minister for Family Affairs, Hannelore Roensch, who in 1994 intended to reduce tax pressure on families with children. Unfortunately she 'framed' her project as 'punishment' for the childless families who should pay higher taxes, rather than framing it as tax reduction for families with children. Unsurprisingly, she had to leave office.

In the arena of tax behaviour, most research on biases and heuristics is related to prospect theory, framing effects and risk-seeking in cases of a possible loss, and risk avoidance in cases of a possible gain (e.g., Carroll, 1987, 1992; Casey and Scholz, 1991; Copeland and Cuccia, 2002; Cullis and Lewis, 1997; Elffers and Hessing, 1997; Hasseldine, 1998a; Hasseldine and Hite, 2003; King and Sheffrin, 2002; Kirchler, Maciejovsky and Weber, 2005; McCaffery and Baron, 2003; Reckers, Sanders and Roark, 1994; Robben *et al.*, 1990a, 1990b; Roberts, Hite and Bradley, 1994; Schepanski and Kelsey, 1990; Schepanski and Shearer, 1995; Seidl and Traub, 2001, 2002; Schmidt, 2001; Traub, 1998, 1999, 2000; Weigel, Hessing and Elffers, 1987; Yaniv, 1999; for a review on prospect theory and political science see Mercer, 2005).

Prospect theory (Kahneman and Tversky, 1979; Tversky and Kahneman, 1992) attempts to reconcile theory and behavioural reality in decision-making. It pays attention to gains and losses with respect to a reference point rather than to total wealth, assumes that subjective decision weights replace probabilities, and that loss aversion rather than risk aversion is an overriding concept. In their 1979 work, Kahneman and Tversky proved in numerous experiments that the assumptions of the neoclassical economic model are frequently violated in practice. The authors confronted their participants with various situations, offering them two prospects to choose from. The results indicate that people tend to favour prospects whose outcome is certain, while rejecting prospects whose outcome is only probable, in the domain of gains. When asked to choose between (a) receiving a guaranteed payment of 3,000 monetary units and (b) receiving a payment of 4,000 monetary units with a probability of 80% or no payment at all otherwise, the majority of the respondents chose the first alternative even though the expected outcome of the second was higher (i.e., 3,200 monetary units). Conversely, individuals confronted with loss situations tend to favour the probable prospect over the certain one. When asked to choose between (a) a loss of

4,000 monetary units with a probability of 80% or no loss at all otherwise, and (b) a sure loss of 3,000 monetary units, the majority chose the first alternative. It can be concluded that when a prospect is positive, individuals seek to avoid risks, whereas when a prospect is negative they engage in risky behaviour in an attempt to reduce the threatened loss.

Human decision-making is assumed to involve two phases: editing and evaluation. The major component of the editing phase is coding. This refers to the perception of outcomes as gains or losses relative to a subjective reference point, instead of in terms of the final state of wealth. Thus, contrary to the assumptions of standard economic decision theory, preferences are not invariant to different representations of the same problem. A further component of the editing phase is combination, i.e., simplifying choice options by combining the probabilities of identical outcomes. Segregation is the separation of the certain component of lotteries from risky components. For example, the chance of winning a sum of 500 money units with probability p = .80 or of winning 300 units with probability p = .20, is decomposed into a sure gain of 300 and an 80% chance of winning an additional 200 units. Further components of the editing phase are cancellation, simplification and detection of dominance. Probabilities of outcomes are often rounded to 'prominent' figures, and alternatives that are perceived as dominated by other alternatives are often rejected without further consideration. In the evaluation phase, decision-makers evaluate edited prospects, choosing the one with the highest value. Outcomes are defined and evaluated relative to a subjective reference point that may represent the status quo of the individual's current wealth and marks the borderline between loss and gain. Sometimes, however, outcomes are evaluated in reference to some other points that may differ from the status quo, such as aspiration levels or asset positions of significant others. According to prospect theory, the value function is concave in gains and convex in losses, with additional gains or losses having diminishing impact. Furthermore, the function is steeper in losses than in gains, which indicates that losses loom larger than gains (see figure 18).

The central implication of the value function is the principle of loss aversion. People are risk-averse for gains with high probabilities and for losses with low probabilities, risk-seeking for gains with low probabilities and losses with high probabilities. If losses are experienced or expected, people take risks to repair or prevent the loss; on the other hand, in gain situations decision-makers are risk averse. The assertion that losses loom larger than gains has also received support in neuropsychological experiments which show more intense activity in specific areas of the human brain when people are informed about losses than gains (Gehring and Willoughby, 2002).

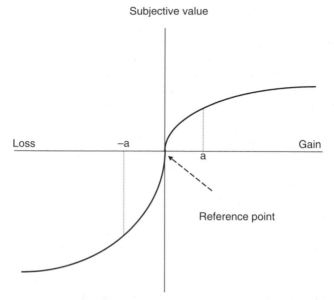

Figure 18: Value function in prospect theory

Kahneman and Tversky (1979) showed also that individuals tend to be inconsistent in the decisions they make if the context of a situation changes. Depending on the wording of a decision task, people perceive prospects as losses or gains, and preference orders may consequently be reversed. Starting from Tversky and Kahneman's 1981 Asian disease problem,[1] such framing effects have frequently been confirmed. The framing refers to a purely rhetorical change in the description of a

---

[1] The Asian disease problem refers to the framing of the following options and people's choices:

Task 1: Imagine that the US is preparing for the outbreak of an unusual Asian disease, which is expected to kill 600 people. Two alternative programmes to combat the disease have been proposed. Assume that the exact scientific estimates of the consequences of the programmes are as follows:

If Programme A is adopted, 200 people will be saved.

If Programme B is adopted, there is a one-third probability that 600 people will be saved and a two-thirds probability that no people will be saved.

If you were the government official making the decision, which programme would you adopt?

Task 2: Imagine that the US is preparing for the outbreak of an unusual Asian disease, which is expected to kill 600 people. Two alternative programmes to combat the disease have been proposed. Assume that the exact scientific estimates of the consequences of the programmes are as follows:

constant reality. The fact that different descriptions of an otherwise unchanged problem affect individual judgments and choices violate the principle of invariance in the economic theory of rationality.

It should be mentioned that descriptions or frames are operationalised differently in decision research in general, and in tax research in particular. Lewin, Schneider and Gaeth (1998) classify three types of framing effects in the literature: risky choice framing; attribute framing; and goal framing. Risky choice framing refers to events with alternatives with different risk levels, such as the Asian disease problem, with sure outcomes or events happening with a certain probability, and presentation of the situation in term of positive or negative outcomes (Tversky and Kahneman, 1981). Attribute framing refers to framing of single attributes. For instance, in marketing research, consumers may be asked to evaluate food that is presented either as 80% lean or 20% fat. Goal framing refers to stressing positive consequences of performing a behaviour or negative consequences of not performing the behaviour. For instance, participants in tax research may be presented with scenarios describing either the consequences of compliance or the consequences of evasion and detection. Most studies in the arena of tax behaviour and framing have focused on risky choice frames.

Risk-seeking in perceived loss situations, and risk avoidance in gain situations, as well as framing effects, have been widely studied in the tax arena. The frequently posed question was how equitable people would judge taxes and how they would behave if taxes were neither presented nor perceived as a loss, but instead as a gain. It can be assumed that risk propensity changes and, consequently, audit probability and fines receive changing weight in considerations regarding tax evasion. If taxes are perceived as a loss, the tendency to repair the loss and willingness to take higher risks should lead to higher evasion as compared to taxes perceived as a gain and covarying risk aversion.

Given that most taxpayers pay a lump sum of income tax when filing their taxes at the end of the year, they have either paid too much or not

If Programme C is adopted, 400 people will die.

If Programme D is adopted, there is a one-third probability that nobody will die and a two-thirds probability that 600 people will die.

If you were the government official making the decision, which programme would you adopt?

The alternatives A and B represent positive framing of the problem (200 people will be saved for sure). The alternatives C and D represent negative framing of the problem (400 people will die for sure). People choosing between alternatives A and B usually take the sure option, alternative A. People choosing between alternatives C and D usually avoid the sure negative event, taking the risky option D.

enough tax and have either a refund or balance due. Those taxpayers who have a refund due may perceive their tax refund as a gain, whereas those whose tax liability actually paid is lower than the liability determined by the tax office, and who thus have additional tax payments due, may perceive the taxes due as a loss and try to repair it by not reporting income or overstating expenditures. Elffers and Hessing (1997) offer the following description of the taxpayer's thought progression during the tax-filing process (cf. Carroll, 1992):

Imagine the following situation. When a taxpayer has finished filling in his tax return form, he quickly calculates what the completed form means in his case. If he concludes that too much money has been withheld, he can expect a refund; he is 'on the verge of gain'. In that case he will opt for the safe, risk-free strategy to collect that profit; he signs the form and puts the envelope in the post. But imagine that he sees from his calculations that it is going to be different; not enough has been withheld and he will have to make an additional payment! The taxpayer is disappointed; for he is 'on the verge of loss'. He comes to the conclusion that he will have to do his utmost to fill in the form 'in a better way' to avoid 'the loss'. So he now opts for a more risky strategy, in which he suppresses part of his taxable income, to the verge of or just over the limit of what is permissible. He takes in his stride that, in so doing, he has to play the rules of the game in a 'supply way' to cut his 'loss', accepting that he is taking the risk of being corrected. (Elffers and Hessing, 1997, p. 291)

Cox and Plumley (1988; as quoted in Webley et al., 1991, pp. 83–4) analysed voluntary compliance rates of 50,000 tax returns in 1982. They analysed the relative proportion of taxes owed that had already been voluntarily paid by the taxpayer relative to the total tax liability, and compared the voluntary compliance rate of wage and salary earners with business income earners, expecting either a refund or balance due. As figure 19 shows, the average voluntary compliance rate is higher in the group of wage and salary earners (95%) than in the group of business income earners (below 90%). Compliance increased steadily with the amount of the expected return: if wage and salary earners expected more than $1,000 in taxes due, their compliance rate was 89%; if they expected a refund of $1,000 or more, their compliance rate increased to 96%. In the group of business income earners, the differences were even more pronounced: if taxes due amounted to $1,000 or more, their compliance rate was 70%, whereas it increased to 95% if a refund of $1,000 or more was expected.

The findings by Cox and Plumley lead to the assumption that compliance increases if taxpayers pay sufficiently high amounts in advance and receive a tax refund at the time of filing. Deliberate over-withholding of income taxes may increase compliance and may substitute for costly detection efforts in enhancing compliance, as Yaniv (1999) has shown in an econometric model.

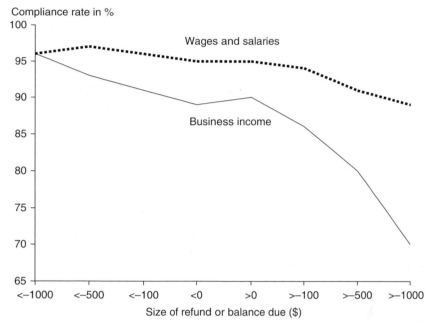

Figure 19: Wage and salary earners' and business income earners' voluntary compliance rates as a function of the size of refund or balance due (Cox and Plumley, 1988; quoted in Webley *et al.*, 1991, p. 84)

Robben *et al.* (1990b) confirmed experimentally the empirical findings for advance tax payments in ten cities in the United States and Europe. Participants engaged in a relatively complex small-business management task – a computer-simulated retail business that sold groceries and household products. Several business-related decisions had to be made during four business periods, and two income tax returns had to be filed. The independent variables manipulated in the experiment were either high or low opportunity to evade, and decision frame. Keeping the overall amount of tax payments and tax refunds identical, half of the participants were informed that they could expect a substantial tax refund, whereas the other half were informed that a considerable tax payment was due on top of already withheld taxes. It was found that non-compliance was more likely to occur, occurred on more occasions and involved larger amounts of money among participants confronting the prospect of an additional tax payment after withholding. Also, evasion, defined as exhibited intentional or erroneous non-compliance and admitted cheating in a post-experimental questionnaire, was significantly higher if a balance was due at the time of filing. Table 12 shows the results by withholding status.

Table 12: *Non-compliance and cheating as a function of withholding status (means and standard deviations in parentheses; Robben et al., 1990b, pp. 355 and 358)*

	Withholding status			
Tax behaviour	Refund		Balance due	
Non-compliance (N = 674)				
Occurrence of non-compliance	0.15	(0.36)	0.22	(0.42)
Frequency of non-compliance	0.27	(0.72)	0.43	(0.95)
Amount index	1486	(5113)	2657	(7328)
Evasion (N = 142)				
Evasion index	0.13	(0.33)	0.31	(0.47)

Elffers, Robben and Hessing (1992) conducted a similar study with withholding status and opportunity to evade as independent variables. People in the high-opportunity condition were found to evade more and to a larger extent than those in the low-opportunity condition, and the over-withholding situation led to less frequent evasion than the under-withholding situation. The prospect of financial loss and increased opportunity to cheat without being detected produced both more frequent and more extensive non-compliance. This corresponds with what was hypothesised and found by Robben (1991) and with what Webley *et al.* (1991) report. In two experiments, participants imagined leading a business, earning income and filing their taxes (Webley *et al.*, 1991). Participants were either in a low-evasion opportunity condition and were presented with three itemised deductions, or in a high-evasion opportunity condition, with six opportunities of deductions. They were informed either that at the end of the year they had a refund due or that they faced an additional tax payment. As in Robben *et al.*'s 1990b study, opportunity and withholding status determined tax compliance. Under the low-opportunity condition, tax evasion was significantly lower than in the high-opportunity condition, and under the condition of refund due, taxpayers were more compliant than under the condition of additional taxes due. A follow-up study confirmed the results with regard to opportunity but not for withholding status. However, when data of those participants who might not have fully understood the instructions were excluded from the analysis, the second study also showed the predicted withholding phenomenon. Support for predictions basing on prospect theory was also reported by Chang, Nichols and Schultz (1987) in a tax-audit lottery field experiment with taxpayers reporting their perceptions of their payments; by Chang and

Schultz (1990); and by Carroll (1992), who analysed the diaries about their tax-related thoughts of taxpayers who expected to receive either a refund or balance due at the time of filing. Schmidt (2001) studied with-holding phenomena and acceptance of certified public accountants' versus non-certified practitioners' aggressive tax advice. He presented partici-pants with scenarios describing either additional taxes due or a refund due. As predicted by prospect theory, taxpayers in a balance-due prepay-ment condition were more likely to agree with aggressive advice, especially from certified public accountants, than taxpayers in a refund-due position.

Schepanski and Kelsey (1990) summarise studies on prospect theory and framing in the arena of tax behaviour. They conclude that general-isability of the framing effect and risk-averse behaviour in gains changing into risk-seeking behaviour if the outcome becomes negative is weak. They argue that it is important to differentiate between actual wealth state and final asset positions and investigate three framing conditions: a loss condition; a refund condition; and a final asset condition. Prospect theory was strongly supported under the conditions of low penalties: participants were more risk-averse in the refund and final asset positions than in the loss condition. Participants were assigned to a loss condition, a refund condition and a final asset condition and instructed to assume they possessed a net worth position amounting to $5,000, $4,300 and $5,000, corresponding to their experimental condition. In the loss con-dition, participants were presented with a situation where the additional tax due was $500 more than what they had been led to anticipate it to be, namely zero. They were asked whether they would pay the additional tax or claim a non-allowable deduction, bringing the additional tax due down to zero. In the refund condition, participants were informed about an unexpected increase in net worth amounting to $700, represented by a refund of withheld taxes. They were also informed that their return included a non-allowable expense deduction that would reduce the refund to $200, if not claimed. Then they were asked to indicate whether or not they would claim the non-allowable deduction. Participants in the final asset position were presented with the same information as those in the loss condition, except that the outcomes were expressed in terms of final net worth states. Under all conditions, non-compliance resulted in a net worth position of $5,000 under the condition of no audit and detec-tion, whereas compliance resulted in a net worth of $4,500. Under the loss condition, participants' attention was directed towards the loss of $500, under the gain situation the focus was on a gain of $700, and under the final asset position, the focus was on final wealth amounting to $4,500. Participants indicated whether they would comply or not and indicated their strength of preference for the alternative chosen. Overall,

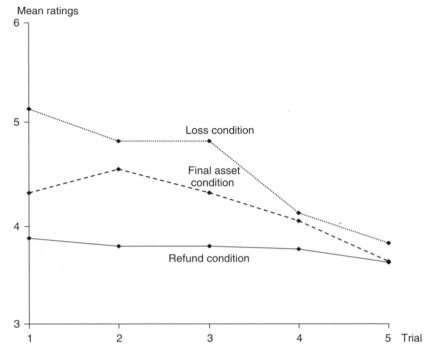

Figure 20: Mean preference ratings for non-compliance under the conditions of loss, refund and final asset position (adapted from Schepanski and Kelsey, 1990, pp. 63 and 65)

participants in each experimental condition evaluated five trials, with varying tax and penalty in the event the non-allowable deduction was detected. Penalty rates varied from 20% in the first trial to 25%, 30%, 35% and 40% in the last trial. In 1990, Schepanski and Kelsey found that non-compliance decreased with the increase of penalty rates. Both the frequencies of choices to evade and the strength of preference were highest in the loss condition and significantly lower in the refund and final asset position. The differences were especially pronounced between loss and refund conditions. Figure 20 shows the mean preference ratings for evasion under the three conditions; table 13 displays the proportions of participants choosing the non-compliant alternative.

In a later experiment, Schepanski and Shearer (1995) tested prospect theory's implications for two possible reference points for taxpayers: current and expected asset positions. They argue that most studies investigated withholding phenomena under the condition of current gains and losses. The reference point was the current asset position with which

Table 13: *Proportion of participants choosing the non-compliant alternative under the conditions of loss, refund and final asset position (adapted from Schepanski and Kelsey, 1990, pp. 64 and 66)*

Trial	Loss condition	Refund condition	Final asset condition
1	.57[a]	.33[b]	.40[b]
2	.48[a]	.32[b]	.44[a]
3	.48[a]	.28[b]	.41[a]
4	.27[a]	.27[a]	.32[a]
5	.22[a]	.20[a]	.21[a]

Note:
Different superscripts indicate significant differences (p < .05) between proportions in the loss conditions and refund condition, and between loss condition and final asset condition

participants compared a balance due or refund. This finding is consistent with the assumption that the status quo is a natural referent and the most likely candidate for the reference point for tax decisions. It is, however, likely that the reference point salient to taxpayers is their expected asset position. If the reference outcome is a taxpayer's expected total liability minus expected amounts withheld at source for the year, a payment due at filing that exceeded what was expected or a refund due that fell short of what was expected would both be framed as losses, while both a payment due less than what was expected at filing or a refund due greater than what was expected would be framed as gains. If expectations are not included in the reference outcome, decisions to comply would be based on current asset position and refunds or additional taxes due. Business students were randomly assigned to four conditions, facing either an unexpected or expected payment, or unexpected or expected refund. As in the former experiment, they indicated their preference for complying or not complying in five trials. Probability of detection varied from 20% in the first trial to 70% in the last trial. Non-compliance decreased with increasing detection probability and the mean preference for non-compliance was significantly higher in the payment condition compared with the unexpected refund condition. No significant differences were found between the expected and unexpected payment conditions (see figure 21). The authors conclude that the reference point taxpayers naturally tend to employ when making tax-reporting decisions is better represented by current asset position than by expected asset position.

Examination of the current cash position and expectations regarding payments or refunds due as two potential reference points in taxpayers' decisions has generally supported the role of cash position, while failing to

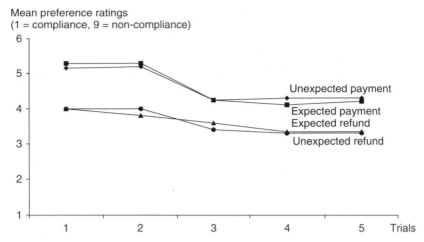

Figure 21: Mean preference ratings for non-compliant versus compliant choice alternatives (adapted from Schepanski and Shearer, 1995, p. 181)

support similar relevance of expectations. Prospect theory does not explicitly address what may serve as a reference point in a decision situation. Results in tax research and other decision areas suggest that the status quo serves as a natural reference point, and further, that individuals quickly adapt to changes in the status quo. Kahneman and Tversky (1979) appealed to the idea of adaptation to understand the role of the status quo as a referent, suggesting that people can be expected to adapt to their current situation over time and treat deviations from their adapted state as gains or losses. Research showed that individuals adapt to general standards of living when evaluating their own happiness (Argyle, 1987). Therefore, it can be expected that adaptation leads to perceptions of gain or loss of cash receipts that, permanently or temporarily, change one's standard. If expectations become meaningful referents via adaptation, Copeland and Cuccia (2002) argue that the construct validity of experimentally assigned expectations is problematic, especially if participants in experiments bring their own salient expectations to the experiment with no opportunity to meaningfully adapt to the experimental manipulations. It is unlikely that individuals adapt to small fluctuations in their cash positions or that tax payments and refunds determined at filing are significant enough to regularly lead to anticipated changes in taxpayers' general living standards. Copeland and Cuccia refer to prior research suggesting that the salient dimensions on which the status quo is evaluated are context-dependent. The attributes of a decision context to which decision-makers adapt, and the levels or conditions of those attributes, can be expected to differ depending on their context-dependent relevance, frequency of occurrence and availability. They expect that taxpayers will adapt to attributes of the tax reporting and filing context that is most relevant to them and with which they have past experience:

> We expect that experienced taxpayers will come to associate certain financial consequences with their tax filing, allowing adaptation to those consequences within the context of the tax reporting experience. In other words, experienced taxpayers are likely to come to expect a given range of financial consequences associated with their annual filing, with those expectations incorporated into their frame of reference. Variance from these expectations will, therefore, contribute to the framing of the current filing as a gain or loss. (p. 504)

The authors state that the use of current cash position as a reference point may be difficult to attribute to adaptation. Nevertheless, it may be a salient referent as it may represent a general aspiration, or the cash itself may have been mentally accounted for so that its receipt or payment represents the gain or loss of a specific consumption opportunity. Indeed, research by Souleles (1999) suggests that tax refunds are consumed soon after they are received. Alternatively, the salience of an infrequent cash payment or refund may be sufficient to make payment or refund salient in the editing phase of tax-reporting decisions. Therefore, Copeland and Cuccia hypothesise that, rather than one feature being relevant in the decision process, both expectations and payment or refund status serve to frame tax-reporting decisions. Taxpayers' reporting decisions should, thus, be framed simultaneously by expectations based on prior filing experiences and current cash position. In their study, Copeland and Cuccia used participants' own prior tax filings to determine expectations and found evidence that expectations and cash position jointly frame the filing decision. This result shows that decision-makers may use multiple reference points. Moreover, consistent with adaptation serving as a mechanism through which expectations frame taxpayers' decisions, they found that the effect attributed to expectations as decision frames decreases when time to adapt to changes from those expectations was allowed. Reactions to variations from expectations were found to wane over time.

Kirchler and Maciejovsky (2001) investigated self-reported tax compliance within the context of taxpayers' previous expected tax payments at filing time (payment or refund), their asset position (expected versus current asset position), and their tax category (self-employed versus business entrepreneurs). The study examined whether different tax categories had an impact on the habitual decision-making framework and hence influenced the reference point employed in the decision process. The reference point employed in decisions where the outcome is uncertain indicates whether the person involved is framing the situation as a gain or a loss. Two major theoretical possibilities within the framework of prospect theory have been discussed to describe a tax-reporting decision: the expected asset position and the current asset position. The former refers to a situation in which the reference outcome would be the taxpayer's expected total tax liability less expected amounts withheld at source for the fiscal year. Accordingly, a payment due at filing that exceeded what was expected or a refund due that fell short of what was expected would both be framed as losses, whereas a payment due that was less than what was expected at filing or a refund due that was greater than what was expected would both be framed as gains. The second theoretical possibility, the current asset position, refers to a situation in which expectations are not included in the reference outcome. Accordingly, taxpayers for whom too little was withheld at the time of filing would have an additional payment due which would be framed as a loss, whereas taxpayers for whom an excess amount was withheld would receive a refund which would be framed as a gain. In these cases, the tax-reporting decision is made when the tax return is filled out. Both possible reference points include the taxpayer's current asset position at filing time. However, the expected asset position also includes the expected year-end settlement amount that is either added to or subtracted from the taxpayer's current asset position (Schepanski and Shearer, 1995). In general, prospect theory is based on the assumption that the reference point, underlying the decision process, corresponds to the current asset position, in which gains and losses coincide with the actual amounts that are received or paid. However, the location of the reference point can be affected by the formulation of the offered prospects and by the expectations of the decision-maker (Kahneman and Tversky, 1979), and actual behaviour depends on the reference point employed in the decision process.

Kirchler and Maciejovsky further examined whether different tax categories (self-employed versus entrepreneurs) have an impact on the habitual decision-making framework and hence influence individual expectations by employing different asset positions. Can the reference point employed in the decision process be manipulated by introducing different tax laws to different people? The expected asset position is the implicit reference point in the 1979 prospect theory account by Kahneman and Tversky. Instead of using the current asset position as a reference point, people should code gains and losses in tax-related decisions to an expectation or aspiration level that differs from the status quo. For example, an unexpected tax withdrawal from a monthly salary check is experienced as a loss, not as a reduced gain. Individuals compare tax outcomes with the neutral reference point in order to make relative decisions, that is, to speak of gains or losses. Taxpayers who receive tax refunds higher than they expected or who actually anticipated a higher tax payment are predicted to frame such outcomes as gains, whereas taxpayers who receive tax refunds lower than they expected or whose tax payments are higher than they expected are predicted to frame such outcomes as losses.

Instead of expected asset position, Schepanski and Shearer (1995) emphasise the current asset position as being employed in tax-related decisions within the framework of prospect theory. Taxpayers for whom too little was withheld are predicted to be surprised by tax payments and to frame them as losses, whereas taxpayers for whom too much was withheld are predicted to be surprised by refunds and to frame them as gains. Decision-making, according to prospect theory, is based on the use of either expected or current asset position. The location of the reference point, and the consequent coding of outcomes as gains or losses, are assumed to be affected either by the formulation of the offered prospects or by the expectations of the decision-maker. In addition, individual expectations should also be determined by the tax code leading to different reference points employed in the decision process. Taxpayers who employ the expected asset position in their tax-related decisions were predicted to be less compliant in the case of an expected payment and more compliant in the case of an expected refund. By contrast, those taxpayers whose reference point is their current asset position are predicted to be less compliant in the case of an unexpected payment and more compliant in the case of an unexpected refund. These assumptions were tested in a sample of self-employed taxpayers and business entrepreneurs. The self-employed, who have the option of choosing the cash receipts and disbursements method, were assumed to employ the current asset position in tax-reporting decisions. Therefore, it was predicted that unexpected payments should lead to low tax honesty, whereas unexpected refunds should lead to high tax honesty. Conversely, business entrepreneurs, who are obliged to use the more restrictive accrual method, think long-term and strategically. Thus, the reference point they employ in making tax-related decisions is their expected asset position. It was predicted that expected payments lead to low tax honesty, whereas expected refunds lead to high tax honesty for this group of respondents. It was found that for the self-employed, an unexpected surprise payment leads to low tax honesty, whereas an unexpected surprise refund leads to high tax honesty. Thus, their self-reported tax compliance can be best described by the current asset position, a fact consistent with the option the self-employed have of choosing the cash receipts and disbursements method instead of the otherwise binding accrual method. The former is characterised by less restrictive accounting principles. By contrast, business entrepreneurs are obliged to use the more restrictive accrual method and have to base decisions on expectations. Therefore, their reference point in making tax decisions can be best described as dictated by their expected asset position. As a result, expected payments are associated with low tax honesty and expected refunds are associated with high tax honesty on the part of these individuals. In situations of unexpected payments and refunds, respectively, business entrepreneurs were risk averse and showed a high level of absolute tax honesty.

Although prospect theory has received considerable support in tax research, several studies suggest limited validity. First, it should be mentioned that risk avoidance in gain situations is unlikely if a gain is very small, and loss aversion seems not likely if the loss is small. Webley et al. (1991) argue that taxpayers behave according to prospect theory when faced with a tax levy that is too high or too low. Schadewald (1989) manipulated the reference point and prepayment conditions, using 70% detection rate. Under this high detection rate, little support for prospect theory was found. Hasseldine and Hite (2003) and Cullis, Jones and Lewis (2006) report gender differences which need to be considered. In tax research, compliance has generally been found to differ between the sexes. Although the results are mixed and much less clear than results regarding, for instance, age, women were more often found to be compliant than men (e.g., Baldry, 1987; Jackson and Milliron, 1986; Lewis, 1982; Webley et al., 1991).

Cullis, Jones and Lewis (2006) conducted a study on framing in the tradition of withholding phenomena with taxes being perceived as a gain or loss. Economics and psychology students completed a short questionnaire designed to assess whether audit probability influences the amount of income declared. Respondents were asked to indicate how much they would declare if the probability of detection was 1%, 5% and 25%, respectively. Further, respondents were asked to imagine themselves as an established trader and whether they would declare their income differently in cases where taxes had not already been deducted compared to respondents where tax had already been deducted based on the previous year's income. Finally, respondents were instructed to behave instrumentally, maximising their profit, or to 'be themselves'. It was found that the detection rates had a major influence on income declared. Income declared increased as the probability of detection increased. With regard to the framing of tax withholding, it was not generally confirmed that more income would be declared when tax has already been deducted based on the previous year's income compared to the condition where tax had yet to be paid for the current year. The framing effect was found only in the samples of economics students and males. Males were much more responsive to framing than females, declaring less when tax was framed as a loss.

Hasseldine and Hite (2003) conducted a study on goal framing and found gender affects responses to positively and negatively framed tax situations. Participants were presented with the conditions outlined in table 14 and asked whether they would include the $500 cash received as income in their federal tax return. Despite almost no risk of being audited, 45% of the participants indicated that they would definitely indicate all their income on their tax return; the average response on the 9-point scale, with low values indicating honesty, was $M = 3.9$ ($SD = 3.2$). While females ($M = 3.8$) were found to exhibit generally more compliant behaviour than males ($M = 4.0$), females were more compliant when the positively framed message was used ($M = 3.4$ versus $M = 4.3$ in the negatively framed condition), whereas males were more compliant when the negatively framed message was used ($M = 3.7$ versus $M = 4.5$ in the positively framed condition). Generally, these results need to be interpreted with caution, as the participants were university employees from just one university. Also, the differences between conditions were small. However, the results indicate that there are limits regarding the application of prospect theory and effects of framing.

Gender differences reported in the studies by Cullis and colleagues and Hasseldine and Hite need to be interpreted with caution. Rather than gender differences, the differences in Hasseldine and Hite's study might be due to differences in self-regulation and regulatory focus of males and females who participated in their study. In particular, the different framing of a loss or gain in the latter study directs participants' attention either to a desirable goal or to an unwanted outcome. Depending on self-regulation and the regulatory focus on promotion or prevention (Higgins, 1998a, 1998b, 2002), people could base their choices either on expected gains or losses. While promotion-oriented people are assumed to regulate their behaviour and choices predominantly on the basis of positive, goal-directed information, prevention-oriented people base their choices predominantly on information useful in avoiding negative outcomes.

Framing effects differ also with regard to taxpayers' tax ethics. In 1994, Reckers, Sanders and Roark examined whether ethical beliefs about tax compliance mediate withholding effects. Arkansas, USA residents participating in the Arkansas Household Research Panel, administered by the University of Arkansas, received a questionnaire with a tax scenario in which a couple with two children was described. They faced either the situation of over-withheld taxes or taxes due, and the option to declare or not to declare revenues amounting to $2,000. Besides manipulating tax withholding, participants were also informed that the marginal tax rates

Table 14: Positively and negatively framed tax scenarios (Hasseldine and Hite, 2003, pp. 530–1)

Positively framed condition	Negatively framed condition
The federal government is concerned that some taxpayers claim too many deductions and do not report all their income when filing their tax returns.	The federal government is concerned that some taxpayers claim too many deductions and do not report all their income when filing their tax returns.
However, if taxpayers like you comply by reporting all your taxable income and by claiming only allowable deductions, then you could gain these advantages:	Therefore, if taxpayers like you do not comply either because you fail to report all your taxable income or you claim more deductions than allowed, then you could suffer these disadvantages:
1. No fines and penalties can be imposed on you.	1. Fines and penalties can be imposed on you.
2. No jail sentences or criminal convictions can be imposed on you.	2. Jail sentences or criminal convictions can be imposed on you.
3. IRS auditors are less likely to audit you.	3. IRS auditors are more likely to audit you.
In short, if you comply, you will not need to worry about any IRS consequences. The IRS will treat you as a compliant taxpayer. The message is clear – if you comply and report all your taxes, in the long run you could gain and not be punished by the IRS!	In short, if you do not comply, you need to worry about IRS consequences. The IRS will treat you as a noncompliant taxpayer. The message is clear – if you do not comply and do not report all your taxes, in the long run you could lose and be punished by the IRS!

Evasion vignette and dependent variable

... Assume that in addition to your regular job at xxx University you are able to make extra money during the year by moonlighting. Further assume that you earned $5,500 during the last tax year and of this amount $500 was paid to you in cash, and the other $5,000 by a single check from a local business. Legally, the cash income of $500 should be included as income in your tax return, but the IRS almost certainly will not audit you and would not know if you do not report the $500 received in cash on your tax return...

If you were faced with the above situation: would you include all of the $500 cash received as income on your federal tax return?

	Definitely yes								Definitely no
	1	2	3	4	5	6	7	8	9

were either 28% or 42%, and asked to indicate on a 6-point scale (1 = not reporting the $2,000 income; 6 = reporting it) how they themselves would behave if they were in the described situation. Moreover, questions on personal tax ethics were presented. Participants who strongly agreed that tax evasion was morally wrong were not influenced by the with-holding frame, while those with low tax ethics indicated not to declare the full income when additional taxes were due at filing. Furthermore, if tax ethics were low, the marginal tax rate influenced compliance, with higher tax rates leading to lower compliance.

In the context of equity theory, King and Sheffrin (2002) tested predic-tions of prospect theory and framing. More specifically, risky choices were studied either in a context-neutral setting or after presenting a scenario in which exchange equity or social comparisons were manipulated. In the scenario manipulating exchange equity, the government had wasted a large amount of money or spent money against the will of voters. This scenario resembles operationalisations of exchange fairness. In one social compari-son scenario, high-income earners' opportunities to evade taxes without punishment were described. This operationalisation corresponds to verti-cal fairness definitions. In the second social comparison scenario, non-allowable tax deductions taken by a co-worker and his brother-in-law in a low audit probability were described. This operationalisation is similar to horizontal fairness or social norms definitions. Table 15 presents a context-neutral risky choice task and the respective choice embedded in the vertical fairness context, along with the percentages of participants choosing the respective options. In these tasks, option A presents the sure gain which, according to prospect theory, participants should prefer over the unsure, but economically more profitable, option B. Options C and D are identical to options A and B, multiplied by 0.25. However, prospect theory predicts that due to a certainty effect participants now prefer D over C. King and Sheffrin argue that according to equity theory, participants should choose B and D because they attempt to counterbalance the inequity in the tax system. In this particular example, predictions of prospect theory were confirmed. This was not the case in the remaining examples used by the authors. Under control conditions, prospect theory was supported; how-ever, responses to the framed questions depicting inequity were more consistent with expected utility theory.

In sum, prospect theory and framing have received considerable sup-port in empirical studies on tax choices and behaviour, but there are also studies delineating the limits of the theory and suggesting differential effects, depending on gender, ethics and fairness. Hasseldine (1998a) provided a summary report on studies on prospect theory and tax-reporting decisions, concluding that withholding phenomena, which by

Table 15: *Context-neutral choice task and choice embedded in a vertical fairness scenario (King and Sheffrin, 2002, pp. 513–14 and p. 518)*

Context-neutral choice task	Choice task embedded in a vertical fairness scenario
	The IRS reports that tax evasion amongst those with income in excess of $100,000 is at an all-time high and the IRS does not have the resources to investigate and punish the evaders. In addition, this year you have high medical expenses that you thought would count for allowable medical deductions, but at filing, you discover that the expenses are not high enough to qualify for deductions. This means that your tax bill is $200 higher than you expected.
Which option would you prefer?	You are preparing your tax return, which of the following options do you prefer?
A: A sure win of $100. (53%)	A: Claiming an allowable tax deduction that will save you $100 in taxes. (65%)
B: An 80% chance of winning $200. (47%)	B: Claiming a 'non-allowable' deduction that nonetheless has an 80% chance of being accepted by the IRS, and which saves you $200 in taxes. (35%)
Now which option would you prefer?	Which of the following options do you prefer?
C: A 25% chance of winning $100. (7%)	C: Claiming a deduction that has a 25% chance of being accepted by the IRS which saves you $100 in taxes. (32%)
D: A 20% chance of winning $200. (93%)	D: Claiming a deduction that has a 20% chance of being accepted by the IRS which saves you $200 in taxes. (68%)

the majority of published studies are empirically supported, provide the tax authorities with a simple strategy to increase compliance:

> If prospect theory is applicable ... then an option for tax policy makers arises ... increasing the amount of withholding tax deducted from source income such as wages and salaries to put more individuals into the domain of gains, (i.e. in a refund-due prepayment position), and therefore have fewer risk seeking individuals evading tax ... tax agencies should continue policies which discourage under-withholding ... Whether individuals would eventually shift their reference points (and by how much) after several years of tax refunds is unclear, but is certainly possible. (p. 504)

5   Self-employment and taxpaying

Most psychological studies on tax behaviour concentrate on income tax and determinants of compliance. The more tax knowledge possessed by taxpayers, the more positive these taxpayers' attitudes, the higher their ethical beliefs, the stronger their social norms and conviction of a fair tax system, and the stronger the deterrence in terms of audits and sanctions of evasion (e.g., Webley, 2004). Also, perceived opportunities not to comply determine tax behaviour. However, opportunities vary considerably and are definitely higher among the self-employed and entrepreneurs.

Opportunity to evade was found to be the most probable and relevant determinant of non-compliance (e.g., Antonides and Robben, 1995; Groenland and van Veldhoven, 1983; King and Sheffrin, 2002; Lewis, 1982; Robben et al., 1990b; Slemrod, Blumenthal and Christian, 2001; Vogel, 1974; Wallschutzky, 1984; Webley et al., 1991). It can be expected, therefore, that the self-employed and entrepreneurs are more prone to tax evasion than employed people earning a salary. Also, cash economy activity is more prevalent among the self-employed. On the other hand, Ahmed and Braithwaite (2005) argue that a number of studies have described small-business owners as law-abiding, responsible and ethical, and as taking their tax obligations seriously (e.g., Brown, 1985; Cunningham and Lischeron, 1991). Moreover, their personal characteristics have been portrayed as ambitious, hard-working, coura-geous and individualistic (C. J. Collins, Hanges and Locke, 2004; DeCarlo and Lyons, 1979; Verheul, Uhlaner and Thurik, 2005). In their study on issues of deterrence, tax morale, fairness and the work practices of Australian small-business taxpayers, Ahmed and Braithwaite (2005) found that small-business taxpayers were similar to and different from taxpayers employed in the private sector and those working for non-profit or govern-ment organisations. On a vast number of attitudinal variables, small-business taxpayers were much the same as other taxpayers. In terms of law abidingness and respect for authority, small-business taxpayers were no different from anyone else. They seemed to have a great deal in common with wage and salary earners in the private and public sectors. The major differences were found in regard to tax-related activities, work practices and tax morale. Small-business taxpayers clearly felt disgruntled. They were less often in the situation where they received a tax refund on submitting their annual income tax return, and they felt less competent and less independent in preparing their income tax return. Small-business owners were more likely to acknowledge that they evaded tax and they expressed a keen interest in tax avoidance and tax-effective planning by using tax practitioners. The issue of taxes is important to small-business owners (Rogoff and Lee, 1996), especially during the start-up phase. Besides economic performance, business vitality, development capacity and a fair tax and fiscal system are important in decision-making. Also provision of incentives as well as business and personal tax reductions are often claimed (Corman, Lussier and Nolan, 1996).

In the same study, Ahmed and Braithwaite (2005) found small-business taxpayers more likely to have experienced conflict with or sanctioning by the tax office, and they admitted to paying less than their fair share of tax. Small-business owners were more aware than others of the tax office's authority to enforce compliance. Thus, this study provides support to previous findings that small-business owners take their responsibilities to obey the law seriously. Differences in tax morale, however, became evident when the focus shifted from paying tax as an obligation under the law to paying tax as a social obligation to society. As Ahmed and Braithwaite conclude, the argument for paying tax in western democracies is to contribute to the government's communal pot so that services can be universally provided as well as extra support as a safety net for those in need. Ideologically, small-business owners were less comfortable with this arrangement than others. They were more supportive of government that does not interfere in the economic and social order, adopting values of independence and self-sufficiency.

Since salaries are frequently taxed on source, opportunities to decide to pay or not to pay taxes due are limited. Self-employed people and entrepreneurs, however, receive their income gross and need to pay taxes out-of-pocket. With regard to the reference point in taxpaying decisions – discussed above – paying out-of-pocket is more likely to be perceived as a loss of one's money than receiving net income without ever holding gross income in one's hands. In other words, the self-employed and entrepreneurs collect their gross income and pay their income tax at the end of the business year. Besides perceiving out-of-pocket payments as a loss, business people may also perceive taxes as a limitation of their entrepreneurial freedom. In a study on social representations of taxes, entrepreneurs associated loss of freedom to invest their money in their own business with the stimulus word 'tax'. More than civil servants, blue- and white-collar workers and students, entrepreneurs think of bureau- cracy, disincentive to work and limitation of their entrepreneurial freedom when confronted with 'taxes' (Kirchler, 1998).

Kirchler and Berger (1998) investigated determinants of self-reported compliance by asking 86 self-employed Austrians and 151 tax auditors to complete a questionnaire on Machiavellianism as a personality trait, perceived limitation of one's freedom to dispose of one's income, vertical justice, tax mentality and morale and intended compliance in three scenarios which described the possibility not to declare total income and to overstate deductions at tax filing. The self-employed had the impression that vertical justice was low; their tax mentality and morale were lower than in the sample of tax auditors, while their intention not to comply was higher. Perceived limitation of freedom was high, ranging significantly above the mid-point of the five-point answering scale. In the sample of the self-employed, non-compliance was found to depend on tax morale. Tax morale was found to be positively related to age and neg- atively related to Machiavellianism. The older the self-employed were and the less Machiavellian their personality, the higher was self-reported compliance. Perceived limitation of freedom was found to depend on school education and Machiavellianism: the less educated and the more Machiavellian a participant was, the stronger the perceived limitation of freedom, and consequently, the lower the tax mentality. In the sample of tax auditors, those loading low on Machiavellianism were highly com- pliant (see figure 22).

Taxes are perceived as limiting one's freedom to make autonomous decisions about one's own income and investments in one's own busi- ness. Self-employed people and entrepreneurs seem to perceive taxes as a loss of money they already possess and perceive their freedom to decide about their finances as threatened and restricted.

People often respond to restrictions, real or perceived, on their free- dom by undertaking actions to re-establish their lost freedom. Brehm (1966) has developed a theory based on the notion that people want to re-establish their threatened freedom. According to his reactance theory, people display a concern for independence by resisting the attempts of others to limit their freedom of decision. Brehm suggests that a person who has a set of free behaviour alternatives 'will experience reactance whenever any of these behaviours is eliminated or threatened with elimi- nation' (p. 4). Reactance may result from a possible loss of control over events or a reduction of choice alternatives and develop into a motive to resist if the individual perceives a chance to re-establish his or her former situation (Wortman and Brehm, 1975). People can re-establish their

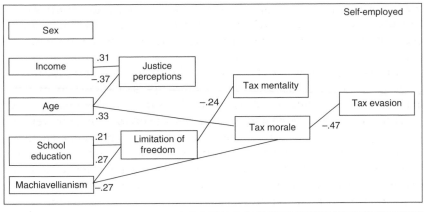

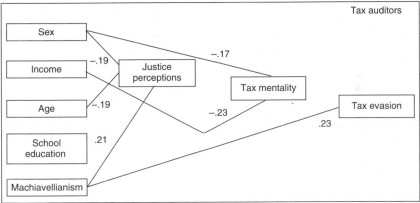

Figure 22: Structural model of determinants of non-compliance of self-employed people and tax auditors (beta weights) (Kirchler and Berger, 1998)

freedom by choosing the opposite behaviour to what is desired by the manipulative source. Perceived limitation of freedom can also be re-established by accepting the observed opposition or resistance of other people who suffer from a limitation of their freedom. If people perceive taxes as a loss of freedom, they are likely to develop reactance. Reactance can be conceived as motivation to re-establish freedom by developing negative attitudes towards the government and taxes in general. Moreover, reactance may manifest itself by decreasing tax morale, and those who have the opportunity to evade taxes by exaggerating costs and lowering income may be inclined to change their behaviour and avoid or evade taxes (Pelzmann, 1985).

The greater a person's motivation to control his or her choices, the more intense reactance should be. In 1999, Kirchler investigated whether the loss of previously possessed money leads to more intense negative feelings than loss of money which a person never had in his or her hands, i.e., money withheld from the gross income at source. It can be assumed that especially entrepreneurs, who take the risk of establishing an enterprise, perceive taxes as a severe reduction of their profit and investment possibilities. Since entrepreneurs have more opportunities to avoid and/ or evade taxes, reactance motives may lead to such behaviour tendencies.

The more experience an entrepreneur has accumulated over time, the more certain he or she is that the firm will continue to operate despite high taxes, and the more he or she has adapted to the national tax system, the lower reactance should be. Entrepreneurs not only have greater opportunities to evade than other categories of taxpayers, but during the start-up phase of their enterprise they may have stronger motives to respond by reactance. Opportunities and reactance motives together would explain entrepreneurs' admittance of more frequent evasion than workers (43% versus 13%; Wallschutzky, 1984).

Kirchler's study also investigated entrepreneurs' reactance to taxes as dependent on the length of time an enterprise has existed. It was hypothesised that experiences of limited freedom through taxes lead to reactance. Reactance manifests itself by negative attitudes towards taxes, low tax morality and avoidance of taxes. Reactance was hypothesised to depend on the number of years an entrepreneur has run his or her firm. Since age of respondents was expected to be correlated with length of time running an enterprise, age was controlled in the analysis.

Kirchler developed a questionnaire which was completed by 128 Austrian entrepreneurs to assess (a) perceived loss of freedom due to tax obligations, (b) attitudes towards tax evasion, (c) moral standards with regard to taxpaying, (d) actions to reduce or avoid taxes, and (e) demographic characteristics.

The relationships between duration of enterprise, age of respondents, loss of freedom, attitudes, morality and actions were studied simultaneously within a structural equation model. From a conceptual point of view, the model assumed that duration of enterprise and age of the employer determine perceived loss of freedom, as well as other variables expressing attitudes towards and behaviour with regard to taxes. Loss of freedom itself should lead to attitudes favouring tax evasion, lower moral standards and to approval of tax-reducing actions. Also, attitudes and low morality should be correlated with tax-avoiding actions. Figure 23 represents the results of a model that explains variance of reactance. Duration of running an enterprise had a significant effect on perceived loss of freedom through tax regulations. Loss of freedom was significantly related to anti-tax behaviour. Anti-tax behaviour was found also to

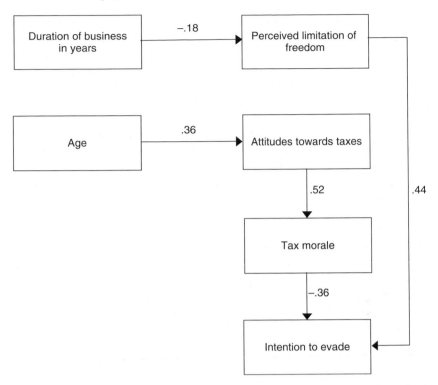

Figure 23: Structural relationship between duration of running a business, age of respondents, perceived limitation of freedom, attitudes towards taxes, tax morale and intention to evade (Kirchler, 1999)

depend on tax morale and attitudes towards taxes. Age of respondents had a significant effect on tax attitudes, with attitudes becoming more favourable as taxpayers age.

Length of running a business determines perceived restriction of one's freedom and reactance motives and intention to evade taxes. As Pelzmann (1985) also emphasises, loss of freedom and reactance motives determine tax behaviour intentions, and persons who establish a small or medium business, or take the risks of investing in a new branch, experience intense reactance. Perceived restriction of one's own freedom of choice was directly linked to behaviour tendencies. No causal link was found between perceived freedom and anti-tax attitudes and morale. Perceived loss of freedom and reactance seem to decrease after years of experience with one's own firm and perhaps trust in the profitability of one's business. Over time, adaptation to the tax system as well as a separation of gross income from net income and taxes into separate (mental) accounts are likely to occur (Adams and Webley, 2001). Interestingly, in Kirchler's 1999 study, perceived loss of freedom did not correlate with age. As expected, older participants were more likely to have run their firms for a greater number of years than younger participants. The correlation between years in business and perceived loss of freedom remains almost identical if age of the respondents is held constant (i.e., a partial correlation was conducted between years in business and perceived loss; age was held constant).

Limitation of personal freedom of choices and/or actions, even if necessary for establishing public goods, may have the exact opposite effect from those desired. Individuals who experience loss of freedom may successfully escape the perceived pressures. However, it is not necessary that people themselves perceive loss of their freedom. Even if they observe the loss of others' freedoms, they may act in a way to restore the freedom. It is as if people observing others losing their freedom anticipate that they themselves might lose their freedom in the future. As a consequence, they react against the constraints in advance (Brehm, 1966). Perhaps citizens' resistance to condemning tax evasion and self-employed taxpayers' reluctance to pay taxes can be explained, at least in part, as a restoration of observed limitation of freedom.

Self-employed workers and entrepreneurs were found to be particularly ambitious and hard-working. If tax rates increase, work engagement may suffer especially in the group of small-business owners. This is likely because higher income due to hard work is cut by taxes, and thus time spent on work is worth less, while the relative value of leisure time is increasing. Moreover, the self-employed may be less compliant if they work hard and if tax rates are high, in order to counterbalance income cuts (Calderwood and Webley, 1992).

J. H. Collins, Murphey and Plumlee (1990) found evidence of a positive relationship between work effort and non-compliance opportunities. Taxpayers with a non-compliance opportunity seem to work harder than those without an under-reporting opportunity. Considering reported relationships between hard work, tax rate and opportunity not to comply, it may be expected that hard work would be positively related to legal or illegal reductions of one's tax obligations.

If high tax rates and low opportunities to avoid taxes are related to less hard work, one might also expect a causal relationship between hard work and tax non-compliance: people working hard may try to avoid or to evade taxes more often than people working less hard. Higher non-compliance of the hard-working might also be a strategy to re-establish fairness with regard to taxpayer–government exchanges. However, this conclusion does not seem to hold. Self-employed people and entrepreneurs working hard for their money are not more likely to evade taxes than those with low work effort. Kirchler *et al.* (2005) investigated experimentally whether effort while earning one's income is a relevant factor for taxpayers' compliance decisions and, if so, whether it is high or low effort that leads to non-compliance.

Within the framework of taxpaying as a decision under uncertainty, it is of interest to investigate whether propensity to take the risk of evasion changes if, prior to the decision, high effort was put in earning the income to be declared. From a strict economic perspective, the source of income should not alter its subjective valuation, and sunk costs like prior investments of effort should not affect actual decisions. Behavioural research, however, has demonstrated that both assumptions are wrong. First, money earned by one's own effort or skills is evaluated higher than had it been gained by chance or luck (Loewenstein and Issacharoff, 1994) and is less readily spent than windfall gains (Arkes *et al.*, 1994). Second, sunk costs do affect decision-makers, as seen in an increase in their willingness to take risks they would otherwise forgo had they not incurred these costs (Arkes and Blumer, 1985; Thaler, 1980; Thaler and Johnson, 1990). For the context of tax evasion, the effort put into earning an income can be experienced as sunk costs. In line with source dependence and sunk cost effects, it would therefore be expected that more effort (i.e., more sunk costs) should lead to higher subjective valuation of one's earnings and, consequently, to non-compliance.

Recent research on the effect of sunk costs indicates, however, that in some cases, earlier expenditure of resources can also reduce risk-seeking. For example, Garland, Sandefur and Rogers (1990) presented geologists with oil exploration scenarios and found that higher sunk costs – previously drilled dry wells – resulted in reduced likelihood to authorise the next drill. A study by Zeelenberg and van Dijk (1997) asked participants to imagine that they had invested time and effort in a job and were offered a gamble over their payment. Participants were more willing to take risks when they were offered the gamble without prior investment. Zeelenberg and van Dijk conjecture that in some cases, people feel that they have 'too much invested to gamble'. While most prior research on sunk costs had focused on financial investments, Zeelenberg and van Dijk (1997) argued that individuals experiencing behavioural sunk costs develop a certain expectancy or aspiration level (Helson, 1964; Weiner, 1996) for (financial) compensation for their behavioural effort. If a safe option is given, which is able to satisfy the aspiration level, it will be chosen, while additional, but risky, gains from the gamble are forgone. Accordingly, in the context of tax evasion these considerations seem to imply that high effort invested to earn one's income would lead to less risk-seeking, that is, less evasion.

The previous paragraphs briefly reported findings from behavioural decision-making research that yielded two contradicting predictions on the effects of hard versus easy work on tax compliance. Kahneman and Tversky's (1979) prospect theory, the state-of-the-art model of decision-making, allows the analysis of the basic processes underlying the proposed hypotheses for compliance decisions under influence of high versus low effort. Taxpayers have their gross income in their pockets and have to pay taxes directly out of it. Assuming that this status quo is used as the reference point, taxpayers face a choice of either a sure loss (i.e., reporting honestly), a gamble between no loss and a smaller loss (under-reporting and not being detected), or a larger loss (under-reporting and being detected). Prospect theory predicts risk-seeking for such a framing, since all outcomes occur in the domain of losses. From this starting point, two potential mechanisms need to be considered, which could explain the controversial findings reported above: (a) a change in the slope of the value function; and (b) a change in the reference point.

(a) If effort changes the slope of the value function, risk-seeking could be more or less pronounced for a given tax decision. A steeper slope of the function increases convexity when evaluating the outcomes of a given gamble, and therefore increases the risk-seeking tendency. These considerations are exemplified in figure 24. Function V represents a value

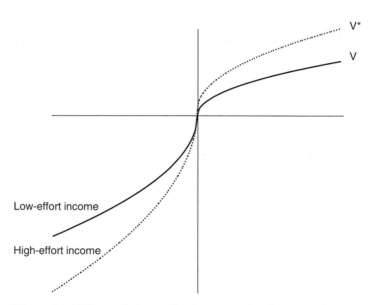

Figure 24: Effects of change in slope on value functions in prospect theory

function for low-effort income. High-effort changes the function, resulting in value function V⋆ with a steeper slope. In V⋆, subjective valuation of an outcome is higher than in V, and also the difference between the subjective value of a given gamble and the subjective value of the sure outcome increases, which implies more risk-seeking in the high-effort income value function V⋆.

(b) The status quo is not necessarily the reference point. It has been suggested that aspiration levels could also function as reference points. Kahneman and Tversky (1979, p. 286) in their original paper on prospect theory stated, 'there are situations in which gains and losses are coded relative to an expectation or aspiration level that differs from the status quo'. Heath, Larrick and Wu (1999) discussed the notion that goals can serve as reference points in more detail. For compliance decisions it is plausible to assume that taxpayers who put different efforts into earning their income adapt to different reference points. It can be assumed that high effort induces the setting of an aspiration level for an expected net income that serves as a reference point in the decision. Low effort, on the other hand, should decrease the likelihood that taxpayers think about how much income will remain after paying taxes. Therefore, taxpayers should evaluate their decision outcomes from their usual reference point, namely the gross income they have already in their pocket. Figure 25 shows feasible effects of adapting to different reference points. Value function V for low-effort income implies the gross income as reference point (R). Value function V⋆ is based on the decision-maker's aspiration

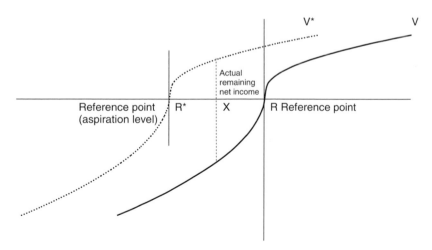

Figure 25: Effects of a shift in reference point on value functions in prospect theory

level and the expected net income as reference point (R*). If outcome X, which represents the actual remaining net income in the case of honest declaration, is valued, this outcome is always in the loss domain for value function V, but in the gain domain for value function V* if the aspiration level is lower than X. Consequently, a reference point R results in risk-seeking, and a reference point R* in risk aversion. However, if the aspiration level R* is higher than X, X is also in the loss domain, resulting in risk-seeking behaviour for reference point R.

These hypotheses and their underlying decision mechanisms were investigated by Kirchler, Maciejovsky and Schwarzenberger (2005) in two experiments. Participants were instructed to take the role of architects who were competing for building projects. Each project was described as lasting one year; every participant ran through three business years. After a neutral control condition, the architect's work in the project was described as easy or hard, depending on the experimental condition. At the end of that year participants were informed about their gross income and were required to file their tax report. The tax rate in all conditions was 50%, audit probability amounted to 15.3%, and fines in the case of detected evasion were twice the evaded amount.

Aggregate tax evasion in the first experiment amounted to 21% of the overall taxes due in the control condition, to 25% in the low-effort condition, and to 18% in the high-effort condition. These percentages represent how much tax was not collected by tax authorities from their point of view. Highest evasion occurred in the low-effort condition. A high level of aggregate evasion could mean either that many taxpayers evaded small parts of their income, or that a few evaded a large amount of taxes. Regarding individual tax honesty, the overall level of participants reporting their full income was rather high. In the control condition, 59% reported their income honestly, while 41% understated their income. In the low-effort condition, 54% understated their income, and in the high-effort condition, 42% understated their income. Tax reporting changed significantly over the three conditions. While only 2% of participants filed an honest tax report in the low-effort condition and were dishonest in the high-effort condition, 14% showed the opposite behaviour pattern, being dishonest in the low-effort condition and honest in the high-effort condition. Dishonest tax reporting was more likely in the low-effort condition than in the high-effort condition. Moreover, the amount of evaded tax was higher if work effort was low. Table 16 shows individual tax honesty patterns.

In the second experiment, design and procedure were the same as in the first experiment. In this study participants were also asked what they expected to earn in each period. The responses were used as proxies for

Table 16: *Individual-level tax honesty by control and experimental conditions (Kirchler et al., 2005)*

| Control | Condition | | f | % |
	Low-effort	High-effort		
Honest	Honest	Honest	51	40.5
Honest	Honest	Dishonest	2	1.6
Honest	Dishonest	Honest	10	7.9
Honest	Dishonest	Dishonest	11	8.7
Dishonest	Honest	Honest	4	3.2
Dishonest	Honest	Dishonest	1	0.8
Dishonest	Dishonest	Honest	8	6.3
Dishonest	Dishonest	Dishonest	39	31.0
			126	100.0

participants' aspiration levels. On the aggregate level, results of the first experiment were replicated: the level of tax evasion was 23% in the control condition; 26% in the low-effort condition; and 24% in the high-effort condition. With regard to individual tax honesty, 52% of participants under-reported their income in the control condition. In the low-effort condition, 57% under-reported, and in the high-effort condition, 58% under-reported. Over the three conditions, individual tax honesty did not vary, whereas amounts of evaded tax were slightly higher in the low-effort condition than in the high-effort condition.

Unsurprisingly, aspiration levels were higher in the high-effort condition than in the low-effort condition. The aspiration level was differentially related to tax evasion behaviour. In the low-effort condition, participants who evaded taxes stated similar aspiration levels as those participants who reported honestly. In the high-effort condition, however, participants who evaded taxes stated a higher aspiration level than those who had reported honestly. The aspiration level was also differentially related to severity of tax evasion: while in the low-effort condition, the correlation between relative aspiration level and tax evasion severity was not significant, in the high-effort condition, a higher aspiration level was correlated significantly with the amount of evaded tax. These results indicate complex interrelations between effort, aspiration level and tax behaviour. In general, the findings of Kirchler *et al.* (2005) seem to suggest that high effort evokes higher risk aversion and therefore diminishes the propensity to evade taxes. The aspiration level as subjective threshold for a satisfying income seems to mediate this effect. It may serve as an alternative reference point in the evaluation of outcomes.

If one's aspiration level can be satisfied by the safe option, that is paying taxes honestly, and the risky option offers a better outcome, but concurrently bears the risk of falling below one's expectations, the sunk cost effect can reverse and lead to risk-averse behaviour, i.e. tax compliance.

The study shows that work effort and aspiration levels are important in explaining tax behaviour. It may, therefore, be advisable for tax authorities to take into account taxpayers' aspiration levels on their net income. Assuming that aspiration levels can be influenced, media and other communication channels may help keep taxpayers' aspirations at a modest level. Second, since auditing all tax files is too costly, it may be advisable to audit reports on easily earned money (e.g., capital gains) rather than income earned through blood, toil, sweat and tears, or auditing files selected at random.

Besides income tax, business corporations also pay and collect excise, payroll, property and sales taxes such as Value Added Tax and General Sales Tax. Webley (2004) summarised results of studies conducted on corporate income tax non-compliance, employer evasion of unemployment insurance taxes and Value Added Tax. With regard to corporate income tax, it seems that compliance is associated with being a publicly traded company and belonging to a highly regulated industry, such as banks and insurances. Unemployment insurance non-compliance was mainly associated with wrongly classifying employees as independent contractors. In many countries, businesses collect sales tax and they act as remittance agents for some withholding taxes, such as personal income tax, employee payroll taxes, etc. (Webley, 2004). According to Christensen, Cline and Neubig (2001), US businesses either pay or collect 84% of total taxes. The variety of taxes places a considerable burden on businesses and creates possibilities of non-compliance. Research on taxes collected and paid by businesses and non-compliance is scarce, as Webley summarises in his 2004 report on tax compliance by businesses. Together with his associates, he conducted studies on Value Added Tax compliance. Compliance and non-compliance were both measured as taxpayers' self-reported compliance, and as compliance observed by the tax authority after inspection. Interestingly, there were many differences between compliant and non-compliant taxpayers if self-reported compliance was used as a dependent variable, but there were few differences if the results of inspections were taken to separate the groups into compliant, mildly non-compliant and seriously non-compliant taxpayers. Besides being younger and more egoistical, feeling less guilty if Value Added Tax was not paid, believing that tax was unfair and friends would not disapprove of tax evasion, self-reported non-compliers had also less accurate knowledge about Value Added Tax and thought the money was coming from their own business funds. In the group of inspected evaders, penalties for late payments were more frequent, and taxpayers were less satisfied with the quality of service from the tax office.

Adams and Webley (2001) interviewed three groups of business people (restaurant proprietors, flooring and furnishing proprietors and builders). They found five emergent factors regarding Value Added Tax: feelings of inequity; negative perceptions of tax authorities; the significance of sanctions; morality; and mental accounting of collected taxes. While there were a number of similarities with income tax compliance, the question of ownership of Value Added Tax in relation to the psychological phenomenon of mental accounting is of particular interest. The interviewed business people differed in the way they perceived Value Added Tax monies collected. While some perceived the money as belonging to the business or themselves, others perceived it as money belonging to the state. Shefrin and Thaler (1988) propose, in respect of personal finances, that people hold mental accounts that operate independently of one another. Usually people avoid tapping into resources that are assigned to different mental accounts. People seem to be unwilling to use the money that they had assigned to household expenditure for other expenditure, such as daily consumption. According to Thaler (1985), individuals and organisations implicitly or explicitly develop a plan regarding their future financial transactions, assign a budget to each category of expenditure and manage their financial transactions accordingly. The cognitive representation of these plans and categories are so-called mental accounts, functioning as frames of reference for financial decisions. Adams and Webley's study also investigated whether business people psychologically separated money owed to the Value Added Tax into separate accounts from money from business turnover. Their findings suggest that the majority of business people perceive the money they collect forms part of their business turnover rather than money paid by the customers to be passed on to the tax office. Only a minority believe that Value Added Tax is not their money, and keep it in a separate mental account. It can be expected that, in general, it is hard to pay the collected money to the tax office especially if it is perceived as personal income and not kept in a separate mental account. If ownership of collected Value Added Tax is not perceived, and the money is mentally assigned to a separate account, transferring it to the tax office may be perceived as less of a loss.

In sum, tax evasion of self-employed business people and entrepreneurs seems to be significantly higher than that of employed income earners. Furthermore, legal tax avoidance seems to be higher. McBarnett (1992) emphasises that corporate crime is not the only

because they do not have the opportunity or knowledge to do so. Other taxpayers are willing and able but do not dare to evade. Still other taxpayers are willing and able to evade and, if the risk of being caught and fined is perceived as low, they will evade.

Interaction between tax authorities and taxpayers is determined by both parties' basic assumptions about the others' goals and strategies. If tax authorities perceive taxpayers as rational agents interested in maximising their individual profit, then it is likely that they assume the role of 'hunters' or 'cops', applying strategies to catch the 'robbers'. On the other hand, taxpayers perceiving themselves as being persecuted may adopt the respective role and try to escape by using creative constructions of non-compliance and making use of loopholes in the tax law, or by taking the risk of evading if it pays. An example of the circular relationship between control, sanctions and the development of more sophisticated strategies to escape the authorities is provided by the following text in an Austrian newspaper (*Die Presse*, 4 August 2006, p. 15):

1.31 billion Euros of tax fraud detected
  We want to demonstrate that evasion does not pay, declares Grasser [Austrian Minister of Finance]. Control as a "prevention strategy". Grasser implicitly admits that the deterrence is not effective ... Grasser will take rigorous steps by increasing controls, "until the drastic measures show effect" and impostors desist from fiddling. "Smugglers become smarter and smarter", say investigators.

If tax authorities believe in taxpayers' willingness to comply with the spirit and letter of the law and accept that the complexity of tax law may lead to mistakes in tax filings both to the advantage and disadvantage of taxpayers, they may develop the role of advisors with the principal goal of assisting in preparing correct tax reports and supervising taxpayers. On the taxpayers' side, this approach is likely to elicit perceptions of empathy and fair treatment, which is likely to be reciprocated by fair behaviour and compliance. This latter perception of taxpayers should not be judged as naive and blind to deviant behaviour. No doubt, besides a majority of taxpayers who are willing to pay their taxes correctly, there are non-cooperative citizens who must be aware that tax authorities 'hide an iron fist in a velvet glove' and are ready to use it without hesitation if the tax law is violated. In other words, a duality of deterrent fears and civic obligations as motivation to comply is required.

Under the assumption of rational, utility-maximising taxpayers who are not willing to pay their fair share voluntarily, it is necessary to stem the flow of tax evasion by audits and fines. Since administration of the tax system is costly, and audits are a relevant cost factor, it is necessary to apply effective audit schemes (J. H. Collins and Plumlee, 1991). Yitzhaki and Vakneen (1989) calculated that administrative compliance costs amount to 5–10% of the tax revenue. Evaders must be detected by applying effective strategies to select reports with a high probability of being faked, to detect so-called 'ghosts', that is, individuals who fail to comply with their income tax filing requirements completely, and to employ inspectors who are not susceptible to bribes, or to control the inspectors by other inspectors.

Many approaches to developing strategies to detect evaders are reminiscent of a 'cops and robbers' orientation or 'hunter' tradition with taxpayers being the thieves and tax inspectors the cops trying to catch them. Erard and Ho (2001) and Yaniv (2003) conducted studies on 'ghosts', about whom nothing is known, and whom the tax agency is unable to track down through audit strategies based on reported income. Empirical studies were conducted and models offered which suggest using the prosperity of citizens as a signal of evasion. According to Erard and Ho, non-filing is more prevalent among self-employed individuals, and within occupations where income may be more easily concealed from the tax authority, such as the cash economy. In addition, for taxpayers with incomes near the filing threshold, the burden associated with completing a return appears to serve as a deterrent to filing.

In attempting to increase the effectiveness of tax audits, some countries anticipate tax evasion and award a bonus to informants and to tax inspectors which is proportional to the taxes collected by the inspector. Taxpayers often believe that tax auditors have a strong agenda to ensnare people (Adams and Webley, 2001). Yaniv (2001) writes that the average bounty provided by the US IRS was generally assumed to be higher than 10%. However, in recent years, it was actually less than 2% of the amount recovered in taxes and fines. According to Vasina (2003), this approach to providing financial incentives for the successful detection of evasion seems to boost the collection rate by reducing the incentives to accept bribes by inspectors, and creates incentives for tax inspectors to work conscientiously. Tax evasion in Russia is widespread, estimated to be no less than 40% of Russia's GDP, and corruption in the tax administration is a serious problem. Corruption is associated with low salaries of tax inspectors and causes serious problems in establishing an effective tax system. Creating incentives for 'successful' audits may be useful in a system with high evasion rates; however, this strategy also creates a 'cop-like' mentality with tax officials 'hunting' the evaders rather than a customer-relations approach, which aims at fair interaction between tax officials and taxpayers. In 2003, Fjeldstad and Tungodden reported on recent literature on tax administration in poor countries, suggesting that there are virtues in allowing fiscal corruption. By strengthening the bargaining power of corrupt tax inspectors, it is argued that tax evasion may be reduced and tax revenues increased. However, the authors argue that this intriguing paradox does not justify policies that stimulate corruption: first, while an increase in corruption may raise revenue in the short run, the opposite will be the case in the longer run. Second, the instrumental value of reducing corruption goes far beyond its effects on tax evasion and tax revenues. Accepting corruption as a policy strategy to increase tax revenues may undermine values of democracy and good governance. Third, eliminating corruption should be considered an end in itself.

The 'cops and robbers' or 'hunt and control' approach is not only costly and of uncertain effect, it also raises the question of how to control the controllers. For instance, Vasin and Navidi (2003) constructed a game-theoretical model describing the interaction of tax inspectors and taxpayers and how to control inspectors.

A more successful approach to detecting potential evaders is the application of knowledge accumulated in studies of behavioural economics and economic psychology and the selection of tax reports on the base of this knowledge. Above all, it is important to take into account that the perception of taxpayers by tax authorities and the resulting style of interaction determine the relationship between tax authorities and taxpayers. Even more promising is an approach that is directed towards enhancing voluntary compliance. From an exchange perspective, the style of interaction determines the contractual relationship between the involved parties, which shapes tax morale and, consequently, the willingness to comply. If tax authorities treat taxpayers as fair partners rather than unwilling participants in a relationship where tax authorities have legal and expert power, mutual respect and honesty are likely to result.

It is not easy to establish a cooperative contractual relationship or psychological contract when the tools to enforce tax payments applied by tax authorities are predominantly control and punishment. This is especially true as taxpayers do not seem to agree on the appropriate punitive response for criminal activity (Durham, 1988). Respectful, client-oriented interaction and acknowledgement of individuals' rights often remain the only possible means to create an empathic understanding which is apt to increase trust, tax morale and voluntary compliance (Feld and Frey, 2002; Frey, 2003; Tyler, 1990). Experimental work by Alm, Jackson and McKee (1990) provides evidence that tax compliance tends to be higher when taxpayers are aware of a direct link between their tax payments and the provision of a desirable public good. Considerable sociological work suggests that taxpayers are more likely to report honestly if they feel that they are being treated courteously and respectfully by the tax agency. Consistent with this perspective, Frey (1992) argues that tight monitoring and heavy punishment of non-compliant citizens can crowd out tax morale and ultimately result in greater non-compliance (cf. Feld and Frey, 2005b). Cialdini (1996) stresses the fact that monitoring not only makes people feel observed and controlled but also leads to the impression of not being trusted.

The tradition of perceiving taxpayers as unwilling to comply if they have a promising chance to cheat, and the necessity of making evasion impossible and avoidance difficult in order to secure a fair tax system, has led to the development of strategies that detect non-compliant taxpayers. Given the high costs of audits and a generally high compliance rate, randomly selecting reports for audits is not efficient. In place of random selection, the US IRS selects income tax returns for audit using formulas based on findings in tax research, taking into account the attributes of returns having a tax adjustment and those having no tax adjustment. Reinganum and Wilde (1988) call the formula for audit selections one of the best-kept secrets in the US Government. The formula used to select returns for scrutiny is based on a series of special line-by-line audits conducted as part of the Taxpayer Compliance Measurement Program, and is designed to predict, for any given return, the forthcoming additional tax and penalty that can be expected to result from an audit; that is, it is based on a 'yield criterion', and thus not directed towards enhancing voluntary compliance.

Before describing recent developments in countries exhibiting a shift from a 'cops and robbers' mentality towards customer orientation, highly creative, promising and rather humorous approaches to selecting faked reports shall be presented.

Nigrini (1996, 1999) presents a technique that could supplement audit selection formulas by applying Benford's Law. He focuses on the digits used in income and deduction numbers and draws conclusions about the extent of apparent manipulation of tax reports. Intuitively, most people assume that in a string of numbers sampled randomly from some body of natural numbers, the first non-zero digit could be any number from 1 to 9 and all nine numbers would be regarded as equally probable. This assumption is, however, wrong. The evasion detection model is based on Benford's Law, which provides the expected frequencies for the digits in tabulated data and compares them with frequencies of digits in numbers reported in tax files. If expected and reported frequencies more or less match, a report is probably honest; otherwise, if frequencies are significantly different, the report is likely to be faked.

Studies on accounting data (see Carslaw, 1988; Thomas, 1989) have shown that managers tend to round up income numbers when these numbers are below cognitive reference points, which leads to the appearance of digits at the first, second, etc. position of a number which differ

Table 17: *Probability of appearance of digits in leading position, second and third position of naturally occurring amounts (Benford, 1938)*

Digit	Leading position	Second position	Third position	Fourth position
0		0.11968	0.10178	0.10018
1	0.30103	0.11389	0.10138	0.10014
2	0.17609	0.10882	0.10097	0.10010
3	0.12494	0.10433	0.10057	0.10006
4	0.09691	0.10031	0.10018	0.10002
5	0.07918	0.09668	0.09979	0.09998
6	0.06695	0.09337	0.09940	0.09994
7	0.05799	0.09035	0.09902	0.09990
8	0.05115	0.08757	0.09864	0.09986
9	0.04576	0.08500	0.09827	0.09982

Note:
The number 9876 has four digits, with a 9 as the first digit, 8 as the second digit, 7 as the third digit and 6 as the fourth digit. The table indicates that under Benford's Law the expected proportion of numbers with a first digit 9 is 0.04576 and the expected proportion of numbers with a third digit 7 is 0.09902.

from the probability of appearance observed by Benford in 1938. Prices of consumer goods also violate Benford's Law (el Sehity, Hölzl and Kirchler, 2005). The same should be true for numbers in tax reports if reports are faked. Contrary to intuition, the occurrence of the digits 0 to 9 at the first, second, etc. position in natural numbers is not equally likely. Especially in the first position the distribution is skewed: numbers start with the digits 1 or 2 more often than with the digits 8 or 9. This phenomenon was first noted by Newcomb in 1881 and rediscovered in 1938 by Benford, after whom it was subsequently termed. The distribution of the first digits can be described through a logarithmic function; formally, the relative frequency of a specific digit a in the first place of a number is $F_a = \log_{10}[(a+1)/a]$ (Benford, 1938, p. 554). The frequencies calculated by this formula fit closely with the empirical frequencies compiled from diverse data sets such as addresses, river lengths or molecular weights. The digit 1 occurs with a relative frequency of about .30, the digit 2 with a relative frequency of about .18, and the digit 9 with a relative frequency of about .05. Not only the first digit, but also digits in later positions can be described by such a function (Benford, 1938; Hill, 1995). From the third position onward, however, the distribution becomes very similar to a uniform distribution (see table 17). Various explanations for the peculiar logarithmic distribution of first digits have been suggested. As recently as 1995, Hill provided a statistical proof showing that unbiased sampling from a mixture of probability distributions results in the logarithmic distribution. Hill's approach also explains the finding that data sets being compiled from diverse subsets or being influenced by a variety of factors follow Benford's Law quite well.

To illustrate Benford's Law, Mark Nigrini offered the following example: if the Dow Jones stock averages 1,000, the first digit would be 1. To get a Dow Jones average with a first digit of 2, the average must increase to 2,000, and getting from 1,000 to 2,000 is a 100% increase. If the Dow Jones went up 20% per year, it would take five years to get from the first digit 1 to the first digit 2. However, if the Dow Jones started with the first digit 5, it requires only one 20% increase to get from 5,000 to 6,000, and this is achieved in one year. Once the Dow Jones has reached 9,000, it takes only an 11% increase or just seven months to reach the 10,000 mark, which starts again with the digit 1. At that point we start with the first digit 1 once again. Once again the number must double before reaching 2 as the first digit. In financial settings, numbers frequently develop over time due to interest rates, inflation, or other relative factors. Geometric growth such as inflation produces a data set that follows Benford's Law (Benford, 1938; Nigrini, 1999). For example, consider a retail price of 1 and an annual inflation rate of about 2.3% (i.e., the price increases tenfold in 100 years). Only after 30 years would the price change its first digit to 2; then it would need another 18 years to change its first digit to 3. Once the first digit is 9, it would change to 1 within less than five years. The relative number of years the price has a certain first digit (0.30, 0.18 ... 0.05) follows the logarithmic distribution and is invariant whatever the rate of inflation, the dimension of the price scale or the initial price. The number 1 predominates at every step of the progression, as it does in logarithmic sequences. As Nigrini puts it, 'the persistence of a 1 as a first digit will occur with any phenomenon that has a constant (or even an erratic) growth rate' (1999, p. 80).

The income tax agencies of several nations are using detection software based on Benford's Law, and it is proving to be a potential tool to detect evasion in combination with other factors included in audit selection formulas.

Another approach to detecting evaders may be taken less seriously: in social psychology, there is a tradition of name letter effects which assumes that there is a tendency to evaluate alphabetical letters in one's name, especially initials, particularly favourably; name initials may even predict behaviour, such as career choices (Hodson and Olson, 2005). In 1996, two tax researchers under the pseudonyms Thomas M. Lochbuy and Russel J. O'Rourke published a humorous paper in the *Australian Tax Review* dealing with the tradition of name-letter effects. The paper introduced 'meta-alphabetological analysis and a new internal validity dimension of research designing: hemispheric balance, which can successfully be applied for identifying tax cheats'. Tax evaders in the United States were shown to be significantly more likely to be persons with surnames starting with the letters B and W than to have surnames starting with any other letter. Taxpayers with surnames starting with the letter V were found to be especially honest. The authors might have thought, 'nomen est omen', and they went on to observe the frequency of appearance of first letters in more than 1.6 million American and Australian taxpayer surnames. The actual data regarding the incidence with which individuals in alphabetic clusters of surnames were caught for tax cheating were compared against the predicted incidence of such occurrence. T-tests were used to identify alphabetic surname clusters where the frequency of tax cheats was significantly different from the frequency with which such alphabetic clusters occurred in the community. Since no differences in frequencies of surname letters were observed between American and Australian samples, data were pooled. Table 18 shows the

Table 18: *Frequency of surname first letter (percentages) in census data and tax evader data (Lochbuy and O'Rourke, 1996, p. 81)*

Surname letter	Frequency of surname letter		Surname letter	Frequency of surname letter	
	Census data	Evader data		Census data	Evader data
A	5.38	4.05	N	2.93	1.56
B**	6.90	12.05	O	2.78	1.90
C	5.41	7.02	P	5.38	3.78
D	5.80	4.85	Q	0.30	0.01
E	2.72	2.46	R	4.36	4.27
F	3.17	3.50	S	9.46	10.19
G	4.99	4.67	T	4.64	3.51
H	4.57	7.66	U	0.98	0.19
I	1.39	0.59	V***	2.53	0.65
J	2.09	2.31	W**	3.12	7.23
K	6.11	4.44	X	0.09	0.01
L	4.91	4.45	Y	1.36	0.94
M	6.61	6.91	Z	2.02	1.13

Note:
**Significantly greater proportion of evaders than proportion of general public at $p < .01$ level;
***Significantly smaller proportion of evaders than proportion of general public at $p < .001$ level.

frequency of surname letters in census data and evader data. No doubt, people with surnames starting with B or W are suspect. It remains to be shown whether honesty changes when a woman changes her maiden name!

It is not easy to persuade all taxpayers to comply. Although evasion may not be the predominant problem, as empirical research has shown, problems with legal forms of tax avoidance and corporate crime (cf. Simpson, 2002) are increasing with the emergence of the multinational global economy, electronic commerce, etc. Administration of tax systems has become more difficult and has policy implications that affect the national economy through decisions made by businesses on the basis of tax policy. Traditional regulatory styles of tax authorities have focused on command and control with almost automatic application of penalties for evasion. For example, the US IRS has often relied on over-zealous enforcement or undue punishment for securing compliance (Payne, 1993, as quoted in James and Alley, 2002). At the same time, prosecution power has not always been used effectively, 'with a history of slap-on-the-wrist prosecutions that rarely touch major evaders or avoiders' (V. Braithwaite, 2003b, p. 1). The control style of interaction and application of indiscriminate punishments has failed and has been heavily criticised by citizens. The US IRS, the Australian Taxation Office and tax authorities in many other countries were accused of being rude, abusive or unhelpful (Job and Honaker, 2003; Job, Stout and Smith, 2007). Job and Honaker (2003) summarise claims as follows: accusations of excessive and unfair use of power were balanced with claims that the tax office was 'out of touch' and 'lacked understanding' of 'commercial reality'. There were suggestions that the tax office's actions were 'morally wrong' and that a tax office's poor use of penalties '"threatened the integrity of the tax system"' (p. 112). Niemirowski and Wearing (2003) found that Australian taxpayers were only moderately satisfied with tax authorities' service and not convinced that tax authorities were helpful when dealing with enquiries about tax returns, or equitable in their treatment of taxpayers. A 'cops-and-robbers' perspective feeds distrust: J. Braithwaite (2003) quotes a survey commissioned by the Australian Taxation Office which showed low trust in the tax institution. Results indicated that only 32% of taxpayers believed tax laws were effective in making sure large companies paid their share of tax, and only 20% believed that the tax office did a good job of stopping tax avoidance.

The theory of regulation contends that regulation exists to benefit the regulated (Pelzman, 1976; Stigler, 1971). Since the 1990s there have been signs of fundamental change in the approach of tax agencies with respect to taxpayers (J. Braithwaite, 2005; V. Braithwaite, 2003b; James and Alley, 2002). With the emergence of New Public Management (Andrews, 2003; Gruening, 2001; Horton, 2003), tax authorities have become aware of the necessity to consider taxpayers as customers. Instead of control and unreasonable severity, an approach leading to a 'cops and robbers' mentality, an approach characterised by education and support is more promising in persuading taxpayers to comply. Tax advisors and tax officers play a key role in securing overall compliance. Should they develop an adversarial relationship through a 'cops and robbers' mentality, characterised by poor communication skills, lack of technical and legal knowledge, and inconsistency in punishment, current and future tax compliance may decrease (Hansford and Hasseldine, 2002). Tax authorities of Australia, France, Sweden, the UK, the US and many other countries are reconstructing their approaches to taxpayers by treating them as clients, addressing their needs and improving fiscal consciousness. Further innovations in government infrastructure and services have also been made to improve tax adherence (Owens and Hamilton, 2004). The US IRS has taken a carrot-and-stick approach towards improving tax compliance. According to Dalton (1994), the agency now offers assistance to all delinquent taxpayers who file on their own initiative before the US IRS notifies them of the unfiled returns. One of the special assistance measures provides the taxpayers with copies of old tax forms and records of previous years' income reported to the agency. The US IRS also helps taxpayers in negotiating instalment agreements, penalty abatements and compromise offers. Lastly, the non-filer initiative gives assurances that there will be no criminal prosecution of non-filers as long as the income in question is derived from legal sources and the taxpayers initiate contact with the US IRS. On the other hand, if taxpayers continue to evade payment of their taxes despite these incentives, the agency will mount an aggressive campaign of investigation and criminal prosecution against the persons involved.

James and Alley (2002) and James et al. (2003) summarise some experiences with tax reform in Australia, France, Japan, New Zealand, the UK and USA, and their changes from a command-and-control perspective to the recognition of the importance of voluntary compliance and customer service orientation. In the United States, views of people interested in tax administration regarding the US IRS's organisational goals and useful strategies to reach them were collected and categorised. Table 19 shows the twelve categories of strategies to promote voluntary compliance, as reported by James et al. (2003).

Strategic planning incorporates taxpayers' subjective concepts of taxation and their behaviour (Niemirowski and Wearing, 2003). Taxpayers' cooperation with tax institutions and compliance with tax law is

Table 19: *Strategies to reach customer orientation (James et al., 2003)*

1. Training
   This should include customer service training and cross-functional training for employees so they have an understanding of the entire system of tax administration.
2. Public relations
   There should be better publicity about how the tax system works, how taxpayers benefit by complying and how the IRS deals with abuses of the system.
3. Automation
   This should be used in order to identify non-compliance.
4. Simplification and fairness
   Simplification is necessary because continuous changes and complexity in tax law have a negative effect on compliance. Also the law should be applied consistently.
5. Personnel issues
   There is a need for a highly skilled and trained workforce which has multi-functional talents. There will be fewer low-skilled employees.
6. Organisational structure
   This should be arranged so that taxpayers' issues or problems can be resolved through a single point of contact. There is also a need for specialisation so that expertise of particular industries may be developed to improve dealings with taxpayers, and there should be better customer service.
7. There should be increased cooperation with state, local and foreign governments.
8. Taxpayer service and education
   There should be more assistance for small businesses to help them comply, more 'preventative' education for the public and increased awareness of tax responsibilities in schools.
9. Compliance efforts should be coordinated.
10. Positive incentives to comply
    There is a need to devise ways (not necessarily monetary) to recognise compliant behaviour and to reward those who submit tax returns and pay their tax on time.
11. A more organised approach to influence legislation
    The revenue service should become a taxpayers' advocate in the legislature for simplification and fairness.
12. Inculcate in citizens a sense of responsibility toward taxes. There is a need for citizens to understand and accept their responsibilities of compliance. There is also a need to publicise the tax burden carried by compliers versus the burden that would be carried if everyone complied. Students should be educated early in their tax responsibilities.

predominantly determined by the institutions' rules and regulations. Murphy (2004b) argues that threat and coercion as regulatory tools are not only expensive to implement, but can actually produce the opposite behaviour from that sought. The latter point further emphasises the importance of relational issues in building trust in the institution. Tyler and De Cremer (2006), discussing promotion of cooperation in groups, organisations and societies, conclude that the use of incentives and sanctions can effectively shape cooperative behaviour.

However, although effective, rewards and punishments are not a particularly efficient mechanism for shaping behavior. First, their impact on behavior is marginal. Further, these effects are costly to obtain, because organizations must commit considerable resources to the effective deployment of incentive and sanctioning systems. For these reasons, the adequacy of instrumental approaches to motivating cooperation has been questioned within law ... and management. ... (p. 429)

The authors continue by focusing on social psychological factors which can supplement instrumental motivations in securing cooperation. One type of social motivation relevant to cooperation is identification with the group, organisation or society. When people identify with their group, motives are transformed from the personal to the group level and the interests of the group become individuals' self-interests. It is important to motivate people to activate ethical motivations to support group policies, to feel a sense of personal responsibility and obligation to support group decisions and to uphold moral values relevant to the group or society. To encourage identification with groups and society and to activate moral motives, Tyler and De Cremer (2006) propose in particular fair procedures.

The fairness of procedures is linked to: (a) opportunities for voice and participation; (b) the quality of decision-making – neutrality, accuracy, consistency of rule application; (c) the quality of interpersonal treatment – respect for rights, treatment with dignity and respect; and (d) judging that the authorities have trustworthy and benevolent motives. All of these factors distinctively shape procedural fairness judgments. Further, these social influences act in addition to the instrumental effects traditionally studied by economists. (p. 430)

Similarly, Torgler (2003c) stresses the importance of trust in the political and legal system to enhance compliance (see also Kramer and Tyler, 1996; Tyler, 2001a). Trust is inversely related to resistance and depends mainly on aspects of procedural fairness, perceptions of fair and trustworthy treatment, neutrality, respect, consultation and outcome favourability (Murphy, 2003b).

The Australian Taxation Office underwent significant reforms aimed at building a voluntary compliance culture by taking a proactive role based on characteristics which V. Braithwaite summarises as:

(a) professional, responsive, fair, open, and accountable in helping taxpayers comply with their tax obligations; as well as (b) effective in bringing to account those who intentionally avoided their obligations. Through adopting such practices, the intent was that the tax office earns (c) the trust, support and respect of the community. [A] Taxpayers' Charter ... articulated 12 rights of taxpayers and committed tax officers to treating taxpayers fairly and reasonably, to explain decisions, assist with questions, and provide reliable information, to respect taxpayer privacy, to keep the taxpayers' compliance costs to a minimum, and to be accountable, if necessary, through independent review. The taxpayers' obligations, articulated also in the Charter document, were four-fold and involved being truthful in dealings with the tax office, keeping records in accordance with the law, taking reasonable care in preparing tax information, and lodging tax returns and required documents by the due date. (V. Braithwaite, 2003b, p. 1)

Ayres and Braithwaite (1992) proposed a new approach to ensuring business compliance with regulatory rules. Their approach of responsive regulation is presented in the form of a pyramid with cooperative strategies of self-regulation at the bottom and severe sanctions and incapacitating of wrongdoing at the top (figure 12). This model underlies the Australian Taxation Office Compliance Model, which considers various scientific approaches to tax behaviour and is based on the empirical fact that most taxpayers are compliant either by moral conviction and acceptance of social norms or because they lack opportunities to evade or fear being caught and fined. The model recognises that legal sanctions are not sufficient to enforce compliance. Instead, it focuses on education, persuasion and dialogue as strategies to gain compliance. However, in the case of persistent non-cooperation, economic and legal sanctions come into operation. The regulatory pyramid has three sides: regulatory strategies, enforcement strategies and motivational postures of taxpayers. At the lowest level of regulation, applicable to most taxpayers, is education and advice about tax regulations and record keeping. Responsive regulation consists of educating and delivering services to taxpayers willing to comply. Taxpayers who take tax officials' authority seriously, who are open to admitting wrongdoing, willing to correct their mistakes and subsequently meet the law's expectations are likely to display motivational postures of commitment or capitulation and to be willing to report their income correctly (V. Braithwaite, 2003a, 2003b). The regulatory task consists of educating, delivering service and providing the necessary support. Taxpayers are perceived as trustworthy and must be treated with respect. More demand is made on tax officials as taxpayers put more social distance between themselves and the authority. V. Braithwaite (2003b) characterises taxpayers' motivational postures at the next stage as capitulation rising into resistance. Capitulation describes giving in to authority because it is there and it is legitimate. Compliance would not occur without the presence of the authority. When taxpayers become angry with the authority, they move to resistance. On the side of regulation, enforced self-regulation is required when capitulation is the observed behaviour. Examinations of businesses become necessary and records are reviewed, with the focus on education. If taxpayers are not willing to cooperate, if there are discrepancies between the tax declaration and records, or if they resist tax laws, command regulation should be applied by audits without punishment or with discretionary punishment. On the top of the pyramid-like-compliance model is a cohort of taxpayers who are disengaged. These taxpayers have such contempt for the tax system that chances of persuasion to make them compliant are low. In such difficult cases, non-discretionary command regulation should be applied by incapacitating taxpayers' ability to evade. Prosecution, imprisonment and taking away a licence to practice appear to be effective strategies of non-discretionary command regulation (V. Braithwaite, 2003b).

The shift from a command-and-control style of regulation to a more persuasive and responsive style is not easy, as the Australian experience demonstrates. Traditions of rigid bureaucracy have favoured an inflexible style of regulation, but the perception of taxpayers as 'utility-maximising thieves' had to be replaced by a perception of taxpayers as customers, and regulatory responsibilities needed to be adopted correspondingly. In cooperation with the Australian National University (for descriptions and evaluations see V. Braithwaite, 2003d), training programmes were applied to explain the spirit of responsive regulation and to raise tax officials' awareness of the principles and practices of responsive regulation. Job, Stout and Smith (2007) describe the change processes and training as interactive and include tax-specific case studies to demonstrate both poor and preferred methods of enforcement. For instance, the innovative advanced pricing programme used for transnational corporations demonstrated how cooperative approaches can gain higher returns than audits. Over a period of eighteen months, awareness training was provided on a face-to-face basis for more than 3,000 staff members. The principles of responsive regulation were incorporated into the corporate plans, training packages for staff, staff performance assessments, recruitment selection criteria and in the day-to-day operations of the field staff. Besides outlining problems encountered with regard to tax officials' perceptions of legitimacy of the new administrative approach, Job, Stout and Smith (2007) report on organisational barriers, individual tension and general resistance which had to be overcome to successfully implement the new responsive regulation philosophy in the Australian and New Zealand tax administration. Furthermore, successful implementation often required the persuasion of tax officials to accept the necessity of culture change in order to enhance taxpayers' compliance. Despite encountering resistance to organisational change, and the difficulties of evaluating change processes and their effects in the long run, the 'new culture' of customer relationship orientation is more promising in enhancing cooperation and voluntary compliance than the traditional perception of taxpayers as egoistic utility-maximisers with no feelings of responsibility to the community.

7   Cautious conclusions

Tax non-compliance is a universal phenomenon. It takes place in all societies, in all social strata, in all professions, in all industries, in all religions and in virtually all economic systems. Scholars as far back as Plato wrote about the phenomenon. In the fifteenth-century Ducal Palace of Venice, there is a stone with a hole in it, through which people could inform the Republic about tax evaders (Adams, 1993; Tanzi and Shome, 1994). Governments as far back as ancient Egypt have struggled to maintain compliance with tax laws. Indeed, it has been suggested that tax resistance has played a significant role in the collapse of several major world orders, including the Egyptian, Roman, Spanish and Aztec empires (Erard, 1997). It is therefore surprising how little attention this phenomenon had received until recent years. Only during the past twenty-five years has the subject of tax compliance come into its own as a research area within economics. Since then, the number of studies on tax behaviour has significantly increased, as has the diversity of methods used to study evasion. This, however, is also an issue of concern since the results obtained by different measures are heterogeneous, due to difficulties of measurement, because 'individuals often undertake substantial efforts to conceal their evasion' (Andreoni, Erard and Feinstein, 1998, p. 836), but also to methodological biases. Moreover, most findings originate from studies conducted in the United States, which limits generalisability of results. Few studies focus on cultural differences, and rarely have differences between tax systems been addressed.

7.1   Methodological concerns

Studies on tax compliance have employed various research methods. Results depend on definitions of concepts, operationalisation and methods applied. Not surprisingly, the arsenal of methods, sampling techniques, operationalisations of variables and uneven use of self-reported and observed tax non-compliance has been extensively discussed (e.g., Fischer, Wartick and Mark, 1992; Gërxhani, 2006; Groenland, 1992; Torgler, 2002;

182

Webley *et al.*, 1991). In their review of the literature on detection probability and compliance, Fischer, Wartick and Mark (1992) summarise insights stemming from analytic studies in the field of microeconomic decision theory. Here mathematical models of tax evasion are developed, predominantly examining the impact of audit probability, fines in cases of evasion, tax rate and income. The models are highly stylised analyses that fail to incorporate many facets of taxpayers' realities. For instance, in economic theory, taxpayers' income function considers financial profit as the only argument for predicting taxpayers' behaviour. Psychological variables, such as fairness considerations, social norms, attitudes, etc., are not considered in the economic income function. Moreover, taxpaying is conceived as an act occurring within a singular period of time; neither experiences with past audits nor the relationship between taxpayers and tax authorities are considered. Although mathematical models provide valuable insights into compliance behaviour and may be highly sophisticated, they reduce taxpayers' goals to purely financial profit and consider only a handful of taxpayer realities, which results in predictions of tax compliance that are virtually never sufficient as a guide to policy.

Microeconomic models are frequently tested with data taken from the US IRS 'Taxpayer Compliance Measurement Program' data pool. This data pool – described as 'the best data set in the world' (Slemrod, 1992, p. 3) and 'among the best available for studying tax non-compliance' (Andreoni, Erard and Feinstein, 1998, p. 836) – includes estimates of the voluntary compliance rate of audit classes and aggregate data on numerous taxpayer characteristics. In 1992 Fischer, Wartick and Mark reviewed several studies using the data pool and came to the conclusion that, in light of the difficult modelling issues inherent in these studies, many results are inconsistent and highly sensitive to the assumptions underlying the theoretical models. With regard to the impact of audit and detection probability on tax compliance, the results provide conflicting evidence.

The difficulty of obtaining 'hard' empirical data on tax compliance has led researchers to generate their own data via surveys and experimental simulation (Baldry, 1987). Economic psychological approaches particularly rely on surveys. In surveys, taxpayers are asked to self-report their evasion activities. Although surveys are usually an economic way to collect data, they have several shortcomings which limit generalisability of findings (e.g., Wilson and Sheffrin, 2005). Reliability and validity of measures, especially construct validity, constitute major problems with the approach. For instance, honesty and perfect recall are required if answers in surveys can be trusted as accurately reflecting tax compliance. Researchers in the Netherlands conducted highly relevant studies on the methodologies used in tax evasion research (e.g., Antonides and Robben, 1995; Elffers, Weigel and Hessing, 1987; Elffers, Robben and Hessing, 1991, 1992; Hessing *et al.*, 1988; Hessing, Elffers and Weigel, 1988), comparing self-reports and behavioural data obtained from tax authorities. Hessing *et al.* (1988) explored the limitations of self-reports as substitutes for observation of tax evasion behaviour and found negligible correspondence between respondents' self-reports of tax evasion and officially documented behaviour. Non-significant correlations were obtained despite the fact that all government claims against the respondents had been settled, unprotested, before the study began and despite the respondents' awareness that the accuracy of their self-reports could be checked against their tax records. The results of the study suggest that different explanatory variables may be correlated with each type of behavioural measure: attitudes toward the tax non-compliance measures and subjective norm measures exhibited significant correlations with the self-report data but not with officially documented behaviour, and measures of more broadly focused personal dispositions predicted actual behaviour but not self-reports. Having observed a lack of association between self-reported evasion behaviour and officers' classifications, Elffers, Weigel and Hessing (1987) studied data generated from self-reports, tax officers' classifications and experimental methods on the same sample of taxpayers (see table 5). Not only was the lack of association between self-reported behaviour and officers' classifications replicated, but also the evasion in the experiment did not correlate with either of these. The authors concluded that tax evasion consists of at least three conceptually independent aspects that need to be assessed by three independent measures, which leads to the conclusion that self-reported tax evasion is not a proxy of observed evasion. The correlation between self-reports and observed behaviour seems to be especially poor in the field of tax non-compliance. Hessing's research team (1993) studied self-reported and officially documented unemployment benefit fraud and found that in this field, self-reports and official reports correlate higher than in tax evasion studies.

While the Dutch studies bear ground for serious concern, Hite (1988) reports a positive relationship between results obtained by different measures. She determined whether self-reported taxpayer compliance rates and hypothetical reporting decisions corresponded to government-reported compliance rates and whether self-reported compliance rates corresponded to hypothetical reporting decisions. The relationships were low but positive.

Problems of measurement originate from different sources. First, it is not always clear what is understood as non-compliance, evasion or avoidance. While non-compliance represents the most inclusive conceptualisation referring to the failure to meet tax obligations whether that failure is intentional or not, evasion and cheating refer to a deliberate act of non-compliance that results in the payment of less tax than actually owed, whether or not the behaviour eventuates in subsequent conviction for tax fraud. Tax evasion behaviour, then, is a more restrictive term which excludes inadvertent non-compliance resulting from memory lapses, calculation errors, inadequate knowledge of tax laws, etc. (Elffers, Weigel and Hessing, 1987). Ordinary taxpayers participating in a survey may also have problems understanding tax issues, as was found in studies on taxpayers' preferences for progressive or flat tax (e.g., Roberts, Hite and Bradley, 1994; Seidl and Traub, 2002), or they are not interested in the issue and lack the motivation or ability to correctly recall their experiences. Moreover, wording is of eminent importance in surveys and in experimental settings. For instance, Green, Kahneman and Kunreuther (1994) investigated sensitivity of survey measures of willingness to pay for public goods. Visitors to a science museum were asked about funding two projects either by donations or by means of a tax increase. Willingness to pay was substantially reduced by a seemingly innocuous reminder about how many individuals would be affected by a tax or would be asked to contribute to a given cause. Subtle changes in question order and wording can affect the nature of the responses. Moreover, the perspective taken by respondents seems to play a role in attributions of causes of non-compliance. If respondents are asked about their own tax behaviour, they tend to attribute evasion to external factors, whereas they attribute evasion to internal factors if they assume the role of other taxpayers (Hite, 1987).

Second, tax officials may not always be able to correctly detect intentional and non-intentional acts and, thus, may be unable to distinguish between fraud and taxpayers' errors. In his 2004 studies on Value Added Tax, Webley confirmed that objective and self-report measures do not correspond. He concludes that self-report measures are an indication of who has committed, and who is likely to commit, deliberate acts of non-compliance. Thus, self-reports are useful to assess actual and potential evasion. Objective measures are an indicator of who has been detected for non-compliance by inspectors. Clever evaders may avoid being defined as non-compliant, while some unintentionally careless taxpayers may be defined as evaders. Indeed, Elffers, Robben and Hessing (1991) studied the processing of Dutch tax returns by tax officers, which were subsequently submitted to a reassessment analysis by independent tax officers. Independent tax officers and teams of three Dutch officers judged tax returns, errors and evasion independently, and only reached an agreement rate of approximately 50%.

Third, variables that influence intentional evasion behaviour may be quite irrelevant for explaining inadvertent non-compliance, and with respect to income taxes, evasion in the form of deliberately under-reporting income may depend on variables different from those determining claiming unwarranted deductions.

In economics, experiments are becoming increasingly accepted methods to test theoretical predictions in a controlled field (Davis and Holt, 1993). From these experiments, causality conclusions are drawn, which lead to problems in survey research. In the early 1960s and 1970s, laboratory experiments were first used to study economic behaviour (Siegel and Fouraker, 1960; V. L. Smith, 1962, 1964) and, in the late 1970s, tax behaviour (e.g., Friedland, Maital and Rutenberg, 1978; Spicer and Becker, 1980; Webley, 1987; see also Alm, 1991; Webley et al., 1991). Experiments can be perceived as a link between models and the 'real world' (Guala and Mittone, 2005). Experimental analysis of taxpayers' reporting behaviour allows control over a complex environment and isolation of some aspects of taxpayers' behaviour, which are manipulated to test specific predictions deriving from a theoretical model.

The value of inferences that can be drawn from experiments is dependent on how the individual interprets the experimental situation and what goals individuals try to achieve (Alm, 1991). It must be the case that participants prefer more of the rewards provided in experiments and their decisions and behaviour must be related to those rewards, so that participants recognise that their actions affect their outcome. Moreover, rewards must be large enough to offset any subjective costs that participants place on participation in the experiment. However, the magnitudes of gains and losses faced by participants are often too small, and thus, irrelevant to them, creating the perception among participants that experimental studies are 'games'.

Experiments have to be administered in a uniform and consistent manner to allow replicability. They should not be excessively long and instructions should be easily understandable, ensuring that participants fully comprehend the experimental scenario and do not lose motivation. Moreover, instructions should be phrased in a neutral way, excluding examples that may cause anchoring effects. Researchers must also ensure that participants believe that the procedures described to them are the actual procedures followed. All these criteria are important for ensuring the experimenter's control over participants' preferences and preventing participants from developing different mental representations of the experimental conditions or different mental scripts (Alm, 1991).

In summary, experimental approaches have the potential to address some of the weaknesses of other methods, although experimental situations often appear artificial and lack ecological validity. Experimental approaches have been frequently criticised as lacking validity. With regard to internal validity, inferences about a causal relationship between independent and dependent variables must be accurate; investigated higher-order constructs must be operationalised appropriately so that they are reflected in the experimental treatments; and external validity, that is, generalisabilty of causal relationships, must be assured (Fischer, Wartick and Mark, 1992). If experiments are applied to test theoretical assumptions, and internal and external validity as well as construct validity are established, experiments add valuable insight to the findings obtained in studies employing other methods.

7.2   Summary of research findings

There is little dispute that the shadow economy has increased and that the high levels of income tax avoidance are a growing cause for concern. Yet it is tax non-compliance, which is not necessarily illegal, that poses a much larger problem than does illegal behaviour. Most citizens accept legal non-compliance, and many may legally avoid taxes. However, illegal non-compliance (evasion) is quite contained. The percentage of taxpayers evading taxes is much smaller than one would expect based on assumptions and predictions made by the standard economic model of tax behaviour (e.g., Andreoni, Erard and Feinstein, 1998; Porcano, 1988).

The growing problem has stimulated research on tax behaviour in the social sciences. One of the most significant determinants of tax non-compliance has been detected to be inherent in tax law, namely its complexity. Complexity and uncertainty in tax law have received much attention, and endeavours to simplify the law have been undertaken in most industrialised countries. Frequently, there was little success in reducing complexity by trying to reformulate tax laws, and thus the debate is shifting from reformulating specific, particularly complex rules which often lead to uncertainty, to establishing general principles which are perceived as more promising guidelines for tax behaviour (J. Braithwaite, 2005).

The present economic-psychological review aims at summarising and integrating findings of tax research and presenting innovative research with the hopes of drawing practical conclusions. According to Wearing and Headey (1995), in contrast to compliant taxpayers, the would-be tax evaders seem to have less confidence in the efficacy of the social system, less confidence in the institutions of society, more dissatisfaction with the economy and its management, more dissatisfaction with the equity between consumption taxes and investment expenditures, and seem to be characterised by a lower sense of personal competence, less economic knowledge, a dependence on private (non-commercial) sources for financial services and a lower sense of well-being. Studies also suggest that individuals report more income in response to: decreased tax rates, increased penalty rates, greater audit probability, increased feelings of fair treatment, increased influence on how to spend tax revenue and increased rewards for honest tax payments. Moreover, a majority of participants are honest, probably because they follow social norms and are convinced that one should pay one's share. In this review, research on behavioural economics and economic psychology has been classified into two main thematic fields: (a) individual and social representations of tax issues; (b) tax behaviour as the result of a decision process. Two additional sections focus on the specificity of tax behaviour of the self-employed and entrepreneurs and on the interaction between taxpayers and tax authorities.

With regard to interaction between taxpayers and tax authorities, two approaches have been distinguished: (a) a 'cops and robbers' approach, based on the assumption that taxpayers are unwilling to pay their tax share, and try to avoid taxes legally whenever possible or to illegally evade taxes if it is profitable to do so; (b) a 'service and client' approach, which assumes taxpayers to be cooperative citizens who are willing to comply if they understand tax laws and perceive the law and the procedures of taxpaying to be fair. In this review, we assumed that taxpayers react differently depending on perspective and approach taken by the tax authorities. They either comply voluntarily or as the result of enforcement. As long as interaction is based on a positive, trusting foundation as argued in procedural justice theories, it can be hypothesised that taxpayers are willing to comply voluntarily, without considering what alternative provides the best individual profit. A 'cops and robbers' relationship, on the other hand, is likely to provoke more 'rational', egoistic behaviour, or at least an attempt to behave rationally in terms of egoistic profit maximisation. When taxpayers start thinking about incentives for evading, they face an explicit decision whether to comply or to take the risk to evade taxes with the possibility of saving money or, in the case of detection and fines, of losing money. It can be hypothesised that determinants of compliance, collected under the heading 'decision-making' or under the title 'social representations', assume different importance. In the case of voluntary compliance, subjective tax knowledge, attitudes, norms and fairness may play a major role, whereas in the case of enforced compliance, audits and fines may prove useful in obligating citizens to pay their share. The relationship between voluntary compliance and social representations is assumed to be circular: social representations which determine trust lead to voluntary compliance, and voluntary compliance stabilises trust and cooperation. Also, the relationship between enforced compliance and the audits and fines that determine the state's power to enforce compliance is circular: a powerful but not trustworthy authority enforces compliance through control and sanctions, and control and sanctions breed distrust, which results in extensive decisions to maximise one's own profit. Before elaborating on which variables might influence tax behaviour under different tax authorities' perspectives and interaction approaches, the two interaction styles are summarised.

7.2.1   *Interaction between tax authorities and taxpayers*

Administration of the tax system is costly, and audits are a relevant cost factor. Therefore, effective audit schemes are a necessity, and only those efficient in identifying evaders should be applied. Many strategies approach evasion detection with a 'cops and robbers' orientation, with taxpayers being the thieves and tax inspectors the cops trying to catch them. From such a perspective, it is important to detect individuals with identities and characteristics shrouded in mystery, so-called 'ghosts', about whom nothing is known and whom the tax agency is unable to track down through audit strategies based on reported income. It is also relevant to increase the effectiveness of tax audits by awarding a bonus to informants and to tax inspectors. The 'cops and robbers' approach is not only costly and of doubtful effect, it also raises the question of how to control the controllers. Moreover, this approach may seem useful in limiting tax evasion by constraining taxpayers to follow the letter of the law, but it is surely not adequate to limit tax avoidance and to motivate taxpayers to voluntarily follow the spirit of the law. With statistics on tax evasion and avoidance leaving no doubt that avoidance and corporate crime (Simpson, 2002) are by far a greater problem than individual income tax evasion, another approach to tax enforcement is clearly necessary.

It is important to take into account that the perception of taxpayers and the resulting style of interaction determine the relationship between tax authorities and taxpayers. From an exchange perspective, the style of interaction determines the 'psychological contractual relationship' between the involved parties, which shapes tax morale and consequently willingness to comply. If tax authorities treat taxpayers as fair partners rather than inferiors unwilling to pay their share, especially in a relationship where tax authorities have legal and expert power, mutual respect, honesty and trust are likely to result.

With the emergence of New Public Management tax authorities have also become aware of the necessity to consider taxpayers as customers. Instead of using control and unreasonable severity, which provokes a 'cops and robbers' mentality, an approach characterised by education and support is more promising in the endeavour to persuade taxpayers to comply. In 1992, Ayres and Braithwaite proposed a new approach to ensure business compliance with regulatory rules. Their approach of responsive regulation is presented in the form of a pyramid with cooperative strategies of self-regulation at the bottom and severe sanctions and incapacitating of wrongdoing at the top. The model recognises that legal sanctions are not sufficient to enforce compliance. Rather, it focuses on education, persuasion and dialogue as strategies to gain compliance. However, in the case of voluntary and repeated non-cooperation, economic and legal sanctions come into operation.

Tax authorities of various countries are reconstructing their approaches to taxpayers by treating them as clients and addressing their needs and improving fiscal consciousness. James *et al.* (2003) report strategies to promote voluntary compliance, including: training of tax officers; improved public relations; simplification of tax laws and procedural fairness; organisational improvement to offer effective advice and problem resolution; and improving citizens' awareness with regard to their tax responsibilities. Strategies to promote voluntary compliance shall shift from command and control strategies of audits and fines which breed distrust in authorities to changes of taxpayers' social representations in order to establish a trustful relationship.

Introducing a new approach is not easy, and resistance to changing processes in organisations is likely to result. The proposed new culture of a customer relations orientation is, however, more promising in enhancing cooperation, creating a cooperative tax climate and increasing voluntary compliance than was the traditional perception of taxpayers as egoistic utility maximisers.

Tax authorities adopting a 'cops and robbers' perspective, who exert sharp control and apply severe punishment in cases of evasion, are likely to contribute to the creation of a climate in which taxpayers are perceived as 'enemies' whose illegal behaviour requires prosecution. On the other hand, taxpayers may themselves assume the role of the hunted. Rather than perceiving tax authorities as accomplishing a relevant task for the welfare of the community, taxpayers may perceive the authorities as hunters from whom taxpayers need to escape. Perceived peril of persecution and prosecution is likely to corrupt taxpayers' willingness to voluntarily comply. Rather than perceiving interaction processes with the authorities as supportive and fair, taxpayers may consider possibilities to legally avoid paying taxes, or, if it pays, to evade. It might be assumed that, under these circumstances, taxpayers are trying to make a (rational) decision, choosing the option that promises the highest individual profit, rather than considering their tax share as a fair contribution to the public good. If this assumption is correct, tax behaviour shall be best explained as the outcome of a decision process. Variables described in the decision-making chapter may best describe compliance. Indeed, it is not voluntary cooperation that requires audits and punishment, but rather endeavours of individual profit maximisation. Tax policy must consider when and how often to control taxpayers, and how to frame taxes in order to reduce taxpayers' perception of loss and reluctance to pay their share. While a 'cops and robbers' climate might make the losses from paying taxes more salient, evoking thoughts of possible gains from evasion and a (rational) decision on these two prospects, a 'service and client' approach emphasises the gains from paying taxes for the collective as a whole. Moreover, the latter establishes a relationship built on trust and cooperation, which leads to voluntary cooperation. The change of focus from the individual to collective welfare makes egoistic utility maximising less likely. A 'service and client' atmosphere may lead to taxpayers adopting completely different attitudes. Taxpayers should be cooperative and willing to comply, as directed by their (social) representations of the government and of taxation: taxpayers should be motivated to pay taxes correctly when the tax law is intelligible, when it can be acted upon easily, when the government policy meets citizens' acceptance, when tax mentality is positive, when personal and social norms favour cooperation, and when distribution of taxes is perceived to be fair and procedures are just. Voluntary compliance should depend on those variables summarised in chapter 3. If taxpayers are treated as equal partners, if they understand tax law and agree with the government activities in general and with fiscal policy in particular, if taxes are perceived as fair and tax-collection procedures are transparent and perceived as just, it can be assumed that taxpayers behave as cooperative citizens. In these circumstances, intrusive audits and severe punishments would undermine their voluntary cooperation rather than educating them to become honest taxpayers.

In the final chapter, a model is presented which recognises and accommodates both enforced and voluntary compliance rates, depending on the power of the state and tax authorities to audit and fine evading taxpayers on one hand, and on favourable social representations of taxation and trust in tax institutions on the other hand. As the model heavily relies on the findings presented in chapters 3, 4 and 5, those findings are summarised.

7.2.2   *Social representations of taxes*

Individual and social representations of taxes refer to knowledge, thoughts and beliefs, feelings and evaluations, norms, fairness perceptions, motivational tendencies and, in general, citizens' tax morale. Although empirical studies lack findings of a strong relationship between individual and social representations and tax behaviour, there is no doubting Schmölders (1960) conclusion that 'the state is mirrored in citizens' minds', an idea key to understanding what citizens approve and disapprove of in tax politics and which arguments lead to acceptance of tax non-compliance, to acceptance of non-cooperation between citizens and the community, and opposition to prosecution of evasion. In everyday life taxes may not be a hotly disputed issue. Nevertheless, people periodically try to make sense of their contributions to the community, namely when taxes are due, when government spending is contested or when new taxes are introduced. Moreover, the public discussion of taxation issues leads individuals to evaluate fiscal policy, tax rates and the use of taxes for the provision of public goods, as well as the interaction between themselves and tax authorities. Eventually, motivation to comply or not to comply develops with implications for subsequent behaviour.

Tax law is complex. Most people are neither interested in nor have a proper understanding of the law. They often have only vague guesses about the taxes they pay. Poor understanding or misunderstanding breeds distrust and opposition. Traditional assumptions link low tax knowledge with non-compliance. It was, however, also argued that lack of knowledge leads to uncertainty, and people's risk aversion may increase in situations of uncertainty. Indeed, Beck, Davis and Jung (1991) found that income uncertainty can increase reported income. Snow and Warren (2005) showed that an increase in taxpayers' uncertainty about the amount of tax evasion an audit can detect increases compliance of prudent taxpayers. Caballe and Panades (2005) conclude that effects of uncertainty about audit costs are generally ambiguous. Nevertheless, it can be generalised that most survey studies confirmed a positive relationship between tax knowledge, subjective understanding and favourable tax attitudes.

People's attitudes, judgments and behaviour intentions are more affected by what they think than what actually is (Lewis, 1978). Since tax laws are criticised as being too complex to be fully understood by ordinary taxpayers, representations and evaluations of taxes are mainly a product of myths. Unsurprisingly, associations with taxes are often negative. Representations about taxation are, however, different in different taxpayer groups: while most people recognise the need for contributing to the public budget and are aware of public goods, taxes are perceived as a loss of personal freedom to decide how to invest one's own money, as contributions without a fair return, or as a repeated request from government to plug the gaps in the state's finances caused by inefficient management by politicians.

Studies on tax psychology often focus on attitudes and tax compliance. Within the frame of the theory of planned behaviour (Fishbein and Ajzen, 1975) and the theory of reasoned action (Ajzen, 1991), attitudes are – among norms and perceived control of behaviour or perceived opportunities of avoidance – determinants of intentions of behaviour. People avoiding their tax payments were frequently judged rather positively, as quite intelligent and hard-working. This result is not surprising, since work and achievement are fundamental values in societies with a Christian tradition, and wealth is perceived as a consequence of hard work and discipline. Some types of shadow work may be perceived as a virtue rather than a vice, especially if it is hard work. In such cases, keeping what one has earned may not be judged as criminal behaviour. On the other hand, taking advantage of public goods to which one is not entitled is judged as incorrect and condemned.

Besides attitudes as clusters of beliefs and evaluations, norms and level of control determine behaviour intentions. Like attitudes, norms have received considerable attention in tax research. However, the conceptualisation and use of norms as predictors of tax compliance has produced mixed outcomes. There is considerable overlap between perceived personal norms, values and a person's tax ethics, which convey a moral imperative that one should deliberately comply with social norms, usually defined as prevalence or acceptance of tax evasion among a reference group (Wenzel, 2005b). Personal norms reflect a taxpayer's tax ethics and are related to moral reasoning, authoritarianism and Machiavellianism, egoism, norm dependency, and values. The more developed a person's moral conscience, the more honest a person is, the less egoistical and Machiavellian, the more pronounced a person's social and cooperative values are, the stronger their religious beliefs are, and the more likely a person is to feel shame and guilt, the more likely it is that that person complies with the law.

Social norms are a function of an individual's perceived expectation that one or more relevant referents would approve of a particular behaviour and the extent to which the individual will be motivated to comply with such a referent's beliefs. The relevance of social norms is generally supported in empirical studies on tax evasion. If taxpayers believe that non-compliance is a widespread and socially accepted behaviour, then it is more likely that they too will not comply. The relationship between social norms and tax compliance intentions is, however, complex. Wenzel (2004a) argues that social norms should elicit concurring behaviour when taxpayers identify with the group to whom the norms are ascribed. Taxpayers then internalise the social norms and act accordingly. However, when identification is weak, social norms should be ineffective or even counterproductive. Also, in Wenzel's work personal norms involving a strong taxpaying ethic take precedence over social norms.

Norms are conceived as behaviour standards at three levels: the individual, the social reference group and the national level. On the individual level, norms define internalised standards on how to behave; in one's social setting, norms determine the behaviour of a social group, e.g., friends and acquaintances, vocational groups. Finally, on the national level, norms become cultural standards, often mirrored in the actual law. Research on tax compliance has focused on personal ethics and subjective perception of behavioural habits in taxpayers' reference groups. On the cultural level, norms have been addressed mainly under the term tax morale (Schmölders, 1960) and civic duty (Frey, 1997), and also under the term cultural norms. Cultural norms and societal institutions are perceived as important in determining tax compliance (Mumford, 2001).

In the attitude–behaviour approach to tax behaviour, opportunity in terms of probability of cash receipts and non-withholding at source is conceived perhaps as the most important situational constraint (Weigel, Hessing and Elffers, 1987). Generally, greater opportunity is correlated positively with non-compliance.

When citizens are asked what they think about the tax system, most often fairness concerns are communicated. As a consequence, Andreoni, Erard and Feinstein (1998) claim that incorporating moral and social dynamics into economic theory is essential. The most frequent differentiation in tax compliance research referred to exchange equity with the government and equity of one's contributions relative to the contributions of other taxpayers. Wenzel (2003) provided a conceptual framework for justice and fairness considerations based on conceptual distinctions made in social-psychological justice research. In social psychology, three areas of justice are differentiated: (a) distributive justice refers to the exchange of resources, both benefits and costs; (b) procedural justice refers to the processes of resource distribution; and (c) retributive justice refers to perceived appropriateness of sanctions in cases of norm-breaking. The central retributive questions refer to attributions of responsibility for wrongdoing, the restoration of damages for wrongful behaviour and the punishment a norm-breaker deserves.

With regard to distributive justice, comparisons are made on different levels. At an individual level, research on horizontal fairness considers the distribution of resources between taxpayers of comparable income groups. If an individual's perceived tax burden is heavier than that of comparable others, tax evasion is likely to increase. Besides horizontal fairness, vertical fairness and exchange fairness may be a taxpayer's major concern. If taxpayers disapprove of government spending and perceive the exchange with the government as unjust, tax evasion is likely to increase. At the societal level, taxpayers may evaluate the fairness of the tax system. There is evidence that suggests that the structure of taxes has an influence on people's willingness to comply. On the societal level, especially questions regarding progressive, regressive or flat taxes are important. Depending on question-formats, taxpayers seem to prefer progressive taxes and evaluate it more just than flat or regressive taxes.

In tax research, procedural justice is of inestimable importance. On the individual level, procedural justice refers to the quality of treatment in interaction between taxpayers and authorities, the quality of information provided by tax authorities, the extent to which compliance and admin- istration costs are imposed on taxpayers as well as the dynamics of allocation of revenues. Access to and provision of information related to the tax law and explanations for a tax law change can increase fairness perceptions. It seems that information which reduces tax law complexity and non-transparency leads to perceptions of greater fairness. Efficiency of interactions between taxpayers and tax authorities, the length of queues at information desks and satisfaction with audit treatment all seem to determine perceptions of procedural justice. At the individual level, fair treatment of individual taxpayers and the culture of interaction are relevant aspects of fairness and justice perceptions and the building up of trust. On the group and societal level, procedural fairness concerns the neutrality of tax officers regarding cohorts such as occupational groups or income groups. The perception that certain groups of people have more liberty leads to the perception of unfair treatment. If tax authorities and officers treat taxpayers equally, in a respectful and responsible way, trust in the institution and cooperation is likely to increase on individual, group and societal levels. Tax non-compliance can be the result of disapproval of government policy. Experimental work by Alm, Jackson and McKee (1990) also provides similar evidence: tax compliance tends to be higher when taxpayers are aware of a direct link between their tax payments and the provision of a desirable public good. Considerable sociological work suggests that taxpayers are more likely to report honestly if they feel that they are being treated courteously and respectfully by the tax agency. Consistent with this perspective, Frey (1992) has argued that tight moni- toring and heavy punishment on non-compliant citizens can crowd out tax morale and ultimately result in greater non-compliance.

Similar to procedural justice, retributive justice has received relatively little attention in the field of tax compliance. Retributive justice is closely related to the interaction between tax authorities and taxpayers, as is procedural justice. Retributive justice incorporates norms associated with the rigidity of audits and the responsibility for wrongdoing, the restoration process and the appropriateness of penalties in cases of norm-breaking. Unreasonable and intrusive audits and unfair penalties lead to negative attitudes toward the tax office and taxes in general. Also, tax amnesties trigger concerns about retributive justice, particularly if amnesties are perceived as legalising illegal behaviour and favouring the wealthy who resisted compliance.

Justice research has not always yielded consistent evidence for the impact of justice perceptions on tax compliance. The cause is mainly that different aspects of justice and fairness were investigated, operationalisation and measurement of justice are heterogeneous and inter-individual and situational differences, such as the tax climate, were largely neglected. As Wenzel (2002) shows, fairness judgments are not stable but depend on the object of comparison and on taxpayers' identification with a social group or category to which justice refers. Justice concerns seem to be especially strong if taxpayers identify with their nation and the tax-collecting government.

Subjective constructs of tax phenomena and collective sense-making are based on subjective tax knowledge, myths and legends, on subjective constructs and evaluations in terms of attitudes, on perceived and internalised norms, perceived opportunities not to comply, and on fairness perceptions. The condensation of knowledge, attitudes, norms, opportunities and fairness considerations yields the motivation and drive of taxpayers to behave honestly. V. Braithwaite (2003a) refers to the aggregation of subjective constructs and socially shared beliefs and evaluations as motivational postures. The concept of motivational postures as 'interconnected beliefs and attitudes that are consciously held and openly shared with others' includes individuals' attitudes toward the government, the tax system, other taxpayers and individual and social norms (V. Braithwaite, 2003a). Tax morale and civic duty are the aggregate of citizens' beliefs and evaluations of the state and taxation. While at the individual level, motivational postures are among the factors driving compliance and non-compliance, at the social or national level, tax morale and civic duty are the motivational forces leading to or deterring from engagement in the shadow economy, tax evasion and avoidance.

Motivational postures determine the way taxpayers position themselves in relation to tax authorities. They influence cooperation and non-compliance, and are useful parts of justification processes. Five motivational postures have been identified (V. Braithwaite, 2003a; V. Braithwaite et al., 1994). Commitment and capitulation reflect an overall positive orientation towards tax authorities, whereas resistance, disengagement and game-playing reflect a negative orientation. V. Braithwaite (2003a) found that different motivational postures can be held simultaneously – they are not stable individual characteristics, and taxpayers do shift between them. Commitment and capitulation were the most frequent encountered motivational postures in surveys conducted in Australia. Resistance, game-playing and disengagement were found less frequently. Moreover, commitment and capitulation were negatively related to evasion and tax avoidance, whereas the other three postures were positively related.

On the aggregate societal level, tax knowledge, attitudes, norms, perceived opportunity, fairness considerations and motivational postures contribute to tax morale. Tax morale implies the intrinsic motivation to comply. Tax morale was coined in 1960 by Schmölders, who defined it as an 'attitude of a group or the whole population of taxpayers regarding the question of accomplishment or neglect of their tax duties; it is anchored in citizens' tax mentality and in their consciousness to be citizens, which is the base of their inner acceptance of tax duties and acknowledgment of the sovereignty of the state' (pp. 97–8). The importance of tax morale and its impact on the shadow economy and tax non-compliance has been widely supported by empirical research.

7.2.3 Deciding to pay taxes

If tax payments are perceived as a social dilemma situation, the optimal strategy for rational individuals is to evade. Such rational behaviour leads to the worst outcome for the commons and ultimately for each individual. Therefore, taxpayers need to be forced to cooperate by control mechanisms and severe fines in case of non-cooperation. The neoclassical economic approach to tax behaviour starts from this assumption. In their seminal works, Allingham and Sandmo (1972) and Srinivasan (1973) start with the assumption that taxpayers have the choice between two main strategies: (a) declare the actual income, or (b) declare less than the actual income. When selecting the latter strategy, the payoff will depend on whether or not the taxpayer is investigated by the tax authorities. If taxpayers are not investigated, they are clearly better off than under the first strategy. If they are investigated and evasion is detected, they are worse off. Taxpayers are assumed to engage in maximising income by making a decision under uncertainty. Audits and sanctions in cases of evasion are perceived as the dominant instruments to ensure cooperative behaviour.

Studies on the impact of audits on compliance found that tax resistance is not strongly related to self-reported tax evasion or compliance behaviour. With regard to objective audit probabilities and subjectively perceived probabilities, Andreoni and colleagues concluded their 1998 review stating that audit probabilities have little effect on compliance and perhaps the effect of subjective audit and detection probabilities is mediated via psychological variables, such as moral obligations.

> The studies discussed ... indicate that individuals generally make poor predictions of the probability of audit and magnitude of fines from tax evasion. Moreover, there is consistency between their sense of a moral obligation to be honest and the tendency to overestimate the chance of being caught. Perhaps as a consequence, a high subjective probability of detection is associated with significantly more compliant behaviour. (p. 846)

The authors concluded their discussion on prior audits, emphasising the importance of considering why audits have very little specific deterrent value:

> One possible explanation is that audits may not turn out as badly as taxpayers initially fear. For example, if an audit fails to uncover existing non-compliance or if a substantial penalty is not applied to discovered non-compliance, a taxpayer may conclude that it pays to cheat. Alternatively, perhaps taxpayers do find audits to be a negative experience, but the impact of this experience is to make them want to evade by more in the future in an attempt to 'get back' at the tax agency. (Andreoni, Erard and Feinstein, 1998, p. 844)

Sequences of audits have been largely neglected in empirical research. It remains unclear whether audits lead to, e.g., (a) higher subjective estimations of audits in the future and therefore to higher compliance, or (b) subjective concepts of specific patterns of audit probabilities and speculation on audit occurrences in future years, and thus to strategic compliance behaviour, or (c) learning how to cleverly evade in order to escape the auditors, and thus to non-compliance, or (d) feelings of revenge to get back what the tax office took in upcoming years. The effect of audits and learning is acknowledged in few publications on tax compliance, and presumptions about the effect of audits, detection of irregularities and eventually fines are at least twofold. It can be hypothesised that – if it changes at all – compliance could increase or decrease after audits. Taxpayers may put effort into making sense of their experiences with tax authorities; they may try to predict audits and understand tax auditors' strategies and consequently learn how to deal with tax authorities effectively. If tax compliance is perceived as learned behaviour, then the question arises how often and when audits should be made and fines executed, or when audits and rewards should be provided in case of proven honesty. If tax authorities chose not to audit taxpayers randomly but followed reinforcement schedules to improve cooperation and reward honest taxpayers rather than punishing evaders, inspections might be more effective. Based on the findings by Mittone (2006), it can be assumed that tax compliance behaviour results in part from learning processes. Whether this is indeed the case still needs to be investigated.

With regard to fines, theoretical economic analyses of the effect of audits and fines suggest unequivocally that increases in audit probabilities and fines decrease evasion. The empirical research, on the other hand, does not yield clear results. Fischer, Wartick and Mark (1992) concluded their review on the experimental literature on the relationship between audit and detection probabilities and taxpayer compliance by emphasising the inconsistency of findings: some experiments failed to detect a significant positive relationship; other studies, attempting to determine the relative effectiveness of increased detection probability versus fines, provided weak evidence that fines were more effective, while other studies concluded that detection probability was more effective. Despite mixed results, the weight of evidence seems to support the conclusion that there is a positive relationship between detection probability and compliance.

Theoretical analyses of tax behaviour predict that high tax rates act as a disincentive to work. The argument states that increasing the tax rates for the more affluent will induce them to work less, which will generate less wealth for them and also negatively affect the economy as a whole. According to the 'substitution hypothesis', higher tax rates lower the costs of leisure, and consequently people will reduce their work engagement. According to the 'income effect hypothesis', however, the opposite should be true: higher rates of taxation reduce real income and, thus, people will work more in order to keep their living standards high. Although both hypotheses are theoretically interesting, a clear and strong effect of tax rate changes on work engagement does not seem to exist.

Economic modelling has also focused on income effects. Andreoni, Erard and Feinstein (1998) summarise studies on tax rates and income effects and conclude that the results of analyses of US IRS data, surveys and laboratory experiments are inconclusive. The relationship between income and evasion needs to be investigated further and is perhaps not linear, as many studies implicitly assume.

There are many reasons that can explain why the probability of audits and fines does not have the predicted high effect on tax compliance. First of all, the assumption that taxpayers are trying to avoid taxes if the opportunity presents itself must be doubted, especially if taxpayers trust the government and tax authorities and if the tax climate is favourable. Many studies show that the vast majority of citizens are willing to pay taxes and do not adopt economic decision-making models under uncertainty in order to maximise income. Most taxpayers seem to take for granted the legitimacy of the tax system and its overarching objectives and are probably not engaged in decision-making if the tax climate is characterised by mutual trust. Instead they pay their share without considering possibilities to avoid or evade taxes.

Rational models of decision-making assume the presence of perfect information processing. However, studies in behavioural economics, economic psychology and cognitive psychology present convincing evidence that individuals' information processing capabilities are limited. The more complex a situation is, the more decision-makers deviate from what the rational model predicts and the more inconsistent decisions are likely to be. People use heuristics and are vulnerable to biases. Due to limited understanding of tax issues and lack of interest in the issue, individuals were sometimes found to be inconsistent with regard to their preferences for specific types of tax, regressive, flat or progressive. Depending on the metric, individuals seem to prefer progressive tax if their judgments are based on probabilities, but they like flat tax in situations where tax is presented in absolute amounts of money.

Most research on decision-making biases is related to prospect theory and the tendencies to seek risks in situations perceived as loss and avoid risks in situations of gain. If taxpayers pay a lump sum of income tax when filing their taxes, they have either paid too much or not enough in taxes and will have either a refund or balance due. Those taxpayers who have a refund seem to perceive their tax refund as a gain, whereas those whose tax liability actually paid is lower than the liability determined by the tax office (and thus owe an additional tax payment) seem to perceive the taxes due as a loss and try to repair it by not reporting income or by overstating expenditures. Studies on advance tax payments and refunds or additional taxes due at time of tax reporting show that compliance is more likely to occur among participants confronting the prospect of a tax refund. Also, in the case where withholding leads to a tax refund at the end of the year, fairness judgments are more favourable.

Prospect theory seems to be able to explain, at least in part, decisions to comply or not to comply in view of a taxpayer's current cash position and expected payments or refunds due. However, the impact of current cash position and expected outcomes on tax decisions is complex and seems to vary between taxpayer groups, depending on their experiences. Moreover, predictions of prospect theory and framing effects differ with regard to taxpayers' tax ethics. Taxpayers who strongly agree that tax evasion is morally wrong seem not to be influenced by the withholding frame, while those with low tax ethics may not declare the full income when additional taxes are due at filing.

7.2.4   Self-employment and paying taxes out of pocket

Opportunity to evade taxes is probably the most relevant determinant of non-compliance. Opportunities to evade are high if taxes are not paid at source. Such is the case in groups of self-employed people and business owners. Tax research has particularly singled out those groups paying taxes out of their pocket, mainly small-business owners. Taxes may be perceived as limiting one's freedom to make autonomous decisions about one's income. Whereas employed people get their net income with taxes already subtracted, the self-employed and business owners get their profit and income, respectively, gross and need to pay income taxes 'out of their pockets'. People often respond to restrictions on their freedom or perceived restrictions by undertaking actions to re-establish their lost freedom. Reactance may originate in feared or perceived loss of control over events or a reduction of choice alternatives and develops into a motive to resist if individuals perceive a chance to re-establish their former situation. The self-employed and small-business owners seem to experience taxes as loss of their entrepreneurial freedom, which leads to reactance and the endeavour to cut taxes. The more experience taxpayers have accumulated in the course of time, the more certain they are that the firm will continue to operate despite high taxes. Moreover, the more they have adapted to the national tax system, the less pronounced reactance should be. Self-employed and business owners not only have greater opportunities to evade than other categories of taxpayers, but may also have stronger motives to oppose tax payments during the start-up phase of their enterprise.

Self-employed and small-business owners were also found to be particularly ambitious and hard-working. If tax rates increase, work engagement may suffer. Small-business owners may decide to work less if tax rates increase. High workloads demand higher income, and if there is an increase in tax payments, the remaining income may be inadequate.

Besides income tax, business corporations also pay and collect various other taxes. In many countries, businesses collect sales tax and they act as remittance agents for some withholding taxes, such as personal income tax, employee payroll taxes, etc. The variety of taxes imposes a considerable burden on businesses and creates possibilities of non-compliance. Research on taxes collected and evaded by businesses is scarce, as Webley (2004) summarises in his report on tax compliance by small businesses. Besides being younger and more egoistical, feeling less guilty if tax was not paid, believing that tax was unfair and having friends who would not disapprove of tax evasion, self-reported non-compliers had less accurate knowledge about tax and believed the money was coming from their own business funds. There are a number of similarities with income tax compliance and correct payment of Value Added Tax. In the latter case, the psychological phenomenon of mental accounting was found to be of particular interest. Business people seem to differ in the way they perceive Value Added Tax and tax collected to be transferred to the state. While some may perceive the money as belonging to their business or themselves, others perceive it as money belonging to the state. If business people psychologically put money owed in Value Added Tax into a separate (mental) account from the money generated by business turnover, their compliance is likely to be higher than it would be otherwise.

7.3   The 'slippery-slope model': trust in authorities and voluntary compliance versus power of authorities and enforced compliance

Trust is a critical factor in understanding the origins of civic engagement, cooperation with authorities and compliance. If governmental authorities had to continually explain and justify their actions, their ability to effectively manage public affairs would be greatly diminished. Moreover, because of the costs of monitoring, authorities cannot detect and punish every failure to cooperate. Efficient performance of the state in general and tax authorities in particular depends on individuals' feelings of obligation toward the community, their willingness to comply with authorities' directives and regulations and their willingness to voluntarily defer to tax authorities (Kramer, 1999).

As already explained, tax authorities' orientation towards taxpayers and their interaction style create a tax climate which fosters either resistance and individual profit maximisation or taxpayers' trust in the authorities and the perceived legitimacy of authorities. The consequences of the latter are cooperation and voluntary compliance. Taxpayers accept the legitimacy of tax authorities and trust authorities if they hold motivational postures of cooperation as opposed to resistance (Braithwaite, 2003a; Braithwaite and Wenzel, 2007). Without such a climate, taxpayers dissociate from the state and tax authorities, and do not value public benefits or accept authorities' view of justice. In the language of Braithwaite and Wenzel (2007), taxpayers become dismissive and dissociated.

A 'cops and robbers' approach stimulates a climate of persecution and prosecution, leading ultimately to an unwillingness to cooperate and individual profit considerations, whereas a 'service and client' approach seems likely to change taxpayers' representations and evaluation of taxation, and consequently stimulates trust and a climate of cooperation. When people think their behaviour is under the control of extrinsic motivators, such as tax authorities, intrinsic motivation to comply may be reduced. Thus, surveillance by control and fines 'may undermine individuals' motivation to engage in the very behaviour such monitoring is intended to induce or ensure' (Kramer, 1999, p. 591). Referring to cooperation within organisations, Cialdini (1996) notes, 'monitoring and surveillance systems communicate to employees that they are not trusted, potentially breeding mistrust and resentment in return. When people feel coerced into complying with behavior, they may resist the behavior when they think monitoring is imperfect and they can get away with it. Because of psychological reactance, even honest employees may try to cheat or sabotage monitoring systems' (Kramer, 1999, p. 591). If we apply this statement to tax behaviour, a 'cops and robbers' approach may not only be ineffective with regard to tax compliance, but have corrosive effects: well-intentioned and highly committed citizens may distrust the surveillants and feel impelled to cheat. Systems intended to guarantee trust may, ironically, make it more difficult for citizens to demonstrate their trustworthiness, breed distrust and provoke non-cooperative behaviour.

Interaction processes based on transparency and neutrality of the procedures, trustworthiness of tax institutions and tax authorities and respectful, polite and dignified treatment of taxpayers are likely to enhance voluntary compliance. Voluntary compliance is assumed to be especially related to taxpayers' social representations and determined by them. A climate of cooperation is likely if government policy is accepted and trusted, personal and social norms are favourable to cooperation and tax burden and tax procedures are perceived as fair.

If the climate is hostile, government institutions – if they have legitimate and expert power – can enforce compliance. Taxpayers who are unwilling to pay their taxes, but are threatened by audits and fines, need to carefully consider what option to choose: the safe option to pay their tax share, accepting the loss of some money, or deciding for the risky option with the possible benefit of tax savings or the possible cost of detection and fines. Under such circumstances, extensive decision-making processes are likely to occur, with taxpayers carefully considering the value of their options. Audit probability, fines, tax rates, income effects, assumed strategies used by the authorities and chances to escape them, framing effects and withholding phenomena, etc. are presumed to be meticulously considered when deciding how to deal with one's income and with tax authorities. People with many opportunities to evade or to avoid their taxes are likely to cut their share if it pays, that is, if the power of tax authorities to control and fine in the case of evasion is weak. In the case of strong power to enforce tax payments, that is, high audit rates, high detection probability as well as severe fines, and unequivocal tax laws forbidding tax avoidance, taxpayers are constrained to comply. It can be expected that the weight of determinants of compliance differs depending on tax climate. Hence, empirical studies should reveal different determinants in operating depending on the predominant climate – determined by trust in authorities and power of authorities – of the society or laboratory environment. This would explain why empirical studies sometimes confirm a strong deterrent effect of audits and fines, and in other circumstances these effects are low or even opposite to the predictions.

If the climate is friendly and taxpayers trust the authorities, compliance is likely to occur voluntarily, independent of tax authorities' power to enforce compliance (e.g., Bergman, 2002; Feld and Frey, 2005a; Frey, 2003). A friendly climate is likely to be related to perceived legitimacy of tax authorities. According to Tyler (2006),

Legitimacy is a psychological property of an authority, institution, or social arrangement that leads those connected to it to believe that it is appropriate, proper, and just. Because of legitimacy, people feel that they ought to defer to decisions and rules, following them voluntarily out of obligation rather than out of fear of punishment and anticipation of reward. Being legitimate is important to the success of authorities . . . since it is difficult to exert influence over others based solely upon the possession and use of power. Being able to gain voluntary acquiescence from most people, most of the time, due to their sense of obligation increases effectiveness during periods of scarcity, crisis, and conflict. (p. 375)

Taxpayers may perceive paying taxes as a civic duty and cooperate with government institutions to the benefit of the community. In a climate of mutual trust, audits and sanctions are likely to have no effect or possibly corrupt cooperation. A 'service and client' approach is characterised by clear and understandable regulations, transparency of procedures, neutrality, respect and politeness with regard to taxpayer treatment as well as support. Procedural fairness perceptions are at the base of a climate of trust, which is assumed to enhance taxpayers' voluntary cooperation. Rather than meticulously deciding what option promises the highest individual profit, subjective understanding of tax law, attitudes towards the government, personal and social norms, perception of distributive fairness and procedural justice are likely to affect taxpayers' motivation to meet tax requirements. On the aggregate level, high tax morale and a strong sense of civic duty ensure citizens' willingness to cooperate with the state spontaneously, rather than engaging in complex decision-making with the aim of maximising egoistic profit.

Figure 26 displays these assumptions graphically in a three-dimensional space with power of the state and trust in authorities as dimensions determining voluntary or enforced compliance. The figure presents the 'slippery slope' from voluntary to enforced compliance to non-compliance. It is assumed that compliance can result under the condition of strong power of the state as well as under the condition of trust in authorities. On one hand, if tax authorities have the power to enforce compliance and if taxpayers decide on how to increase their individual profit come to the conclusion that it does not pay to evade, enforced compliance is high. If

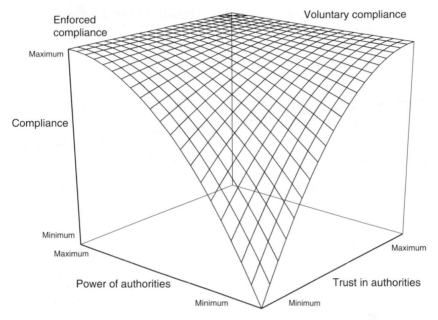

Figure 26: Determinants of compliance depending on the power of the state and trust in authorities: the 'slippery-slope model'

trust in authorities is low, and if the power of the authorities is weak, it is likely that citizens seek opportunities to avoid or evade taxes. On the other hand, voluntary compliance is high if interaction with authorities is trustful and if citizens understand the law and perceive taxes as distributed fairly and procedures as just, if they hold positive attitudes towards the government and have developed favourable personal and social norms, that is, if they have favourable social representations about taxation. The power of the state, expressed by audit frequency and the power to sanction non-cooperation, is ineffectual in this tax climate or may even corrupt compliance.

The curvature of the 'slippery-slope model' results from assumptions of diminishing returns for both power and trust, i.e., a comparable increase in compliance can only be achieved by exceedingly high increases in power or trust. The term 'slippery slope' was chosen to illustrate the potential dynamics inherent in the interplay between trust and audits. High compliance can only be maintained with high levels of trust or power. As soon as trust and power are at intermediate levels, the model suggests that a downward spiral may occur: because trust in the authorities is already undermined, monitoring and audits are seen as signals of a 'cops and robbers' attitude on behalf of the tax authorities and create even more distrust.

Finally, self-employed taxpayers are frequently assumed to egoistically take advantage of their opportunities to cut taxes. Indeed, paying taxes out-of-pocket is more likely to be perceived as a loss than taxes paid at source, and consequently, tendencies to reduce a perceived loss may be strong. However, research has shown that self-employed taxpayers need not be non-compliant. At the beginning of running a business, it may be difficult to keep separate accounts for different money flows, and perceptions of limited freedom to run and invest in one's business may be strong. However, in the long run, these initial problems seem to dissipate, and the self-employed become increasingly compliant. This seems to be especially true if they work hard for their money. If their social representations of taxation are favourable, then there is no basis for assuming self-employed taxpayers to be non-cooperative. Non-compliance may merely be the result of not understanding the tax laws. Again, in a situation of persecution, prosecution and mutual distrust, it is likely that the voluntary willingness to comply vanishes and, rather than feeling a civic duty to pay their share, taxpayers may engage in egoistic profit-maximisation decisions.

At present, there is a need for empirical evidence to support the presented 'slippery slope-model' of voluntary compliance versus enforced compliance as correlated to the interaction style, feelings of mutual trust or distrust and authorities' enforcement power. Moreover, research on the impact of psychological variables on tax behaviour, especially procedural aspects, is still in its infancy (Franzoni, 2000). The proposed model may, however, shed light on the vast empirical research studies that offer conflicting explanations for income tax behaviour, and further serve as a starting point to investigate the numerous effects of different determinants of compliance, depending on authorities' taxpayer orientation, their reactions and the resulting tax climate. The model may also prove to be of practical value in discussions on the power of authorities, taxpayers' trust in authorities and strategies to shift taxpayers from enforced compliance to voluntary compliance through dialogue and support. This model implies the need for a psychological intervention, one that changes social representations of taxation and eventually changes the institutions themselves from a 'command and control'- to a 'service and client'-oriented system characterised by responsive regulation.

References

Abric, J.-C. (1984). A theoretical and experimental approach to the study of social representations in a situation of interaction. In S. Moscovici and R. Farr (eds.), *Social representations* (pp. 223–50). Cambridge: Cambridge University Press.

Adams, C. (1993). *For good and evil: The impact of taxes on the course of civilization.* Lanham, MD: Madison Books.

Adams, C., and Webley, P. (2001). Small business owners' attitudes on VAT compliance in the UK. *Journal of Economic Psychology*, 22(2), 195–216.

Adams, J. S. (1965). Inequity in social exchange. In L. Berkowitz (ed.), *Advances in experimental and social psychology* (vol. II, pp. 267–99). New York, NY: Academic Press.

Agnell, J., and Persson, M. (2000). Tax arbitrage and labor supply. *Journal of Public Economics*, 78(1–2), 3–24.

Ahmed, E. (2004). Validation of the 'Management of Shame State – Shame Acknowledgment and Shame Displacement' (MOSS-SASD) in the context of taxation. Unpublished manuscript. The Australian National University, Canberra, Australia.

Ahmed, E., and Braithwaite, V. (2004). When tax collectors become collectors for child support and student loans: Jeopardizing the revenue base? *Kyklos*, 57(3), 303–26.

(2005). Understanding small business taxpayers: Issues of deterrence, tax morale, fairness and work practice. *International Small Business Journal*, 23(5), 539–68.

Ajzen, I. (1991). The theory of planned behavior. *Organizational Behavior and Human Decision Processes*, 50(2), 179–211.

(1993). Attitude theory and the attitude–behavior relation. In D. Krebs and P. Schmidt (eds.), *New directions in attitude measurement* (pp. 41–57). New York: de Gruyter.

Alexander, C., and Feinstein, J. S. (1987). *A microeconomic analysis of income tax evasion* (Mimeo). Ann Arbor, MI: Michigan Institute of Technology.

Allingham, M., and Sandmo, A. (1972). Income tax evasion: A theoretical analysis. *Journal of Public Economics*, 1(3–4), 323–38.

Alm, J. (1991). A perspective on the experimental analysis of taxpayer reporting. *The Accounting Review*, 55(3), 577–93.

Alm, J., Cronshaw, M. B., and McKee, M. (1993). Tax compliance with endogenous audit selection-rules. *Kyklos*, 46(1), 27–45.

Alm, J., Jackson, B. R., and McKee, M. (1990). *Alternative government approaches for increasing tax compliance* (Mimeo). Boulder: University of Colorado, Department of Economics.

(1992a). Institutional uncertainty and taxpayer compliance. *The American Economic Review*, 82(4), 1,018–26.

(1992b). Estimating the determinants of taxpayer compliance with experimental data. *National Tax Journal*, 45(1), 107–14.

(1993). Fiscal exchange, collective decision institutions, and tax compliance. *Journal of Economic Behavior and Organization*, 22(3), 285–303.

(2005). *Audit information dissemination, taxpayer communication, and compliance behavior*. Retrieved 31 December 2005, from http://aysps.gsu.edu/people/working/AlmJacksonMcKee-DirectversusIndirectEffects-05.18.05.DOC.

Alm, J., Martinez-Vazquez, J., and Schneider, F. (2004). 'Sizing' the problem of the hard-to tax. In J. Alm, J. Martinez-Vazquez and S. Wallace (eds.), *Taxing the hard-to-tax: Lessons from theory and practice* (pp. 11–75). Amsterdam: Elsevier.

Alm, J., McClelland, G. H., and Schulze, W. D. (1992). Why do people pay taxes? *Journal of Public Economics*, 48(1), 21–38.

(1999). Changing the social norm of tax compliance by voting. *Kyklos*, 52(2), 141–71.

Alm, J., McKee, M., and Beck, W. (1990). Amazing grace – tax amnesties and compliance. *National Tax Journal*, 43(1), 23–37.

Alm, J., Sanchez, I., and deJuan, A. (1995). Economic and noneconomic factors in tax compliance. *Kyklos*, 48(1), 3–18.

Alm, J., and Torgler, B. (2006). Culture differences and tax morale in the United States and in Europe. *Journal of Economic Psychology*, 27(2), 224–46.

Anderhub, V., Giese, S., Güth, W., Hoffmann, A., and Otto, T. (2001). Tax evasion with earned income: An experimental study. *Finanz Archiv*, 58(2), 188–206.

Andreoni, J. (1991). The desirability of a permanent tax amnesty. *Journal of Public Economics*, 45(2), 143–59.

Andreoni, J., Erard, B., and Feinstein, J. S. (1998). Tax compliance. *Journal of Economic Literature*, 36(2), 818–60.

Andrews, M. (2003). New public management and democratic participation: Complementary or competing reforms? A South African study. *International Journal of Public Administration*, 26(8–9), 991–1,016.

Angermeier, W. F., Bednorz, P., and Hursh, S. R. (1994). *Operantes Lernen. Methoden, Ergebnisse, Anwendung*. Munich: Ernst Reinhardt.

Antonides, G., and Robben, H. S. J. (1995). True positives and false alarms in the detection of tax evasion. *Journal of Economic Psychology*, 16(4), 617–40.

Argyle, M. (1987). *The psychology of happiness*. London: Methuen.

Arkes, H. R., and Blumer, C. (1985). The psychology of sunk cost. *Organizational Behavior and Human Decision Processes*, 35(1), 124–40.

Arkes, H. R., Joner, C. A., Pezzo, M. V., Nash, J. G., Siegel-Jacobs, K. and Stone, E. (1994). The psychology of windfall gains. *Organizational Behavior and Human Decision Processes*, 59(3), 331–47.

Arrow, K. (1974). *The limits of organization*. New York: Norton.

Ayres, I., and Braithwaite, J. (1992). *Responsive regulation: Transcending the deregulation debate*. New York: Oxford University Press.

Baldry, J. C. (1987). Income tax evasion and the tax schedule: Some experimental results. *Public Finance*, 42(3), 357–83.

(1994). Economic analysis and taxpayer compliance: Time for a new agenda. *Australian Tax Forum*, 11(1), 45–62.

Balestrino, A., and Galmarini, U. (2003). Imperfect tax compliance and the optimal provision of public goods. *Bulletin of Economic Research*, 55(1), 37–51.

Bandura, A. (1977). Self-efficacy: Toward a unifying theory of behavioral change. *Psychological Review*, 84(2), 191–215.

Barber, B. M., and Odean, T. (2004). Are individual investors tax savvy? Evidence from retail and discount brokerage accounts. *Journal of Public Economics*, 88(1–2), 419–42.

Baron, J. (2000). *Thinking and deciding* (3rd edn). New York: Cambridge University Press.

Bartelsman, E. J., and Beetsma, R. M. W. J. (2003). Why pay more? Corporate tax avoidance through transfer pricing in OECD countries. *Journal of Public Economics*, 87(9–10), 2,225–52.

Beck, P. J., Davis, J. S., and Jung, W.-O. (1991). Experimental evidence on taxpayer reporting under uncertainty. *Accounting Review*, 66(3), 535–58.

Becker, G. (1968). Crime and punishment: An economic approach. *The Journal of Political Economy*, 76(2), 169–217.

Benford, F. (1938). The law of anomalous numbers. *Proceedings of the American Philosophical Society*, 78(4), 551–72.

Bergman, M. S. (2002). Who pays for social policy? A study on taxes and trust. *Journal of Social Policy*, 31(2), 289–305.

Bergman, M., and Nevarez, A. (2005). The social mechanisms of tax evasion and tax compliance. *Politica y Gobierno*, 12(1), 9.

Bernasconi, M. (1998). Tax evasion and orders of risk aversion. *Journal of Public Economics*, 67(1), 123–34.

Berti, C., and Kirchler, E. (2001). Contributi e contribuenti: Una ricerca sulle rappresentazioni del sistema fiscale. *Giornale Italiano di Psicologia*, 28(3), 595–607.

Besim, M., and Jenkins, G. P. (2005). Tax compliance: When do employees behave like the self-employed? *Applied Economics*, 37(10), 1,201.

Bitterman, M. (1975). The comparative analysis of learning. *Science*, 188(4,189), 699–709.

Blackwell, C. (2002). *A meta-analysis of tax compliance experiments*. Paper presented at the Annual Meeting of the Public Choice Society and Economic Science Association, San Diego, CA.

Blamey, R., and Braithwaite, V. (1997). The validity of the security-harmony social values model in the general population. *Australian Journal of Psychology*, 49(1), 71–7.

Blau, P. M. (1964). *Exchange and power in social life*. New York: Wiley.

Blickle, G., Schlegel, A., Fassbender, P., and Klein, U. (2006). Some personality correlates of business white-collar crime. *Applied Psychology: An International Review*, 55(2), 220–33.

Blumenthal, M., and Christian, C. (2004). Tax preparers. In H. J. Aaron and J. Slemrod (eds.), *The crisis in tax administration* (pp. 201–29). Washington, DC: Brookings Institution Press.

Bobek, D. D., and Hatfield, R. C. (2003). An investigation of the theory of planned behavior and the role of moral obligation in tax compliance. *Behavioral Research in Accounting*, 15(1), 13–38.

Bogardus, E. S. (1928). *Immigration and race attitudes*. Boston, MA: D. C. Heath and Company.

Bongiovanni, A. (1977). *A review of research on the effects of punishment in the schools*. Paper presented at the Conference on Child Abuse, Children's Hospital National Medical Center, Washington, DC.

Bosco, L., and Mittone, L. (1997). Tax evasion and moral constraints: Some experimental evidence. *Kyklos*, 50(3), 297–324.

Bracewell-Milnes, B. (1979). *Tax avoidance and evasion: The individual and society*. London: Panopticum Press.

Braithwaite, J. (2003). Large business and the compliance model. In V. Braithwaite (ed.), *Taxing democracy. Understanding tax avoidance and evasion* (pp. 177–202). Aldershot: Ashgate.

(2005). *Markets in vice. Markets in virtue*. Leichhardt: The Federation Press.

Braithwaite, V. (1994). Beyond Rokeach's equality–freedom model: Two-dimensional values in a one-dimensional world. *Journal of Social Issues*, 50(4), 67–94.

(1998). The value balance model of political evaluations. *British Journal of Psychology*, 89(2), 223–47.

(2003a). Dancing with tax authorities: Motivational postures and non-compliant actions. In V. Braithwaite (ed.), *Taxing democracy. Understanding tax avoidance and tax evasion* (pp. 15–39). Aldershot: Ashgate.

(2003b). A new approach to tax compliance. In V. Braithwaite (ed.), *Taxing democracy. Understanding tax avoidance and tax evasion* (pp. 1–11). Aldershot: Ashgate.

(2003c). Perceptions of who's not paying their fair share. *Australian Journal of Social Issues*, 38(3), 335–62.

(ed.). (2003d). *Taxing democracy. Understanding tax avoidance and tax evasion*. Aldershot: Ashgate.

Braithwaite, V., and Ahmed, E. (2005). A threat to tax morale: The case of Australian higher education policy. *Journal of Economic Psychology*, 26(4), 523–40.

Braithwaite, V., Braithwaite, J., Gibson, D., and Makkai, T. (1994). Regulatory styles, motivational postures and nursing home compliance. *Law and Policy*, 16(4), 363–94.

Braithwaite, V. and Job, J. (2003). *The theoretical base for the ATO compliance model. Technical Report Research Note 5, CTSI, RSSS, ANU*. Retrieved 12 July 2006, from http://ctsi.anu.edu.au/publications/research%20notes/RN5.pdf.

Braithwaite, V., Schneider, F., Reinhart, M., and Murphy, K. (2003). Charting the shoals of the cash economy. In V. Braithwaite (ed.), *Taxing democracy. Understanding tax avoidance and tax evasion* (pp. 93–108). Aldershot: Ashgate.

Braithwaite, V., and Wenzel, M. (2007). Integrating explanations of tax evasion and avoidance. In A. Lewis (ed.), *Cambridge handbook of psychology and economic behaviour*. Cambridge: Cambridge University Press.

Brandstätter, H. (1994). Determinanten der Steuerhinterziehung: Ergebnisse der experimentellen Psychologie. In C. Smekal and E. Theurl (eds.), *Stand und Entwicklung der Finanzpsychologie* (pp. 213–45). Baden-Baden: Nomos.

Brehm, J. W. (1966). *A theory of psychological reactance*. New York: Academic Press.

Brooks, N., and Doob, A. N. (1990). Tax evasion: Searching for a theory of compliant behavior. In M. L. Friedland (ed.), *Securing compliance: Seven case studies*. Toronto: University of Toronto Press.

Brosio, G., Cassone, A., and Ricciuti, R. (2002). Tax evasion across Italy: Rational noncompliance or inadequate civic concern? *Public Choice*, 112(3–4), 259–73.

Brown, D. (1985). Business ethics: Is small better? *Policy Studies Journal*, 13(4), 766–75.

Burton, H. A., Karlinsky, S. S. and Blanthorne, C. (2005). Perceptions of a white-collar crime: Tax evasion. *American Taxation Association's Journal of Legal Tax Research*, 3(1), 35–48.

Caballe, J., and Panades, J. (2005). Cost uncertainty and taxpayer compliance. *International Tax and Public Finance*, 12(3), 239.

Calderwood, G., and Webley, P. (1992). Who responds to changes in taxation? The relationship between taxation and incentive to work. *Journal of Economic Psychology*, 13(4), 735–48.

Carnes, G. A., and Cuccia, A. D. (1996). An analysis of the effect of tax complexity and its perceived justification on equity judgments. *Journal of the American Taxation Association*, 18(2), 40–56.

Carroll, J. S. (1987). Compliance with the law: A decision-making approach to taxpaying. *Law and Human Behavior*, 11(4), 319–35.

(1992). How taxpayers think about their taxes: Frames and values. In J. Slemrod (ed.), *Why people pay taxes: Tax compliance and enforcement* (pp. 43–63). Ann Arbor, MI: Michigan University Press.

Carslaw, C. A. P. N. (1988). Anomolies in income numbers: Evidence of goal oriented behavior. *The Accounting Review*, 63(2), 321–7.

Casey, J. T., and Scholz, J. T. (1991). Beyond deterrence: Behavioral decision theory and tax compliance. *Law and Society Review*, 25(4), 821–43.

Chan, C. W., Troutman, C. S., and O'Bryan, D. (2000). An expanded model of taxpayer compliance: Empirical evidence from the United States and Hong Kong. *Journal of International Accounting, Auditing and Taxation*, 9(2), 83–103.

Chang, O. H., Nichols, D. R., and Schultz, J. J. (1987). Taxpayer attitudes toward tax audit risk. *Journal of Economic Psychology*, 8(3), 299–309.

Chang, O. H., and Schultz, J. J. (1990). The income tax withholding phenomenon: Evidence from TCMP data. *The Journal of the American Taxation Association*, 12(1), 88–93.

Christensen, K., Cline, R., and Neubig, T. (2001). Total corporate taxation: 'Hidden,' above-the-line, non-income taxes. *National Tax Journal*, 54(3), 495–506.

Christian, C. W. (1994). *Voluntary compliance with the individual income tax: Results from the 1988 TCMP study.* Washington, DC.

Christie, R., and Geis, F. L. (1970). *Studies in Machiavellianism.* New York: Academic Press.

Christopoulos, D. K. (2003). Does underground economy respond symmetrically to tax changes? Evidence from Greece. *Economic Modelling,* 20(3), 563–70.

Chu, C. Y. (1990). Plea bargaining with the IRS. *Journal of Public Economics,* 41(3), 319–33.

Cialdini, R. B. (1993). *Influence. Science and practice.* New York: HarperCollins.
    (1996). Social influence and the triple tumor structure of organizational dishonesty. In D. M. Messick and A. E. Tenbrunsel (eds.), *Codes of conduct* (pp. 44–58). New York: Sage.

Clotfelter, C. (1983). Tax evasion and tax rates: An analysis of individual returns. *The Review of Economics and Statistics,* 65(3), 363–73.

Collins, C. J., Hanges, P. J., and Locke, E. A. (2004). The relationship of achievement motivation to entrepreneurial behavior: A meta-analysis. *Human Performance,* 17(1), 95–117.

Collins, J. H., Milliron, V. C., and Toy, D. R. (1990). Factors associated with household demand for tax preparers. *The Journal of the American Taxation Association,* 12(1), 9–25.

Collins, J. H., Murphey, D., and Plumlee, R. D. (1990). *The taxpayer's dilemma: How hard to work and what to report?* University of North Carolina at Chapel Hill.

Collins, J. H., and Plumlee, R. D. (1991). The taxpayer's labor and reporting decision: The effect of audit schemes. *Accounting Review,* 66(3), 559–76.

Copeland, P. V., and Cuccia, A. D. (2002). Multiple determinants of framing referents in tax reporting and compliance. *Organizational Behavior and Human Decision Processes,* 88(1), 499–526.

Corman, J., Lussier, R. N., and Nolan, K. G. (1996). Factors that encourage entrepreneural start-ups and existing firm expansion: A longitudinal study comparing recession and expansion periods. *Academy of Entrepreneurship Journal,* 1(2), 43–55.

Costa, P. T., and McCrae, R. R. (1992). *Revised NEO Personality Inventory (NEO-PI-R) and NEO Five-Factor Inventory (NEO-FFI) Professional Manual.* Odessa, FL: Psychological Assessment Resources.

Courakis, N. (2001). Financial crime today: Greece as a European case study. *European Journal of Criminal Policy and Research,* 9(2), 197–219.

Cowell, F. A. (1992). Tax evasion and inequity. *Journal of Economic Psychology,* 13(4), 521–43.

Cox, D., and Plumley, A. (1988). *Analyses of voluntary compliance rates for different income source classes.* Washington, DC: International Revenue Service, Research Division.

Cross, R. B., and Shaw, G. K. (1982). The evasion–avoidance choice: A suggested approach. *National Tax Journal,* 34(4), 489–91.

Crush, J. (1985). Colonial coercion and the Swazi tax revolt of 1903–1907. *Political Geography Quarterly,* 4(3), 179–90.

Cuccia, A. D., and Carnes, G. A. (2001). A closer look at the relation between tax complexity and tax equity perceptions. *Journal of Economic Psychology*, 22(2), 113–40.

Cullis, J., Jones, P., and Lewis, A. (2006). Tax framing, instrumentality and individual differences: Are there two different cultures? *Journal of Economic Psychology*, 27(2), 304–20.

Cullis, J., and Lewis, A. (1997). Why people pay taxes: From a conventional economic model to a model of social convention. *Journal of Economic Psychology*, 18(2–3), 305–21.

Cunningham, J. B., and Lischeron, J. (1991). Defining entrepreneurship. *Journal of Small Business Management*, 29(1), 45–61.

Dalton, T. (1994). The new IRS approach to nonfilers and nonpayers. *The CPA Journal Online*, 64 (December), 68–9.

Das-Gupta, A., Lahiri, R., and Mookherjee, D. (1995). Income tax compliance in India: An empirical analysis. *World Development*, 23(12), 2,051–64.

Davis, D. D., and Holt, C. A. (1993). *Experimental economics*. Princeton, NJ: Princeton University Press.

Dawes, R. M. (1980). Social dilemmas. *Annual Review of Psychology*, 31(1), 169–93.

de Juan, A., Lasheras, M. A., and Mayo, R. (1994). Voluntary tax compliant behavior of Spanish income tax payers. *Public Finance*, 49(4), 90–105.

de Rosa, A. S. (1996). *Controversial social representations 'of' and 'around' advertising: How to sell pullovers by provoking discussion on social issues*. Paper presented at the 11th General Meeting of EAESP, Gmunden, Austria.

Dean, P., Keenan, T., and Kenney, F. (1980). Taxpayers' attitudes to income tax evasion: An empirical study. *British Tax Review*, 25(1), 28–44.

DeCarlo, J. F., and Lyons, P. R. (1979). A comparison of selected personal characteristics of minority and non-minority female entrepreneurs. *Journal of Small Business Management*, 17(4), 22–9.

Die Presse (2006). 1,31 Mrd. Euro an Steuerbetrug aufgedeckt. (4 August 2006, page 15).

Dornstein, M. (1976). Compliance with legal and bureaucratic rules: The case of self-employed taxpayers in Israel. *Human Relations*, 29(11), 1,019–34.

(1987). Taxes: Attitudes and perceptions and their social bases. *Journal of Economic Psychology*, 8(1), 55–76.

Duncan, W. A., LaRue, D. W., and Reckers, P. M. J. (1989). An empirical examination of the influences of selected economic and noneconomic variables in decision making by tax professionals. *Advances in Taxation*, 2(1), 91–106.

Durham, A. M. (1988). Crime seriousness and punitive severity: An assessment of social attitudes. *Justice Quarterly*, 5(1), 131–53.

Durkheim, E. (1976 [1898]). Individuelle und kollektive Vorstellungen. In E. Durkheim (ed.), *Soziologie und Philosophie* (pp. 45–83). Frankfurt am Main: Suhrkamp.

Eagly, A. H., and Chaiken, S. (1993). *The psychology of attitudes*. Fort Worth, TX: Harcourt Brace.

Edlund, J. (2003). Attitudes towards taxation: Ignorant and incoherent? *Scandinavian Political Studies*, 26(2), 145–67.

Eichenberger, R., and Frey, B. S. (2002). Democratic governance for a globalized world. *Kyklos*, 55(2), 265–88.

el Sehity, T., Hölzl, E., and Kirchler, E. (2005). Price developments after a nominal shock: Benford's Law and psychological-pricing after the euro introduction. *International Journal of Research in Marketing*, 22(4), 471–80.

el Sehity, T., Kirchler, E., and Muehlbacher, S. (2003). *Rise and decline of social objects: Ten case studies on the social development of meaning*. Paper presented at the IAREP-workshop 'Euro: Currency and symbol', Vienna, Austria.

Elffers, H. (1999). Tax evasion. In P. E. Earl and S.Kemp (eds.), *The Elgar companion to consumer research and economic psychology* (pp. 556–60). Cheltenham: Edward Elgar.

(2000). But taxpayers do cooperate! In M. V. Vugt, M. Snyder, T. R. Tyler and A. Biel (eds.), *Cooperation in modern society. Promoting the welfare of communities, states and organizations* (pp. 184–194). London: Routledge.

Elffers, H., and Hessing, D. J. (1997). Influencing the prospects of tax evasion. *Journal of Economic Psychology*, 18(2–3), 289–304.

Elffers, H., Robben, H. S. J., and Hessing, D. J. (1991). Under-reporting income: Who is the best judge – taxpayer or tax inspector? *Journal of Royal Statistical Society*, 154(1), 125–7.

(1992). On measuring tax evasion. *Journal of Economic Psychology*, 13(4), 545–67.

Elffers, H., Weigel, R. H., and Hessing, D. J. (1987). The consequences of different strategies for measuring tax evasion behaviour. *Journal of Economic Psychology*, 8(3), 311–37.

Erard, B. (1997). Self-selection with measurement errors: A microeconometric analysis of the decision to seek tax assistance and its implications for tax compliance. *Journal of Econometrics*, 81(2), 319–56.

Erard, B., and Feinstein, J. S. (1994a). Honesty and evasion in the tax compliance game. *Rand Journal of Economics*, 25(1), 1–19.

(1994b). The role of moral sentiments and audit perceptions in tax compliance. *Public Finance*, 49 (Suppl.), 70–89.

Erard, B., and Ho, C. C. (2001). Searching for ghosts: Who are the nonfilers and how much tax do they owe? *Journal of Public Economics*, 81(1), 25–50.

Eriksen, K., and Fallan, L. (1996). Tax knowledge and attitudes towards taxation: A report on a quasi-experiment. *Journal of Economic Psychology*, 17(3), 387–402.

Estes, W. (1944). An experimental study of punishment. *Psychological Monographs*, 57 (reprinted in E. Boe and R. Church (1968) (eds.), *Punishment: Issues and experiments* (p. 108–65). New York: Appleton-Century-Crofts.

Etzioni, A. (1988). *The moral dimension. Toward a new economy*. New York: Free Press.

Falkinger, J. (1988). Tax evasion and equity: A theoretical analysis. *Public Finance*, 43(3), 388–95.

(1995). Tax evasion, consumption of public goods and fairness. *Journal of Economic Psychology*, 16(1), 63–72.

Falkinger, J., and Walther, H. (1991). Rewards versus penalties: On a new policy against tax evasion. *Public Finance Quarterly*, 19(1), 67–79.

Fallan, L. (1999). Gender, exposure to tax knowledge, and attitudes towards taxation. An experimental approach. *Journal of Business Ethics*, 18(2), 173–84.

Fehr, E., Fischbacher, U., and Gächter, S. (2002). Strong reciprocity, human cooperation, and the enforcement of social norms. *Human Nature*, 13(1), 1–25.

Fehr, E., and Gächter, S. (1998). Reciprocity and economics. The economic implications of homo reciprocans. *European Economic Review*, 42(3–5), 845–59.

Feld, L. P., and Frey, B. S. (2002). Trust breeds trust: How taxpayers are treated. *Economics of Governance*, 3(2), 87–99.

(2005a). Illegal, immoral, fattening or what? How deterrence and responsive regulation shape tax morale. In C. Bajada and F. Schneider (eds.), *Size, causes and consequences of the underground economy* (pp. 16–37). Aldershot: Ashgate.

(2005b). *Tax compliance as the result of a psychological tax contract: The role of incentives and responsive regulation*. Retrieved 31 December 2005, from http:// www.dur.ac.uk/john.ashworth/EPCS/Papers/Feld_Frey.pdf.

Feld, L. P., and Kirchgässner, G. (2000). Direct democracy, political culture, and the outcome of economic policy: A report on the Swiss experience. *European Journal of Political Economy*, 16(2), 287–306.

Feld, L. P., and Tyran, J. R. (2002). Tax evasion and voting: An experimental analysis. *Kyklos*, 55(2), 197–221.

Ferster, C., Culbertson, S., and Perron Boren, M. (1975). *Behavior principles* (2nd edn). Englewood Cliffs, NJ: Prentice Hall.

Fetchenhauer, D. (2004). *Different perspectives on prosocial and antisocial behavior. Kumulative Habilitation*. Bochum: Ruhr-Universität Bochum.

Fischer, C. M., Wartick, M., and Mark, M. M. (1992). Detection probability and taxpayer compliance: A review of the literature. *Journal of Accounting Literature*, 11(1), 1–46.

Fishbein, M., and Ajzen, I. (1975). *Belief, attitude, intention and behavior: An introduction to theory and research*. Reading, MA: Addison-Wesley.

Fishlow, A., and Friedman, J. (1994). Tax evasion, inflation and stabilization. *Journal of Development Economics*, 43(1), 105–23.

Fjeldstad, O.-H. (2004). What's trust got to do with it? Non-payment of service charges in local authorities in South Africa. *Journal of Modern African Studies*, 42(4), 539–62.

Fjeldstad, O.-H., and Semboja, J. (2001). Why people pay taxes: The case of the development levy in Tanzania. *World Development*, 29(12), 2,059–74.

Fjeldstad, O.-H., and Tungodden, B. (2003). Fiscal corruption: A vice or a virtue? *World Development*, 31(8), 1,459–67.

Franzoni, L. A. (2000). Tax evasion and tax compliance. In B. Bouckaert and G. De Geest (eds.), *Encyclopedia of Law and Economics* (vol. IV, pp. 51–94). Cheltenham: Edward Elgar.

Freiberg, A. (1986). Enforcement discretion and taxation offences. *Australian Tax Forum*, 3(1), 55–91.

French, J. R. P., and Raven, B. H. (1959). The basis of social power. In D. Cartwright (ed.), *Studies in social power* (pp. 150–67). Ann Arbor, MI: University of Michigan Press.

Frey, B. S. (1992). Tertium datur – pricing, regulating and intrinsic motivation. *Kyklos*, 45(2), 161–84.

(1997). *Not just for the money: An economic theory of personal motivation*. Cheltenham: Edward Elgar.

(2003). Deterrence and tax morale in the European Union. *European Review*, 11(3), 385–406.

(2004). Politische Partizipation und Steuermoral. In K. Bizer, A. Falk and J. Lange (eds.), *Am Staat vorbei. Transparenz, Fairness und Partizipation kontra Steuerhinterziehung* (pp. 47–57). Berlin: Duncker und Humblot.

Frey, B. S., and Feld, L. P. (2002). *Deterrence and morale in taxation: An empirical analysis*: Working Paper No. 760. CESifo GmbH.

Frey, B. S., and Weck-Hannemann, H. (1984). The hidden economy as an 'unobserved' variable. *European Economic Review*, 26(1), 33–53.

Friedland, N. (1982). A note on tax evasion as a function of the quality of information about the magnitude and credibility of threatened fines: Some preliminary research. *Journal of Applied Social Psychology*, 12(1), 54–9.

Friedland, N., Maital, S., and Rutenberg, A. (1978). A simulation study of income tax evasion. *Journal of Public Economics*, 10(1), 107–16.

Frijters, P. (2000). Do individuals try to maximize general satisfaction? *Journal of Economic Psychology*, 21(3), 281–304.

Fukuyama, F. (1995). *Trust: The social virtues and the creation of prosperity*. New York: Free Press.

Furnham, A. (2005). Understanding the meaning of tax: Young people's knowledge of the principles of taxation. *Journal of Socio-Economics*, 34(5), 703–13.

Garland, H., Sandefur, C. A., and Rogers, A. C. (1990). De-escalation of commitment in oil exploration: When sunk costs and negative feedback coincide. *Journal of Applied Psychology*, 75(6), 721–7.

Gassner, W. (1983). Steuervermeidung, Steuerumgehung, Steuerhinterziehung. Unpublished manuscript. Vienna University of Economics and Business Administration.

Gehring, W. J., and Willoughby, A. R. (2002). The medial frontal cortex and rapid processing of monetary gains and losses. *Science*, 295(5563), 2279–82.

Gërxhani, K. (2004). Tax evasion in transition: Outcome of an institutional clash? Testing Feige's conjecture in Albania. *European Economic Review*, 48(4), 729–45.

(2006). 'Did you pay your taxes? How (not) to conduct tax evasion surveys in transition countries'. *Social Indicators Research*, 80(4), 555–81.

Gërxhani, K., and Schram, A. (2006). Tax evasion and income source: A comparative experimental study. *Journal of Economic Psychology*, 27(3), 202–22.

Gintis, H., Bowles, S., Boyd, R., and Fehr, E. (2003). Explaining altruistic behavior in humans. *Evolution and Human Behavior*, 24(3), 153–72.

Goldberg, L. R. (1990). An alternative 'description of personality': The Big-Five factor structure. *Journal of Personality and Social Psychology*, 59(6), 1,216–29.

Gouldner, A. W. (1960). The norm of reciprocity: A preliminary statement. *American Sociological Review*, 25(1), 161–78.

Granger, J. (2005). *Focus on compliance issues for the Tax Office in 2005*. Retrieved 5 August 2005, from http://www.ato.gov.au/corporate/content.asp?doc=/content/55484.htm.

Grasmick, H. G., and Bursik Jr, R. J. (1990). Conscience, significant others, and rational choice: Extending the deterrence model. *Law and Society Review*, 24(3), 837–61.

Grasmick, H. G., Bursik, R. J., and Cochran, J. K. (1991). 'Render unto Caesar what is Caesar's': Religiosity and taxpayers' inclinations to cheat. *The Sociological Quarterly*, 32(2), 251–66.

Grasso, L., and Kaplan, S. E. (1998). An examination of ethical standards. *Journal of Accounting Education*, 16(1), 85–100.

Gravelle, H., and Rees, R. (1981). *Microeconomics*. London: Longman Group Ltd.

Green, D. P., Kahneman, D., and Kunreuther, H. (1994). How the scope and method of public funding affect willingness to pay for public goods. *Public Opinion Quarterly*, 58(1), 49–67.

Grimm, O. (2005). Gespenst der Flat Tax geht um. *Die Presse* (12 September), p. 4.

Groenland, E. A. (1992). Developing a dynamic research strategy for the economic psychological study of taxation. *Journal of Economic Psychology*, 13(4), 589–96.

Groenland, E. A. G., and van Veldhoven, G. M. (1983). Tax evasion behavior: A psychological framework. *Journal of Economic Psychology*, 3(2), 129–44.

Gruening, G. (2001). Origin and theoretical basis of New Public Management. *International Public Management Journal*, 4(1), 1–25.

Guala, F., and Mittone, L. (2005). Experiments in economics: external validity and the robustness of phenomena. *Journal of Economic Methodology*, 12(4), 495–515.

Güth, W., and Sausgruber, R. (2004). *Tax morale and optimal taxation*: CESifo Working Paper No. 1284. CESifo GmbH.

Halperin, R., and Tzur, J. (1990). Tax evasion and the low penalty, low audit rate phenomenon. *Journal of Accounting and Public Policy*, 9(3), 179–96.

Hamilton, A. (1999). IRS enforcement drops sharply. *Tax Notes* (8 April), p. 188.

Hansford, A., and Hasseldine, J. D. (2002). Best practice in tax administration. *Public Money and Management*, 22(1), 5–6.

Hardin, R. (1968). The tragedy of the commons. *Science*, 162 (3859), 1243–8.

Haslam, S. A. (2001). *Psychology in organizations: The social identity approach*. London: Sage.

Hasseldine, J. D. (1998a). Prospect theory and tax reporting decisions: Implications for tax administrators. *International Bureau of Fiscal Documentation*, 52(11), 501–5.

(1998b). Tax amnesties: An international review. *Bulletin for International Fiscal Documentation*, 52(7), 303–10.

Hasseldine, J. D., and Bebbington, K. J. (1991). Blending economic deterrence and fiscal psychology models in the design of responses to tax evasion: The New Zealand experience. *Journal of Economic Psychology*, 12(2), 299–324.

Hasseldine, J. D., and Hite, P. A. (2003). Framing, gender and tax compliance. *Journal of Economic Psychology*, 24(4), 517–33.

Hasseldine, J. D., and Kaplan, S. E. (1992). The effect of different sanction communications on hypothetical taxpayer compliance: Policy implications from New Zealand. *Public Finance*, 47(1), 45–60.

Hasseldine, J. D., and Li, Z. (1999). More tax evasion research required in new millennium. *Crime Law and Social Change*, 31(2), 91–104.

Heath, C., Larrick, R. P., and Wu, G. (1999). Goals as reference points. *Cognitive Psychology*, 38(1), 79–109.

Helson, H. (1964). *Adaption-level theory*. New York: Harper and Row.

Herbert, M. (1989). *Discipline: A positive guide for parents*. Oxford: Blackwell.

Hessing, D. J., Elffers, H., Robben, H. S. J., and Webley, P. (1993). Needy or greedy – the social-psychology of individuals who fraudulently claim unemployment benefits. *Journal of Applied Social Psychology*, 23(3), 226–43.

Hessing, D. J., Elffers, H., and Weigel, R. H. (1988). Exploring the limits of self-reports and reasoned action: An investigation of the psychology of tax evasion behavior. *Journal of Personality and Social Psychology*, 54(3), 405–13.

Hessing, D. J., Kinsey, K. A., Elffers, H., and Weigel, R. H. (1988). Tax evasion research: Measurement strategies and theoretical models. In W. F. van Raaij, G. M. van Veldhoven and K. E. Warneryd (eds.), *Handbook of economic psychology* (pp. 516–37). Dordrecht: Kluwer Academic Publishers.

Higgins, E. T. (1998a). From expectancies to worldviews: Regulatory focus in socialization and cognition. In J. M. Darley (ed.), *Attribution and social interaction. The legacy of Edward E. Jones* (pp. 243–69). Washington, DC: APA.

  (1998b). Promotion and prevention: Regulatory focus as a motivational principle. In M. P. Zanna (ed.), *Advances in experimental social psychology* (vol. XXX, pp. 1–46). New York: Academic Press.

  (2002). How self-regulation creates distinct values: The case of promotion and prevention decision making. *Journal of Consumer Psychology*, 12(3), 177–91.

Hill, T. P. (1995). The significant-digit phenomenon. *American Mathematical Monthly*, 102(4), 322–7.

Hite, P. A. (1987). An application of attribution theory in taxpayer noncompliance research. *Public Finance*, 42(1), 105–18.

  (1988). An examination of the impact of subject selection on hypothetical and self-reported taxpayer noncompliance. *Journal of Economic Psychology*, 9(4), 445–66.

  (1989). A positive approach to taxpayer compliance. *Public Finance*, 44(2), 249–67.

  (1990). An experimental investigation of the effect of tax shelters on taxpayer noncompliance. *Public Finance/Finances Publiques*, 45(1), 90–108.

Hite, P. A., and Hasseldine, J. D. (2003). Tax practitioner credentials and the incidence of IRS audit adjustments. *American Accounting Association*, 17(1), 1–14.

Hite, P. A., and McGill, G. A. (1992). An examination of taxpayer preference for aggressive tax advice. *National Tax Journal*, 45(4), 389–403.

Hodson, G., and Olson, J. M. (2005). Testing the generality of the name letter effect: Name initials and everyday attitudes. *Personality and Social Psychology Bulletin*, 31(8), 1,099–111.

Homans, G. C. (1961). *Social behavior: Its elementary forms*. London: Routledge and Paul Kegan.

Horton, S. (2003). Guest editorial: Participation and involvement: The democratisation of new public management? *International Journal of Public Sector Management*, 16(6), 403–11.

Hume, E. C., Larkins, E. R., and Iyer, G. (1999). On compliance with ethical standards in tax return preparation. *Journal of Business Ethics*, 18(2), 229–38.

Hyman, I., McDowell, E., and Raines, B. (1977). Corporal punishment and alternatives in the schools: An overview of theoretical and practical issues.

In J. Wise (ed.), *Proceedings: Conference on corporal punishment in the schools* (pp. 1–18). Washington, DC: National Institute of Education.

IRS (1978). *A dictionary of compliance factors.* Washington, DC: Government Publishing Office.

Jackson, B. R., and Milliron, V. (1986). Tax compliance research: Findings, problems, and prospects. *Journal of Accounting Literature,* 5(1), 125–65.

Jackson, B. R., Milliron, V. C., and Toy, D. R. (1988). Tax practitioners and the government. *Tax Notes* (17 October), pp. 333–8.

James, S. (1998, July). The behaviour of revenue services as a variable in tax administration and taxpayer compliance. Paper presented at the 10th International Conference on Socioeconomics. SASE/SABE, Vienna, Austria.

James, S., and Alley, C. (2002). Tax compliance, self-assessment and tax administration. *Journal of Finance and Management in Public Services,* 2(2), 27–42.

James, S., Hasseldine, J. D., Hite, P. A., and Toumi, M. (2003). *Tax compliance policy: An international comparison and new evidence on normative appeals and auditing.* Paper presented at the ESRC Future Governance Workshop, Institute for Advanced Studies, Vienna, Austria.

Job, J., and Honaker, D. (2003). Short-term experience with responsive regulation in the Australian Taxation Office. In V. Braithwaite (ed.), *Taxing democracy. Understanding tax avoidance and evasion* (pp. 111–29). Aldershot: Ashgate.

Job, J., and Reinhart, M. (2003). Trusting the tax office: Does Putnam's thesis relate to tax? *Australian Journal of Social Issues,* 38(3), 307–34.

Job, J., Stout, A., and Smith, R. (2007). Culture change in three taxation administrations: From command-and-control to responsive regulation. *Law and Policy,* 29(1), 84–101.

Kahneman, D. (1994). New challenges to the rationality assumption. *Journal of Institutional and Theoretical Economics. Zeitschrift für die gesamte Staatswissenschaft,* 150(1), 18–36.

Kahneman, D., Slovic, P., and Tversky, A. (1982). *Judgement under uncertainty: Heuristics and biases.* New York: Cambridge University Press.

Kahneman, D., and Tversky, A. (1979). Prospect theory: An analysis of decision under risk. *Econometrica,* 47(2), 263–91.

(1984). Choices, values, and frames. *American Psychologist,* 39(4), 341–50.

Kaplan, S. E., Reckers, P. M. J., and Reynolds, K. D. (1986). An application of attribution and equity theories to tax evasion behavior. *Journal of Economic Psychology,* 7(4), 461–76.

Kemp, S. (2004). Preferences for funding particular government services from flat or progressive tax. Paper presented at the Joint SABE/IAREP Annual Colloquium, Philadelphia, PA.

Kim, C. K. (2002). Does fairness matter in tax reporting behavior? *Journal of Economic Psychology,* 23(6), 771–85.

King, S., and Sheffrin, S. M. (2002). Tax evasion and equity theory: An investigative approach. *International Tax and Public Finance,* 9(4), 505–21.

Kinsey, K. A., and Grasmick, H. G. (1993). Did the tax reform act of 1986 improve compliance? Three studies of pre- and post-TRA compliance attitudes. *Law and Policy,* 15(4), 239–325.

Kinsey, K. A., Grasmick, H. G., and Smith, K. W. (1991). Framing justice: Taxpayer evaluations of personal tax burdens. *Law and Society Review*, 25(4), 845–73.

Kirchgässner, G., Feld, L. P., and Savioz, M. R. (1999). *Die direkte Demokratie*. Munich: Vahlen.

Kirchler, E. (1997a). Balance between giving and receiving: Tax morality and satisfaction with fiscal policy as they relate to the perceived just distribution of public resources. *Reitaku International Journal of Economic Studies*, 5(1), 59–70.

(1997b). The burden of new taxes: Acceptance of taxes as a function of affectedness and egoistic versus altruistic orientation. *Journal of Socio-Economics*, 26(4), 421–37.

(1998). Differential representations of taxes: Analysis of free associations and judgments of five employment groups. *Journal of Socio-Economics*, 27(1), 117–31.

(1999). Reactance to taxation: Employers' attitudes towards taxes. *Journal of Socio-Economics*, 28(2), 131–8.

Kirchler, E., and Berger, M. M. (1998). Macht die Gelegenheit den Dieb? In *Jahrbuch für Absatz- und Konsumentenforschung* (vol. 44), pp. 439–62.

Kirchler, E., and Hölzl, E. (2003). Economic psychology. *International Review of Industrial and Organizational Psychology*, 18(1), 29–80.

Kirchler, E., and Maciejovsky, B. (2001). Tax compliance within the context of gain and loss situations, expected and current asset position, and profession. *Journal of Economic Psychology*, 22(2), 173–94.

Kirchler, E., Maciejovsky, B., and Schneider, F. (2003). Everyday representations of tax avoidance, tax evasion, and tax flight: Do legal differences matter? *Journal of Economic Psychology*, 24(4), 535–53.

Kirchler, E., Maciejovsky, B., and Schwarzenberger, H. (2005). Specious confidence after tax audits: A contribution to the dynamics of compliance. Unpublished manuscript, University of Vienna, Austria.

Kirchler, E., Maciejovsky, B., and Weber, M. (2005). Framing effects, selective information, and market behavior: An experimental analysis. *Journal of Behavioral Finance*, 6(2), 90–100.

Kirchler, E., Muehlbacher, S., Hölzl, E., and Webley, P. (2005). Effort and aspirations in tax evasion: Experimental evidence. Unpublished manuscript, University of Vienna, Austria.

Kirchler, E., Niemirowski, P., and Wearing A. (eds.) (2006). Shared subjective views, intent to cooperate and tax compliance: Similarities between Australian taxpayers and tax officers. *Journal of Economic Psychology*, 27(4), 502–17.

Kohlberg, L. (1969). Stages and sequences: The cognitive development approach to socialization. In D. Goslin (ed.), *Handbook of socialization theory and research*. Chicago, IL: Rand McNelly.

Kramer, R. M. (1999). Trust and distrust in organizations: Emerging perspectives, enduring questions. *Annual Review of Psychology*, 50(1), 569–98.

Kramer, R. M., and Tyler, T. R. (1996). *Trust in organizations. Frontiers of theory and research*. Thousand Oaks, CA: Sage.

Lamnek, S., Olbrich, G., and Schaefer, W. (2000). *Tatort Sozialstaat: Schwarzarbeit, Leistungsmissbrauch, Steuerhinterziehung und ihre (Hinter) Gruende*. Opladen: Leske + Budrich.

Landsberger, M., and Meilijson, I. (1982). Incentive generating state dependent penalty system: The case of income tax evasion. *Journal of Public Economics*, 19(3), 333–52.

Lang, O., Nöhrbass, K.-H., and Stahl, K. (1997). On income tax avoidance: The case of Germany. *Journal of Public Economics*, 66(2), 327–47.

Lea, S., Tarpy, R. M., and Webley, P. (1987). *The individual in the economy. A survey of economic psychology*. Cambridge: Cambridge University Press.

Lenartova, G. (2003). Prepared tax reform in the Slovak Republic according to the criteria of tax theory and practice. *Ekonomicky Casopis*, 51(6), 664.

Leuthold, J. H. (1983). Home production and the tax system. *Journal of Economic Psychology*, 3(2), 145–57.

Leventhal, G. S. (1980). What should be done with equity theory? New approaches to the study of fairness in social relationships. In K. J. Gergen, M. S. Greenberg and R. H. Willis (eds.), *Social exchange* (pp. 27–55). New York: Plenum.

Lévy-Garboua, L., Masclet, D., and Montmarquette, C. (2005) *A micro-foundation for the Laffer curve in a real effort experiment*. Retrieved 30 March 2006, from ftp://mse.univ-paris1.fr/pub/mse/cahiers2005/Bla05071.pdf.

Lewin, I. P., Schneider, S. L., and Gaeth, G. S. (1998). All frames are not created equal: A typology and critical analysis of framing effects. *Organizational Behavior and Human Decision Processes*, 76(2), 149–88.

Lewis, A. (1978). Perception of tax rates. *British Tax Review*, 6, 358–66.

(1979). An empirical assessment of tax mentality. *Public Finance*, 34(2), 245–57.

(1982). *The psychology of taxation*. Oxford: Martin Robertson.

Liebig, S., and Mau, S. (2005). When is a tax system just? Attitudes towards general principles of taxation and the justice of tax burdens. *Zeitschrift für Soziologie*, 34(6), 468–91.

Lin, W.-Z., and Yang, C. C. (2001). A dynamic portfolio choice model of tax evasion: Comparative statics of tax rates and its implication for economic growth. *Journal of Economic Dynamics and Control*, 25(11), 1,827–40.

Lind, E. A., and Tyler, T. R. (1988). *The social psychology of procedural justice*. New York: Plenum.

Lochbuy, T. M., and O'Rourke, R. J. (1996). Catching tax cheats using meta-alphabetological analysis. *Australian Tax Review*, 25 (June), 79–82.

Loewenstein, G., and Issacharoff, S. (1994). Source dependence in the valuation of objects. *Journal of Behavioral Decision Making*, 7(3), 157–68.

Long, S. B., and Schwartz, R. D. (1987). *The impact of IRS audits on taxpayer compliance: A field experiment in specific deterrence*. Paper presented at the Annual Meeting of the Law and Society Association, Washington, DC.

Long, S. B., and Swingen, J. A. (1991). Taxpayer compliance: Setting new agendas for research. *Law and Society Review*, 25(3), 637–83.

MacCoun, R. J. (2005). Voice, control, and belonging: The double-edged sword of procedural fairness. *Annual Review of Law and Social Science*, 1(1), 171–201.

Malik, A. S., and Schwab, R. M. (1991). The economics of tax amnesties. *Journal of Public Economics*, 46(1), 29–49.

Marshall, R. L., Armstrong, R. W., and Smith, M. (1998). The ethical environment of tax practitioners: Western Australian evidence. *Journal of Business Ethics*, 17(12), 1,265–79.

Mason, R., and Calvin, L. D. (1978). A study of admitted income tax evasion. *Law and Society Review*, 13 (Fall), 73–89.

McBarnet, D. (2001). *When compliance is not the solution but the problem: From changes in law to changes in attitude.* Canberra: Australian National University, Centre for Tax System Integrity.

McBarnett, D. (1992). Legitimate rackets: Tax evasion, tax avoidance, and the boundaries of the law. *The Journal of Human Justice*, 3(2), 56–74.

McCaffery, E. J., and Baron, J. (2003). *Heuristics and biases in thinking about tax.* Retrieved 30 April 2005, from http://papers.ssrn.com/abstract=467440.

   (2004). Framing and taxation: Evaluation of tax policies involving household composition. *Journal of Economic Psychology*, 25(6), 679–705.

McCrae, R. R., and Costa, P. T. (1992). An introduction to the five-factor model and its applications. *Journal of Personality*, 60(2), 175–215.

McKerchar, M. (1995). Understanding small business taxpayers: Their sources of information and level of knowledge of taxation. *Australian Tax Forum*, 12(1), 25–41.

   (2001). The study of income tax complexity and unintentional noncompliance: Research method and preliminary findings. ATAX Discussion paper. University of Sydney, Orange.

Meier, K., and Kirchler, E. (1998). Social representations of the euro in Austria. *Journal of Economic Psychology*, 19(6), 755–74.

Mercer, J. (2005). Prospect theory and political science. *Annual Review of Political Science*, 8(1), 1–21.

Mérö, L. (1996). *Optimal entscheiden. Spieltheorie und die Logik unseres Handelns.* Basel: Birkhäuser.

Messick, D. M., and Brewer, M. B. (1983). Solving social dilemmas: A review. In L. Weeler and P. Shaver (eds.), *Review of personality and social psychology* (pp. 231–240). Beverly Hills, CA: Sage.

Milliron, V. (1988). A conceptual model of factors influencing tax preparers' aggressiveness. In S. Moriarity and J. H. Collins (eds.), *Contemporary tax research* (pp. 1–15). Norman, OK: University of Oklahoma.

Milliron, V., and Toy, D. (1988). Tax compliance: An investigation of key features. *Journal of the American Taxation Association*, 9(2), 84–104.

Mittone, L. (1999). Psychological constraints on tax evasion: An empirical approach. Unpublished Ph.D. thesis, Bristol University.

   (2002). *Individual styles of tax evasion: An experimental study.* Retrieved 30 April 2005, from http://www.inomics.com/cgi/repec?handle=RePEc:wop:uteepu.

   (2006). *Dynamic behaviours in tax evasion. An experimental approach.* Retrieved 30 April 2005, from http://www.inomics.com/cgi/repec?handle=RePEc:wop:uteepu.

Moscovici, S. (1961). *La Psychanalyse, son image et son public.* Paris: Presse Universitaire de France.

(2001). The phenomenon of social representations. In S. Moscovici and
G. Duveen (eds.), *Social representations: Explorations in social psychology*
(pp. 18–77). New York: New York University Press.

Moser, D. V., Evans III, J. H., and Kim, C. K. (1995). The effects of horizontal
and exchange inequity on tax reporting decisions. *Accounting Review*, 70(4),
619–34.

Moser, H. (1994). Zur Kritik der Sprache von Gesetzen. Anmerkungen eines
Sprachwissenschaftlers. In C. Smekal and E. Theurl (eds.), *Stand und
Entwicklung der Finanzpsychologie* (pp. 171–84). Baden-Baden: Nomos.

Mumford, A. (2001). *Taxing culture*. Aldershot: Ashgate.

Murphy, K. (2003a). An examination of taxpayers' attitudes towards the
Australian tax system: Findings from a survey of tax scheme investors.
Australian Tax Forum, 18(2), 209–42.

(2003b). *Preventing widespread resistance to decisions: The role of trust in regulating
taxpayers*. Paper presented at the 28th Annual IAREP Colloquium,
Christchurch, New Zealand.

(2003c). Procedural justice and tax compliance. *Australian Journal of Social
Issues*, 38(3), 379–407.

(2004a). Aggressive tax planning: Differentiating those playing the game from
those who don't. *Journal of Economic Psychology*, 25(3), 307–29.

(2004b). The role of trust in nurturing compliance: A study of accused tax
avoiders. *Law and Human Behavior*, 28(2), 187–209.

Myles, G. D. (2000). Wasteful government, tax evasion, and the provision of
public goods. *European Journal of Political Economy*, 16(1), 51–74.

Nationmaster-Encyclopedia (2005). Retrieved 6 July 2005, from http://www.
nationmaster.com/encyclopedia/Gambler%27s-fallacy.

Newcomb, S. (1881). Note on the frequency of use of the different digits in
natural numbers. *American Journal of Mathematics*, 4(1–4), 39–40.

Niemirowski, P., Baldwin, S., and Wearing, A. (2001). Thirty years of tax compliance research: Of what use is it to the ATO? In M. Walpole and C. Evans
(eds.), *Tax administration in the 21st century* (pp. 199–214). St Leonards:
Prospect Media.

Niemirowski, P., and Wearing, A. (2003). Taxation agents and taxpayer compliance. *Journal of Australian Taxation*, 6(2), 166–200.

Niemirowski, P., Wearing, A. J., Baldwin, S., Leonard, B., and Mobbs, C.
(2002). *The influence of tax related behaviours, beliefs, attitudes and values on
Australian taxpayer compliance. Is tax avoidance intentional and how serious an
offence is it?* Sydney: University of New South Wales.

Nigrini, M. J. (1996). A taxpayer compliance application of Benford's Law.
Journal of the American Taxation Association, 18(1), 72–91.

(1999). I've got your number. *Journal of Accountancy*, 187 (May), 79–83.

Noga, T., and Arnold, V. (2002). Do tax decision support systems affect the
accuracy of tax compliance decisions? *International Journal of Accounting
Information Systems*, 3(3), 125–44.

O'Donnell, E., Koch, B., and Boone, J. (2005). The influence of domain knowledge and task complexity on tax professionals' compliance recommendations. *Accounting Organizations and Society*, 30(2), 145–65.

OECD (2004). Guidance note. Compliance risk management: Managing and improving tax compliance. Retrieved 30 September 2006 from http://www.oecd.org/dataoecd/44/19/33818656.pdf.

Orviska, M., and Hudson, J. (2002). Tax evasion, civic duty and the law abiding citizen. *European Journal of Political Economy*, 19(1), 83–102.

Owens, J., and Hamilton, S. (2004). Experience and innovations in other countries. In H. J. Aaron and J. Slemrod (eds.), *The crisis in tax administration* (pp. 347–88). Washington, DC: Brookings Institution Press.

Park, C. G., and Hyun, J. K. (2003). Examining the determinants of tax compliance by experimental data: A case of Korea. *Journal of Policy Modeling*, 25(8), 673–84.

Paternoster, R., and Simpson, S. (1996). Sanction threats and appeals to morality: Testing a rational choice model of corporate crime. *Law and Society Review*, 30(3), 549–84.

Payne, J. L. (1993). *Costly returns: The burdens of the U.S. tax system*. San Francisco, CA: ICS Press.

Peabody, D. (1985). *National characteristics*. New York: Cambridge University Press.

Pelzman, S. (1976). Toward a more general theory of regulation. *Journal of Law and Economics*, 19(2), 211–40.

Pelzmann, L. (1985). *Wirtschaftspsychologie. Arbeitslosenforschung, Schattenwirtschaft, Steuerpsychologie*. Vienna: Springer.

Pingle, M. (1997). Submitting to authority: Its effect on decision-making. *Journal of Economic Psychology*, 18(1), 45–68.

Pommerehne, W., and Frey, B. S. (1992). *The effects of tax administration on tax morale* (Series II, No. 191): University of Konstanz.

Pommerehne, W., Hart, A., and Frey, B. S. (1994). Tax morale, tax evasion and the choice of policy instruments in different political systems. *Public Finance*, 49 (Suppl.), 52–69.

Pommerehne, W., and Weck-Hannemann, H. (1992). Steuerhinterziehung: Einige romantische, realistische und nicht zuletzt empirische Befunde. *Zeitschrift für Wirtschafts- und Sozialwissenschaften*, 112(3), 433–66.

(1996). Tax rates, tax administration and income tax evasion in Switzerland. *Public Choice*, 88(1–2), 161–70.

Poppe, M. (2005). The specificity of social dilemma situations. *Journal of Economic Psychology*, 26(3), 431–41.

Porcano, T. M. (1988). Correlates of tax evasion. *Journal of Economic Psychology*, 9(1), 47–67.

Porschke, C., and Witte, E. H. (2002). Psychologische Faktoren der Steuergerechtigkeit. *Wirtschaftspsychologie*, 4(1), 34–44.

Rabin, M. (1998). Psychology and economics. *Journal of Economic Literature*, 36(1), 11–46.

Rawlings, G. (2003). Cultural narratives of taxation and citizenship: Fairness, groups and globalisation. *Australian Journal of Social Issues*, 38(3), 269–306.

(2004). Law, liquidity and eurobonds. *The Journal of Pacific History*, 39(3), 325–41.

Reckers, P. M. J., Sanders, D. L., and Roark, S. J. (1994). The influence of ethical attitudes on taxpayer compliance. *National Tax Journal*, 47(4), 825–36.

Reinganum, J. F., and Wilde, L. L. (1985). Income tax compliance in a principal-agent framework. *Journal of Public Economics*, 26(1), 1–18.

(1988). A note on enforcement uncertainty and taxpayer compliance. *The Quarterly Journal of Economics*, 103(4), 793–8.

Richardson, M., and Sawyer, A. (2001). A taxonomy of the tax compliance literature: Further findings, problems and prospects. *Australian Tax Forum*, 16(2), 137–320.

Robben, H. S. J. (1991). *A behavioral simulation and documented behavior approach to income tax evasion*. Deventer: Kluwer.

Robben, H. S. J., Webley, P., Elffers, H., and Hessing, D. J. (1989). A cross-national comparison of attitudes, personality, behaviour, and social comparison in tax evasion experiments. In K. Grunert and F. Ölander (eds.), *Understanding economic behaviour* (pp. 121–34). Dordrecht: Kluwer Academic Publishers.

(1990a). Decision frames, opportunity and tax evasion: An experimental approach. *Journal of Economic Behavior and Organization*, 14(3), 353–61.

Robben, H. S. J., Webley, P., Weigel, R. H., Wärneryd, K. E., Kinsey, K. A., Hessing, D. J., Alvira Martin, F., Elffers, H., Wahlund, R., van Langenhove, L., Long, S. B., and Scholz, J. (1990b). Decision frame and opportunity as determinants of tax cheating: An international experimental study. *Journal of Economic Psychology*, 11(3), 341–64.

Roberts, M. L., and Hite, P. A. (1994). Progressive taxation, fairness and compliance. *Law and Policy*, 16 (January), 27–47.

Roberts, M. L., Hite, P. A., and Bradley, C. F. (1994). Understanding attitudes toward progressive taxation. *Public Opinion Quarterly*, 58(2), 165–90.

Rogoff, E. G., and Lee, M.-S. (1996). Does firm origin matter? An empirical examination of types of small business owners and entrepreneurs. *Academy of Entrepreneurship Journal*, 1(2), 1–17.

Rokeach, M. (1973). *The nature of human values*. New York: Free Press.

Sakurai, Y., and Braithwaite, V. (2003). Taxpayers' perceptions of practitioners: Finding one who is effective and does the right thing? *Journal of Business Ethics*, 46(4), 375–87.

Sandmo, A. (2003). Three decades of tax evasion: A perspective on the literature. Paper presented at the Skatteforum (The Research Forum on Taxation), Rosendal, Norway.

Sanson, A., Montgomery, B., Gault, U., Gridley, H., and Thomson, D. (1996). Punishment and behaviour change: An Australian Psychological Society position paper. *Australian Psychologist*, 31(3), 157–65.

Schadewald, M. S. (1989). Reference point effects in taxpayer decision making. *Journal of the American Taxation Association*, 10(2), 68–84.

Schepanski, A., and Kelsey, D. (1990). Testing for framing effects in taxpayer compliance decisions. *Journal of the American Taxation Association*, 12(2), 60–77.

Schepanski, A., and Shearer, T. (1995). A prospect theory account of the income tax withholding phenomenon. *Organizational Behavior and Human Decision Processes*, 63(2), 174–86.

Schmidt, D. R. (2001). The prospects of taxpayer agreement with aggressive tax advice. *Journal of Economic Psychology*, 22(2), 157–72.

Schmölders, G. (1959). Fiscal psychology: A new branch of public finance. *National Tax Journal*, 12 (December), 340–5.

(1960). *Das Irrationale in der öffentlichen Finanzwirtschaft*. Frankfurt am Main: Suhrkamp.

(1964). *Finanzwissenschaft und Finanzpolitik*. Tübingen: J. c. B. Mohr (Paul Siebeck).

(1970a). *Finanzpolitik* (3th edn). Berlin: Springer.

(1970b). Survey research in public finance: A behavioural approach to fiscal theory. *Public Finance*, 25(2), 300–306.

(1975). *Einführung in die Geld- und Finanzpsychologie*. Darmstadt: Wissenschaftliche Buchgesellschaft.

Schneider, F. (2003). Zunehmende Schattenwirtschaft in Deutschland: Eine wirtschafts- und staatspolitische Herausforderung. *Vierteljahreshefte zur Wirtschaftsforschung*, 72(1), 148–59.

Schneider, F., and Enste, D. (2000). Shadow economies: size, causes, and consequences. *The Journal of Economic Literature*, 38(1), 77–114.

Schneider, F., and Klinglmair, R. (2004). *Shadow economics around the world: What do we know?* Retrieved 25 April 2005, from http://papers.ssrn.com/sol3/papers.cfm?abstract_id=518526.

Scholz, J. T., and Pinney, N. (1995). Duty, fear and tax compliance – the heuristic basis of citizenship behaviour. *American Journal of Political Science*, 39(2), 490–512.

Schwartz, R., and Orleans, S. (1967). On legal sanctions. *University of Chicago Law Review*, 34 (Winter), 274–300.

Seidl, C., and Traub, S. (2001). Taxpayers' attitudes, behavior, and perception of fairness. *Pacific Economic Review*, 6(2), 255–67.

(2002). Die Akzeptanz des deutschen Steuersystems: Eine demoskopische Untersuchung. In E. Theurl and E. Thöni (eds.), *Zukunftsperspektiven der Finanzierung öffentlicher Aufgaben* (pp. 7–27). Vienna: Böhlau.

Seldon, A. (ed.). (1979). *Tax avoision: The economic, legal and moral inter-relationships between avoidance and evasion*. London: Institute of Economic Affairs.

Seligman, M. (1992). *Helplessness*. New York: Freeman.

Shefrin, H. M., and Thaler, R. H. (1988). The behavioral life-cycle hypothesis. *Economic Inquiry*, 26(4), 609–43.

Shelak, B. J. (1997). The impact of the U.S. underground activity. A note relating to the impact on state finances. *Journal of Government Information*, 24(2), 113–17.

Siegel, S., and Fouraker, L. (1960). *Bargaining and group decision making*. New York: McGraw-Hill.

Sigala, M., Burgoyne, C., and Webley, P. (1999). Tax communication and social influence: Evidence from a British sample. *Journal of Community and Applied Social Psychology*, 9(3), 237–41.

Simon, H. A. (1955). A behavioral model of rational choice. *Quarterly Journal of Economics*, 69(1), 99–118.

Simpson, S. S. (2002). *Corporate crime, law, and social control*. Cambridge: Cambridge University Press.

Skinner, B. (1938). *The behavior of organisms*. New York: Appleton-Century Crofts.

Slemrod, J. (1985). An empirical test for tax evasion. *Review of Economics and Statistics*, 67(2), 232–238.

(ed.). (1992). *Why people pay taxes: Tax compliance and enforcement*. Ann Arbor, MI: University of Michigan Press.

Slemrod, J., Blumenthal, M., and Christian, C. (2001). Taxpayer response to an increased probability of audit: Evidence from a controlled experiment in Minnesota. *Journal of Public Economics*, 79(3), 455–83.

Smith, K. W., and Kinsey, K. A. (1987). Understanding taxpaying behaviour: A conceptual framework with implications for research. *Law and Society Review*, 21(4), 639–63.

Smith, K. W., and Stalans, L. J. (1991). Encouraging tax compliance with positive incentives: A conceptual framework and research directions. *Law and Policy*, 13(1), 35–53.

Smith, V. L. (1962). An experimental study of competitive market behavior. *Journal of Political Economy*, 70(2), 111–37.

(1964). Effect of market organization on competitive equilibrium. *Quarterly Journal of Economics*, 78 (May), 181–201.

Snow, A., and Warren, R. S. J. (2005). Tax evasion under random audits with uncertain detection. *Economics Letters*, 88(1), 97–100.

Song, Y.-D., and Yarbrough, T. E. (1978). Tax ethics and taxpayer attitudes: A survey. *Public Administration Review*, 38(5), 442–52.

Souleles, N. (1999). The response of household consumption to income tax refunds. *American Economic Review*, 89(4), 947–58.

Spicer, M. W., and Becker, L. A. (1980). Fiscal inequity and tax evasion: An experimental approach. *National Tax Journal*, 33(2), 171–5.

Spicer, M. W., and Hero, R. E. (1985). Tax evasion and heuristics: A research note. *Journal of Public Economics*, 26(2), 263–7.

Spicer, M. W., and Lundstedt, S. B. (1976). Understanding tax evasion. *Public Finance*, 21(2), 295–305.

Spicer, M. W., and Thomas, J. E. (1982). Audit probabilities and tax evasion decision: An experimental approach. *Journal of Economic Psychology*, 2(3), 241–5.

Srinivasan, T. N. (1973). Tax evasion: A model. *Journal of Public Economics*, 2(4), 339–46.

Stainer, A., Stainer, L., and Segal, A. (1997). The ethics of tax planning. *Business Ethics. A European Review*, 6(7), 213–19.

Stalans, L. J., and Lind, E. A. (1997). The meaning of procedural fairness: A comparison of taxpayers' and representatives' views of their tax audits. *Social Justice Research*, 10(3), 311–31.

Stella, P. (1991). An economic analysis of tax amnesties. *Journal of Public Economics*, 46(3), 283–400.

Stigler, G. (1971). The theory of economic regulation. *The Bell Journal of Economics and Management*, 2 (Spring), 3–21.

Stroebe, W., and Frey, B. S. (1982). Self-interest and collective action: The economics and psychology of public goods. *British Journal of Social Psychology*, 21(2), 121–37.

Strümpel, B. (1966). Disguised tax burden compliance costs of German business men and professionals. *National Tax Journal*, 19(1), 70–77.

(1969). The contribution of survey research to public finance. In A. T. Peacock (ed.), *Quantitative analysis in public finance* (pp. 13–22). New York: Praeger.

Tan, L. M. (1999). Taxpayers' preference for type of advice from tax practitioner: A preliminary examination. *Journal of Economic Psychology*, 20(4), 431–47.

Tanzi, V., and Shome, P. (1994). A primer on tax evasion. *International Bureau of Fiscal Documentation*, 48(6–7), 328–37.

Taylor, N. (2001). Social justice. In R. Brown and S. Gaertner (eds.), *Blackwell handbook of social psychology: Intergroup processes* (pp. 344–64). Oxford: Blackwell.

(2003). Understanding taxpayer attitudes through understanding taxpayer identities. In V. Braithwaite (ed.), *Taxing democracy. Understanding tax avoidance and evasion* (pp. 71–92). Aldershot: Ashgate.

Thaler, R. H. (1980). Toward a positive theory of consumer choice. *Journal of Economic Behavior and Organization*, 1(1), 39–60.

(1985). Mental accounting and consumer choice. *Marketing Science*, 4(3), 199–214.

Thaler, R. H., and Johnson, E. J. (1990). Gambling with the house money and trying to break even: The effects of prior outcomes on risky choice. *Management Science*, 36(6), 643–60.

Thibaut, J., Fredland, N., and Walker, L. (1974). Compliance with rules: Some social determinants. *Journal of Personality and Social Psychology*, 30(6), 792–801.

Thibaut, J., and Walker, L. (1978). A theory of procedure. *California Law Review*, 66(4), 541–66.

Thomas, J. K. (1989). Unusual patterns in reported earnings. *The Accounting Review*, 64(4), 773–87.

Thorndike, E. (1898). Animal intelligence. *Psychological Review Monograph Supplement*, 2(4, Whole No. 8).

Thorndike, J. J., and Ventry, D. J. J. (eds.). (2002). *Tax justice: The ongoing debate*. Washington, DC: The Urban Institute Press.

Thurman, Q., St John, C., and Riggs, L. (1984). Neutralization and tax evasion: How effective would a moral appeal be in improving compliance to tax laws? *Law and Policy*, 6(3), 309–27.

Tibbetts, S. G., Joulfaian, D., and Rider, M. (1997). Shame and rational choice in offending decisions: Tax evasion in the presence of negative income tax rates. *Criminal Justice and Behavior*, 24(2), 234–55.

Torgler, B. (2002). Speaking to theorists and searching for facts: Tax morale and tax compliance in experiments. *Journal of Economic Surveys*, 16(5), 657–83.

(2003a). Does culture matter? Tax morale in an East-West-German comparison. *FinanzArchiv*, 59(4), 504–28.

(2003b). Tax morale in transition countries. *Post-Communist Economies*, 15(3), 357–81.

(2003c). Tax morale, rule-governed behaviour and trust. *Constitutional Political Economy*, 14(2), 119–40.

(2003d). To evade taxes or not to evade: That is the question. *Journal of Socio-Economics*, 32(3), 283–302.

(2005a). Tax morale and direct democracy. *European Journal of Political Economy*, 21(2), 525–31.

(2005b). Tax morale in Latin America. *Public Choice*, 122(1–2), 133–57.

Torgler, B. and Schneider, F. (2004). Does culture influence tax morale? Evidence from different European countries. CREMA Working Paper No. 2004-17. Basel: Center for Research in Economics, Management and Arts.

Traub, S. (1998). The framing of tax reliefs. *Public Finance*, 53(2), 243–62.

(1999). *Framing effects in taxation: An empirical study using the German tax schedule.* Heidelberg: Physica.

(2000). Rahmungseffekte und die Kunst der Besteuerung. *Wirtschaftsdienst. Zeitschrift für Wirtschaftspolitik*, 80(12), 745–50.

Trivedi, V. U., Shehata, M., and Lynn, B. (2003). Impact of personal and situational factors on taxpayer compliance: An experimental analysis. *Journal of Business Ethics*, 47(3), 175–97.

Trivedi, V. U., Shehata, M., and Mestelman, S. (2004). *Attitudes, incentives, and tax compliance.* Hamilton: McMaster University, Department of Economics.

Turner, J. C., Hogg, M., Oakes, P. J., Reicher, S. D., and Wetherell, M. S. (1987). *Rediscovering the social group. A self-categorization theory.* Oxford: Blackwell.

Turner, J. C., and Onorato, R. (1997). Social identity, personality and the self-concept: A self-categorisation perspective. In T. Tyler, R. Kramer, M. Roderick and O. John (eds.), *The psychology of the social self: Applied social research* (pp. 11–46). Hillsdale, NJ: Lawrence Erlbaum.

Tversky, A., and Kahneman, D. (1974). Judgement under uncertainty: Heuristics and biases. *Science*, 185 (4157), 1,124–31.

(1981). The framing of decisions and psychology of choice. *Science*, 211(4481), 453–8.

(1992). Advances in prospect theory: Cumulative representation of uncertainty. *Journal of Risk and Uncertainty*, 5(4), 297–323.

Tyler, T. R. (1990). *Why people obey the law: Procedural justice, legitimacy, and compliance.* New Haven, CT: Yale University Press.

(1994). Psychological models of the justice motive. *Journal of Personality and Social Psychology*, 67(5), 850–63.

(2001a). Public trust and confidence in legal authorities: What do majority and minority group members want from the law and legal institutions? *Behavioral Sciences and the Law*, 19(2), 215–35.

(2001b). Trust and law abidingness: A proactive model of social regulation. *Boston University Law Review*, 81(2), 361–406.

(2006). Psychological perspectives on legitimacy and legitimation. *Annual Review of Psychology*, 57(1), 375–400.

Tyler, T. R., and De Cremer, D. (2006). How do we promote cooperation in groups, organizations, and societies? In P. A. M. van Lange (ed.), *Bridging social psychology. Benefits of transdisciplinary approaches* (pp. 427–33). Mahwah, NJ: Lawrence Earlbaum.

Tyler, T. R., and Degoey, P. (1996). Trust in organisational authorities: The influence of motive attributions on willingness to accept decisions. In R. M. Kramer and T. R. Tyler (eds.), *Trust in organizations: Frontiers of theory and research* (pp. 331–56). Thousand Oaks, CA: Sage.

Tyler, T. R., and Lind, E. A. (1992). A relational model of authority in groups. In M. P. Zanna (ed.), *Advances in experimental social psychology* (vol. XXV, pp. 115–91). San Diego, CA: Academic Press.

Tyszka, T. (1994). *Cognitive representation of economics*. Paper presented at the IAREP/SABE Annual Colloquium, Rotterdam.

Van de Braak, H. (1983). Taxation and tax resistance. *Journal of Economic Psychology*, 3(2), 95–111.

Van Lange, P. A. M., Liebrand, W. B. G., Messick, D. M., and Wilke, H. A. M. (1992). Social dilemmas: The state of the art. In W. B. G. Liebrand, D. Messick and H. A. M. Wilke (eds.), *Social dilemmas. Theoretical issues and research findings* (pp. 3–28). Oxford: Pergamon Press.

Varma, K. N., and Doob, A. N. (1998). Deterring economic crimes: The case of tax evasion. *Canadian Journal of Criminology*, 40(2), 165–84.

Vasin, A. A., and Navidi, K. (2003). Optimal tax inspection strategy. *Computational Mathematics and Modeling*, 14(2), 160–72.

Vasina, P. A. (2003). Optimal tax enforcement with imperfect tax payers and inspectors. *Computational Mathematics and Modeling*, 14(3), 309–18.

Verheul, I., Uhlaner, L., and Thurik, R. (2005). Business accomplishments, gender and entrepreneurial self-image. *Journal of Business Venturing*, 20(4), 483–518.

Vihanto, M. (2003). Tax evasion and the psychology of the social contract. *Journal of Socio-Economics*, 32(2), 111–25.

Vogel, J. (1974). Taxation and public opinion in Sweden: An interpretation of recent survey data. *National Tax Journal*, 27(1), 499–513.

Wahlund, R. (1992). Tax changes and economic behavior: The case of tax evasion. *Journal of Economic Psychology*, 13(4), 657–77.

Wallschutzky, I. G. (1984). Possible causes of tax evasion. *Journal of Economic Psychology*, 5(4), 371–84.

Walster, E., Walster, G. W., and Berscheid, E. (1978). *Equity: Theory and research*. Boston, MA: Allyn and Bacon.

Wärneryd, K., and Walerud, B. (1982). Taxes and economic behaviour: Some interview data on tax evasion in Sweden. *Journal of Economic Psychology*, 2(3), 187–211.

Wartick, M. (1994). Legislative justification and the perceived fairness of tax law changes: A reference cognitions theory approach. *The Journal of the American Taxation Association*, 16(2), 106–23.

Wearing, A., and Headey, B. M. (1995). *The would-be tax evader: A profile*. Paper presented at the 1995 Compliance Research Conference, Canberra.

Webley, P. (1987). Audit probabilities and tax evasion in a business simulation. *Economics Letters*, 25(3), 267–70.

    (2004). Tax compliance by businesses. In H. Sjögren and G. Skogh (eds.), *New perspectives on economic crime* (pp. 95–126). Cheltenham: Edward Elgar.

Webley, P., Cole, M., and Eidjar, O.-P. (2001). The prediction of self-reported and hypothetical tax-evasion: Evidence from England, France and Norway. *Journal of Economic Psychology*, 22(2), 141–55.

Webley, P., Robben, H., and Morris, I. (1988). Social comparison, attitudes and tax evasion in a shop simulation. *Social Behaviour*, 3(3), 219–228.

Webley, P., Robben, H. S. J., Elffers, H., and Hessing, D. J. (1991). *Tax evasion: An experimental approach*. Cambridge: Cambridge University Press.

Weck-Hannemann, H., and Pommerehne, W. (1989). Einkommenssteuerhinterziehung in der Schweiz: Eine empirische Analyse. *Schweizerische Zeitschrift für Volkswirtschaft und Statistik*, 125(4), 515–56.

Weigel, R. H., Hessing, D. J., and Elffers, H. (1987). Tax evasion research: A critical appraisal and theoretical model. *Journal of Economic Psychology*, 8(2), 215–35.

Weiner, B. (1996). Level of aspiration. In A. Manstead and M. Hewstone (eds.), *The Blackwell Encyclopedia of social psychology* (p. 362). Oxford: Blackwell.

Welch, M. R., Xu, Y. L., Bjarnason, T., and O'Donnell, P. (2005). 'But everybody does it . . .': The effects of perceptions, moral pressures, and informal sanctions on tax cheating. *Sociological Spectrum*, 25(1), 21–5.

Wenzel, M. (2000). Justice and identity: The significance of inclusion for perceptions of entitlement and the justice motive. *Personality and Social Psychology Bulletin*, 26(2), 157–76.

(2001). A social categorisation approach to distributive justice: Social identity as the link between relevance of inputs and need for justice. *British Journal of Psychology*, 40(3), 316–35.

(2002). The impact of outcome orientation and justice concerns on tax compliance: The role of taxpayers' identity. *Journal of Applied Psychology*, 87(4), 629–45.

(2003). Tax compliance and the psychology of justice: Mapping the field. In V. Braithwaite (ed.), *Taxing democracy: Understanding tax avoidance and evasion* (pp. 41–69). Aldershot: Ashgate.

(2004a). An analysis of norm processes in tax compliance. *Journal of Economic Psychology*, 25(2), 213–28.

(2004b). A social categorisation approach to distributive justice. *European Review of Social Psychology*, 15(7), 219–57.

(2004c). Social identification as a determinant of concerns about individual-, group-, and inclusive-level justice. *Social Psychology Quarterly*, 67(1), 70–87.

(2004d). The social side of sanctions: Personal and social norms as moderators of deterrence. *Law and Human Behavior*, 28(5), 547–67.

(2005a). Misperception of social norms about tax compliance: From theory to intervention. *Journal of Economic Psychology*, 26(6), 862–83.

(2005b). Motivation or rationalisation? Causal relations between ethics, norms and tax compliance. *Journal of Economic Psychology*, 26(4), 491–508.

Williamson, M. R., and Wearing, A. J. (1996). Lay people's cognitive models of the economy. *Journal of Economic Psychology*, 17(1), 3–38.

Wilson, J. L. F., and Sheffrin, S. (2005). Understanding surveys of taxpayer honesty. *Finanzarchiv*, 61(2), 256.

Witte, A. D., and Woodbury, D. F. (1985). The effect of tax laws and tax administration on tax compliance: The case of the US individual income tax. *National Tax Journal*, 38(1), 1–13.

Worsham, R. G. (1996). The effect of tax authority behaviour on taxpayer compliance: A procedural justice approach. *Journal of American Taxation Association*, 18(2), 19–39.

Wortman, C., and Brehm, J. W. (1975). Responses to uncontrollable outcomes: An integration of reactance theory and the learned helplessness model. In L. Berkowitz (ed.), *Advances in experimental social psychology* (vol. VIII, pp. 277–336). San Diego, CA: Academic Press.

Yaniv, G. (1990). Tax evasion under differential taxation. The economics of income source misreporting. *Journal of Public Economics*, 43(3), 327–37.

(1994). Tax evasion and the income tax rate: A theoretical re-examination. *Public Finance*, 49(1), 107–12.

(1999). Tax compliance and advance tax payments: A prospect theory analysis. *National Tax Journal*, 52(4), 753–64.

(2001). Revenge, tax informing, and the optimal bounty. *Journal of Public Economic Theory*, 3(2), 225–33.

(2003). Auditing ghosts by prosperity signals. *Economics Bulletin*, 8(9), 1–10.

Yitzhaki, S. (1974). A note on income tax evasion: A theoretical analysis. *Journal of Public Economics*, 3(2), 201–2.

Yitzhaki, S., and Vakneen, Y. (1989). On the shadow price of a tax inspector. *Public Finance/Finances Publiques*, 44(3), 492–505.

Zeelenberg, M., and van Dijk, E. (1997). A reverse sunk cost effect in risky decision making: Sometimes we have too much invested to gamble. *Journal of Economic Psychology*, 18(6), 677–91.

Zimbardo, P., and Gerrig, R. (2004). *Psychologie* (16th edn.). Munich: Pearson Studium.

Index

Page numbers in bold refer to figures and tables